The LIGHT from ZION

REVEALING HIDDEN PATHS OF THE KINGDOM.
A POWERFUL MESSAGE FROM 12 RABBIS ABOUT
UNITY, TRUE TREASURES AND GOD'S LOVING HEART.

The LIGHT *from* ZION

gefen ﮔפﬠﬨ
publishing house בית הוצאה לאור
JERUSALEM • NEW YORK   Est. 1981

Oljetreet
PUBLISHING

ROOT
SOURCE

PRESS

ISBN 978-82-998981-3-3

The Bible texts in the introduction part have been reproduced from The
ArtScroll Tanach, with permission of the copyright holders, ArtScroll / Mesorah
Publications, Ltd.

Photo of Jerusalem on the Cover: Kristoffer Undheim
Cover Design: Lisa Hainline
Typesetting: Steve Plummer
Editor: Britt Lode

Co-publisher: www.Root-Source.com

Published in 2016 by Oljetreet Publishing, Norway
www.Oljetreet.no - post@oljetreet.no

1 3 5 7 9 8 6 4 2

Gefen Books
11 Edison Place
Springfield, NJ 07081
516-593-1234
orders@gefenpublishing.com

Gefen Publishing House Ltd.
6 Hatzvi Street
Jerusalem 94386, Israel
972-2-538-0247
orders@gefenpublishing.com

www.gefenpublishing.com

Printed in Israel

The Light from Zion is dedicated to everyone who is waiting for the Kingdom of God to be restored and all glory and gratitude is given to the God of Israel.

It is You Who are my King, O God; command the salvations of Jacob! And to Jerusalem, Your city, may You return in compassion, and may You rest within it, as You have spoken. May You rebuild it soon in our days as an eternal structure, and may You speedily establish the throne of David within it. Blessed are You, LORD, the Builder of Jerusalem.

FOREWORD BY RABBI MOSHE GOLDSMITH

ABOUT A YEAR ago, I received a phone call from a friend asking me if I would speak with a non-Jewish woman from Norway who was interested in talking to a Rabbi. He mentioned to me that he knew her personally and that she was an active supporter of Israel. I agreed, and after our initial email correspondence, a Skype meeting was set up between us.

During our first Skype conversation Britt shared with me that, although she is a Christian, she felt a visceral connection with Torah and admired the way Orthodox Rabbis teach it. She mentioned her belief that the Christian world must be exposed to the powerful messages of Torah teachings, which in her opinion, will lead to Tikun Olam (world rectification). She asked me if I was willing to write a weekly essay on the Parasha which she would translate and circulate on her email list and I agreed.

In a subsequent conversation she mentioned her idea of putting out a book on the weekly Torah portions and asked me if I could finish within a years' time one essay on each Parshah. I told her that a year would not be enough time for me to write and edit all the portions. A few days later, she suggested getting twelve different Rabbis to write a few essays on the weekly portions, which would surely speed up the process in completing a book on the weekly Portions. I expressed my skepticism in the following way: Britt, you'll certainly have a tough time getting twelve Rabbis to agree to participate in such a project."

I was wrong! Due to her amazing enthusiasm and positive attitude she was able to make this happen. Hashem guided her in achieving a difficult task and overcoming the many obstacles that stood in her way.

Aside from the beautiful Torah messages brought down in this book, there's another lesson we shouldn't take for granted—the power of simple faith. It is a pure and uncomplicated faith that must guide us throughout our lives. This is the lesson that Britt Lode teaches through her own example.

Today we have the privilege of living in very special times—where we see an extraordinary awakening on the part of the nations and their need to connect to the light of the Torah. No doubt this is prophecy being fulfilled in our time.

> "Thus says the LORD of hosts: In those days it shall come to pass, that ten men shall take hold, out of all the nations, shall take hold of the hem of a Jewish man, saying: We will go with you, for we have heard that God is with you." (Zachariah 8:23)

When reading this verse it seems superfluous to say "take hold" twice. In my opinion, this is a hint that the nations will be drawn to the Torah through a gradual process. At first, they will take hold of experiments that the prophet chooses not to reveal—the many different pathways that the nations will traverse in their search for Hashem. Ultimately, as the prophet teaches, they will conclude that the answer to their quest lies in their connection with the Nation of Israel.

It is important to stress that this book is not meant for only non-Jewish readers.

I want to end with a supplication: Let it be that the powerful messages in this book reach the heart of millions, bringing them ever closer to the precious light of the Torah.

> "It will come about that In the end of days the mountain of the house of G-D will be established as the chief of the mountains, And will be raised above the hills; And all the nations will stream to it and many nations shall come, and say: "Come, let us go up to the mountain of G-D, to the house of the G-D of Jacob, that He may teach us His ways and that we may walk in his paths." For out of Zion shall come forth the Torah, and the word of G-D from Jerusalem." (Isaiah 2:2-3)

RABBI MOSHE GOLDSMITH
ITAMAR, SAMARIA

FOREWORD by GIDON ARIEL

FROM TIME TO time, a book is published, that in spite of its appearance otherwise, is earth shattering. You are holding such a book.

Truth be told, it is not really this book that is such a game changer, but the very world itself which has shifted so much in recent decades. I am especially alluding to the changes that the Jewish People have undergone, and how those changes impacted the Jews' relationship with the world around them.

There are a number of foundational events in the Biblical account of the Jewish People's history which could be called formative. Certainly the Exodus from Egypt and the Revelation at Sinai would show up on everyone's list; respectively, at these junctures the Children of Israel were emancipated from slavery and received the Torah, the divine document of commandment and relationship with God. Without a unique, unifying thing to do (Torah), and without the ability to do it (freedom), the Jews would at best be a nation like all others, and at worst not exist.

There is however, another verse that proclaims Israel's national establishment:

> "Then Moses and the Levitical priests said to all Israel, "Keep silence and hear, O Israel: this day you have become a people, the people of the LORD your God." (Deuteronomy 27, 9, English Standard Version, slight variation).

This verse is at the same time both explicit and cryptic. On the one hand, it defines the moment of peoplehood; on the other hand, what "day" is it actually referring to? It was spoken towards the end of their 40-year long sojourn in the desert, with no memorable, commemorated event nearby. And that day itself, if identifiable at all, is certainly not observed in any way.

Upon a more careful contextual reading, we can see that this verse is an introduction to the commandment of the ceremony of Mount Grizim and Mount Eival. This ceremony was to take place at the twin peaks of the city of Schchem, known today as Nablus (perhaps because of the difficulty of its pronunciation?), soon after the People's crossing of the Jordan River and their arrival into the Land of Israel. That event can be summed up by its last verse, 26: 'Cursed is he who doesn't confirm the words of this Torah to do them.' All the people shall say, 'Amen.' (World English Bible, replacing the word "law" with "Torah".)

Again, at first reading, this summary and the eleven verses preceding it would point to this event being a recap of the covenant at Sinai. But with other hints in the verses surrounding this one and the story of the actual event at Grizim and Eival, we can come to another, more comprehensive conclusion: This command is meant to consecrate that covenant when all three human aspects of it come together: the Torah of Israel, the People of Israel, and the Land of Israel.

These three components - the Torah, the People, and the Land, are the rope of three strands that cannot be unraveled (see Ecclesiastes 4:12). Even though we were exiled from our beloved Land for two thousand years, this was but a temporary glitch, and our nation never dropped our faith in God's covenant with us.

To return to our original question, what was the formative point of the Jewish People, we can arguably note a verse that brings together these three aspects in a gestative stage:

> "And the LORD said to Abram, "Go forth from your country, and from your place of birth, and from your father's house, to the Land which I will show you..." (Genesis 12:1, original translation)

God directed and commanded about the Land to Abram.

God, Torah, Land, People.

This commandment-covenant about the Land was repeated to Abram's son and grandson, Isaac and Jacob, who together with him comprise the Jewish People's three patriarchs. These three foundational ancestors are our three legged pedestal, whose relationship with God we invoke daily when praying to Him.

But Abram, of course, underwent a metamorphosis himself, when God swore

> "...this is my covenant with you: You will be the father of many nations. No longer will you be called Abram; your name will be Abraham, for I have made you a father of many nations." (Genesis 17:4-5, New International Version)

Notwithstanding some traditional Jewish commentaries assigning the meaning "twelve tribes of Jacob" to the term "multitude of nations," this covenant clearly refers to Abraham's universal legacy. A close reading of Abraham's activities and moral positions throughout the story of his life make it very clear that any subscriber to the ideals of ethical monotheism is his spiritual heir.

Today, we are witness to countless miracles. The industrial revolution, the information age, worldwide independence of nations, educational and political democracy—all these and more are signs of the maturing of the human race. Many of these can be traced back to the first revolutionary, our aforementioned father Abraham. And so his most important innovation—belief in the One True God—must also be included in this list, because more and more people are coming to a considered deep understanding of the importance that belief. And when people consider what is the greatest miracle of them all - the return of the Jewish People from the depths of their exile to their promised Land, as detailed in the Prophets - it is no wonder that so many of these thoughtful believers in the God of Abraham are drawn to His miraculous nation, the Jews, and their miraculous country, the modern State of Israel.

But of course, this development was plainly prophesied in Zechariah 8:23 (original translation):

> "Thus proclaims the Lord of Hosts, in those days, it will happen that ten people from each of all of the languages and cultures of the nations will hold tightly and grab on to the tzitzit (the ritual cloak fringes) of a Jewish person and say we are going to go with you Jews, because we understand that God is with you!"

Which brings us to this book, *The Light from Zion*. My good friend, Britt Lode, is a wonderful example of a person from those nations that Zechariah was talking about. Coming from the nearly Jew-free country of Norway, Britt (whose name, incredibly, means "covenant" in Hebrew!) heard the God of Abraham calling out to her, making it very clear that the way to Him is through His Jewish People. And thanks to the God-directed miracles of telephone, Internet, and Skype, Britt was able to reach out and find Jewish teachers who in turn were open and excited about connecting with and teaching non-Jews like her (a willingness that is no small miracle itself).

I am honored to have taken part in the publication of this book, a 100%

"kosher" presentation of Torah ideas taught by some of the top Torah teachers of our time. While it was Britt's dream to introduce traditional Jewish Torah to the Norwegian public, and in fact she is only publishing this book in English because it is an unavoidable on-the-way benefit of publishing it in Norwegian, I think that *The Light from Zion's* main innovation is its opening up the phenomenon of well known, traditional Israeli Orthodox Jewish teachers teaching Christians and other non-Jews Torah, for out of Zion must come the Torah and the Word of God from Jerusalem.

I translated the word "kanaf" in the prophecy of Zechariah as tzitzit, as opposed to hem, robe, sleeve, garment, etc., as it is usually translated in Christian editions of the Bible. This is understandable, because the concept of tzitzit, as presented in Numbers 15:37-41, is foreign to most Christians.

But besides being the self evident correct meaning of the verse (the word kanaf appears in Numbers 15:38 as it does in Zechariah), there is a fascinating possibility opened up by understanding the nations taking hold of the Jews' tzitzit.

Every tzitzit calls for four fringes, one on each corner of a four-cornered garment. Each fringe has eight strands, for a total of 32 strands per Jew. Zechariah's prophecy, then, assigns 320 non-Jews to every Jewish teacher.

If every Jew in the world entitled to move to Israel as per its Law of Return would do so today, there would be 23 million Jews living in Israel. Let every person alive today - 7.4 billion according to most estimates - grab onto a string of a Jew's kanaf with nine others, and we will see 320 non-Jews—every last one of them!—learning Torah from every Jew.

May it Be God's will that speedily in our day every Jew will recognize and realize his ability and responsibility to return to the Land of his Fathers, to the Torah of his God, and be a light tower of Torah knowledge for every single person on earth and "the earth shall be full of the knowledge of God as water covers the seas."

GIDON ARIEL
MAALE HEVER, HEBRON

The
AARONIC BLESSING

THE LORD SPOKE to Moses, saying,
"Speak to Aaron and his sons, saying: So shall you
bless the Children of Israel, saying to them:

'May the LORD bless you and safeguard you. May
the LORD illuminate His countenance for you and be
gracious to you. May the LORD lift His countenance to
you and establish peace for you.'

Let them place My Name upon the Children of Israel, and
I shall bless them."

NUMBERS 6: 22–27

HEBREW:

וידבר אדוני אל משה לאמר:

דבר אל אהרון ואל בניו לאמור:

כה תברכו את בני ישראל אמור להם:

יברכך אדוני וישמרך: יאר אדוני פניו אליך ויחונך:

ישא אדוני פניו אליך וישם לך שלום:

ושמו את שמי על בני ישראל ואני אברכם:

TABLE OF CONTENTS

Foreword by Rabbi Moshe Goldsmith 7
Foreword by Gidon Ariel 9
The Aaronic Blessing 13

PART 1 - INTRODUCTION

Introduction 21
Acknowledgements 27
Important Details 29
Introduction of Terms 31
The Shabbat Bride 35
The Foundation of the Faith 37

PART 2 - LESSONS
THE BOOK OF GENESIS — BERESHIT

BERESHIT 41
The Creation - Rabbi Gedalia Meyer

NOACH 47
Building a Tower of Hebrew - Rabbi Tuly Weisz

LECH-LECHA 51
What Really Motivates Christians who Support Israel? - Rabbi Tuly Weisz

VAYERA 55
The Secret of How to Find the Entrance to Paradise - Rabbi Chaim Richman

CHAYEI SARAH 59
Guarding the Inner Child - Rabbi Chanan Morrison

TOLEDOT 63
How to be in Love - Rabbi David Aaron

VAYETZE 69
Transformative Torah - Rabbi Yehoshua Friedman

VAYISHLACH 73
Being Here, Feeling There - Rabbi Levi Cooper

VAYESHEV 77
  Why is Life so Difficult? - Rabbi David Aaron

MIKETZ 83
  Insight - Rabbi Zelig Pliskin

VAYIGASH 89
  Yeridah for the Sake of Aliyah - Rabbi Moshe Lichtman

VAYECHI 93
  Revealing the End of Days – Rabbi Chanan Morrison

THE BOOK OF EXODUS - SHEMOT

SHEMOT. 101
  The Very First Righteous Gentiles - Rabbi Tuly Weisz

VA'EIRA 105
  What is a Fitting Legacy for My Children and Grandchildren? - Rabbi Shlomo Riskin

BO 109
  The Exodus - Rabbi Gedalia Meyer

BESHALACH 113
  The Splitting of the Sea and the Resurrection of the Dead - Rabbi Chaim Richman

YITRO 117
  Is it Kosher for Christians to Teach Torah?! - Rabbi Tuly Weisz

MISHPATIM 121
  An Eye for an Eye - Rabbi Chanan Morrison

TERUMAH 125
  Can Man Create Spiritual Reality that Transcends Physical Space? - Rabbi Chaim Richman

TETZAVEH. 131
  When Absence Proves Love - Rabbi Shlomo Riskin

KI TISA. 137
  The Golden Calf - Rabbi Gedalia Meyer

VAYAKHEL. 141
  Vanities and Virtues - Rabbi Shlomo Riskin

PEKUDEI 147
  Insight - Rabbi Zelig Pliskin

THE BOOK OF LEVITICUS - VAYIKRA

VAYIKRA 155
  The Truest and the Hardest Sacrifice: Admission of Guilt - Rabbi Shlomo Riskin

TZAV 159
  Post Prayer Refreshments - Rabbi Levi Cooper

SHEMINI 163
  Above the Rest - Rabbi Moshe Lichtman

TAZRIA 167
  The Power of the Tongue - Rabbi Moshe Goldsmith

METZORA 171
  An Open Heart and a Closed Hand - Rabbi Shlomo Riskin

ACHAREI MOT 177
  Insight - Rabbi Zelig Pliskin

KEDOSHIM 181
  Insight - Rabbi Zelig Pliskin

EMOR 189
  Sefirat HaOmer: What Really Counts - Rabbi Nathan Lopes Cardozo

BEHAR 193
  Bonding or Bondage Why Serve the Divine? - Rabbi David Aaron

BECHUKOTAI 197
  Satisfaction and the Art of Being – Rabbi Nathan Lopes Cardozo

THE BOOK OF NUMBERS - BEMIDBAR

BEMIDBAR 203
  The Disciple as Master - Rabbi Levi Cooper

NASO 207
  Not by Might nor by Power - Rabbi Moshe Lichtman

BEHA'ALOTECHA 211
  Great Dreams - Rabbi Chanan Morrison

SHLACH 215
  The Post-Trauma Victim - Rabbi Yehoshua Friedman

KORACH 219
  Beating Jealousy - Rabbi David Aaron

CHUKAT 223
  The Leader Must Respect His People: Kehal vs. Edah - Rabbi Shlomo Riskin

BALAK 227
The Prophet Balaam - Rabbi Gedalia Meyer

PINCHAS 233
The Perpetuity of Israel and the Danger of Assimilation - Rabbi Moshe Goldsmith

MATOT 237
The Dimensions of Prophecy and the Eternity of the Torah - Rabbi Nathan Lopes Cardozo

MASEI 241
A Match Made in Heaven - Rabbi Moshe Lichtman

THE BOOK OF DEUTERONOMY - DEVARIM

DEVARIM 247
Virtual Walls, Real Unity - Rabbi Levi Cooper

VA'ETCHANAN 251
Wisdom in the Eyes of the Nations - Rabbi Yehoshua Friedman

EIKEV 257
What is Up to God and What is Up to Humans? - Rabbi Shlomo Riskin

RE'EH 263
Experience the World to Come Today - Rabbi Moshe Goldsmith

SHOFTIM 267
The King's Torah Scroll - Rabbi Chanan Morrison

KI TEITZEI 271
The Fight for a 4,000-Year Old Marriage - Rabbi Nathan Lopes Cardozo

KI TAVO 275
There are Hearts of Stone, but there are Stones that are Hearts - Rabbi Moshe Goldsmith

NITZAVIM 281
Free Will - Rabbi Gedalia Meyer

VAYELECH 285
Song and Ecstasy in the Religious Experience - Rabbi Nathan Lopes Cardozo

HAAZINU 289
Insight - Rabbi Zelig Pliskin

V'ZOT HABERACHAH 295
Before the Eyes of All of Israel - Rabbi Chaim Richman

THE HOLIDAYS

ROSH HASHANA 303
  Broken Watches, Broken Souls - Rabbi Levi Cooper

YOM KIPPUR 307
  A Day of Atonement for All - Rabbi Moshe Goldsmith

SUKKOT 313
  The Joy of Hashem's Embrace - Rabbi Chaim Richman

SIMCHAT TORAH 319
  The Unyielding Sefer Torah - Rabbi Nathan Lopes Cardozo

PASSOVER 323
  Destroy Chametz, Gain Freedom - Rabbi Chanan Morrison

SHAVUOUT 327
  A Love Letter from the Divine - Rabbi David Aaron

CHANUKAH 331
  Praise God in The Land - Rabbi Moshe Lichtman

PURIM 335
  "Go Gather All the Jews" - Rabbi Chanan Morrison

TISHA B'AV 339
  A Time to Mourn, a Time to Build - Rabbi Chaim Richman

PART 3 - INTRODUCTION OF THE AUTHORS

RABBI DAVID AARON 346

RABBI DR. NATHAN LOPES CARDOZO 348

RABBI LEVI COOPER 350

RABBI YEHOSHUA FRIEDMAN 352

RABBI MOSHE GOLDSMITH 354

RABBI MOSHE D. LICHTMAN 356

RABBI GEDALIA MEYER 358

RABBI CHANAN MORRISON 360

RABBI ZELIG PLISKIN 362

RABBI CHAIM RICHMAN 364

RABBI SHLOMO RISKIN 366

RABBI NAPHTALI "TULY" WEISZ 368

INTRODUCTION

DEAR READER,

It is a great honor for me to introduce you to this very special book—or I should say this very special book project. As the editor I have been truly immersed in a goldmine, a treasure chamber, whilst preparing this book. By having the opportunity to read and get this close to the wisdom of Torah, it has made me taste its sweet flavors, and "its fruits are better than fine gold, even choice gold, and its produce is choicer than silver. It is more precious than pearls, and all your desires cannot compare to it" (Proverb 8:19 and 3:15)[1]. It is a treasure beyond our understanding and imagination, and I believe it is groundbreaking that so many different rabbis have shared from their wisdom and heart to make this treasure available for both Jews and all nations.

So why do I believe this book is so important?

I grew up in a Christian tradition in Norway, very far from Judaism and Israel. I had the privilege of hearing the stories and words of the Bible from I was born and I grew up with them. As a young adult I began to discover Israel and the Jews—much was thanks to enthusiastic pro Israel preachers I listened to—and I got a desire to study the stories in the Bible in greater depth. What is the Bible really telling us? I discovered that the Bible is the story about the Kingdom of Israel; the Kingdom of God. From the very beginning when God first called Abraham, to the very heights when David and Solomon were the kings of Israel. Then to the downfall when first ten of the twelve tribes were taken captive by Assyria and later on when the last tribe, the tribe of Judah, the Jews, were taken captive by Babylon. Judah came back for a short time, before they had to go out in to Diaspora for a second time, while the ten tribes are still "lost" to this day. It's a dramatic and engaging story full of intrigues, love, jealousy, forgiveness, punishment, promises, disappointment and everything else that life offers us all. What I find most interesting is that this Kingdom, according to the Bible, has not ended. The story is not finished, and the best

---

1 All scriptures are from *The Stone Edition – Tanach* by ArtScroll, slightly changed by replacing HASHEM with the LORD.

part is yet to come! Something more fascinating is that even though Jews and Christians have some differences, we both believe in the God of Abraham, Isaac and Jacob; we both believe in the Word of God and we both have the same goal or vision; we are longing for the redemption and we are waiting for the Kingdom of God—we want to see it restored!

The big question is: how do we get there? For a very long time the Kingdom has lain in ruins, far from the glory it once had. Today, even if we see progress in the right direction—the State of Israel is established, many Jews have moved to Israel, the Hebrew language has been revived, people are searching for the knowledge of Torah and more—the Kingdom is still far from its glorious highlight. The question is; where is the key to the restoration? How can we find the paths that lead to this ancient and mysterious Kingdom? Is it possible to find them? Even if the situation may look dark and impossible, there is still no doubt that the restoration will come, because the word of God talks about it over and over again:

> "For behold, days are coming-the word of the LORD—when I will return the captivity of My people Israel and Judah, said the LORD, and I will return them to the land that I gave their forefathers, and they will possess it." "They will serve the LORD their God and David their king, whom I will establish over them." Jeremiah 30:3, 9 (see also Zechariah 14:9, Isaiah 35:10, Jeremiah 32:37-44, Jeremiah 16:14-15, Amos 9:11-15, Ezekiel chapter 36 and 37.)

I believe the secret to finding the key of the restoration is to look into the past and learn; look at the path that the children of Israel took when they went away from God and to return the same path (Jeremiah 31:20/31:21). "Since the days of your forefathers you have veered away from My laws and you have not observed them. Return to Me and I will return to You! Says the LORD, Master of Legions" (Malachi 3:7). There is no doubt what happened. The children of Israel went away from God and His commandments. The Kingdom became lawless. The people of Israel went off the path, went away from His word, His law, His Torah. The foundations of the Kingdom were destroyed and the result was the end of the Kingdom. God closed and hid the paths of the Kingdom from us, as He says: "I will hedge your ways with thorns, and I will hem her in with a fence, and she will not find her paths" (Hosea 2:8/2:6).

We know that the foundations of every society are made up of its constitution, laws and regulations. They have an important function in stabilizing society so its people can live good and peaceful lives. To respect the laws is also to respect the leader and the leadership in the society. In the Kingdom of God, the laws are even more important because they are an expression of love, it is a Kingdom of love. The Kingdom itself is compared to a marriage and the Ten Commandments are our marriage covenant. The Ten Commandments are also the constitution for the Kingdom. They can be summed up in the royal law: "To love your God with all your heart, with all your soul, and with all your resources," and "to love your neighbor as yourself" (Deuteronomy 6:5 and Leviticus 19:18). The foundation of the Kingdom is love; if you love the King, you will keep His commandments , and that is our way of showing love for our beloved Father (see Exodus 4:22 and Jeremiah 31:9), our Husband (Isaiah 54:5), and our King (Isaiah 43:15). He who cares for all our needs and loves us with an eternal love (see Jeremiah 31:2/31:3). There is absolutely no doubt that He recalls our first love and that He will betroth us to Him forever (Jeremiah 2:2 and Hosea 2:21/2:19). The question is whether we recall our love for Him.

> According to R' Yehudah Halevi (1075-1141), the Torah itself is the king, for it is Israel's ultimate authority. When Scripture laments that there was no king in Israel (Judges 18:1), it means that the people lagged in their obedience to the Torah. Indeed, for one to say that he believes in God but not in His Torah is the same as denying God Himself, for a king without authority is not a king (*The Stone Edition*, Chumash page 1114).

What we need to do is find our way back to our first love. We need to return the same road we came down; we need to ask where to find the good paths. "Thus said the LORD: Stand on the roads and see; ask about the various paths of history, which path is best, and walk on it and find solace for your soul" (Jeremiah 6:16). "Your word is a lamp for my feet and a light for my path" (Psalms 119:105). We need to return to our God, listen to His voice and do everything He has commanded us to do.

> "It will be that when all these things come upon you—the blessing and the curse that I have presented before you—then you will take it to your heart among all the nations where the LORD, your God, has dispersed you; and

you will return unto the LORD, your God, and listen to His voice, according to everything that I command you today, you and your children, with all your heart and all your soul. **Then** the LORD, your God will bring back your captivity and have mercy upon you, and He will gather you in from all the peoples to which the LORD, your God, has scattered you. If your dispersed will be at the ends of heaven, from there the LORD, your God, will gather you in and from there He will take you. The LORD, your God, will bring you to the Land that your forefathers possessed and you shall possess it; He will do good to you and make you more numerous than your forefathers. The LORD, your God, will circumcise your heart and the heart of your offspring, to love the LORD, your God, with all your heart and with all your soul, that you may live" (Deuteronomy 30:1-10).

God wants our obedience and hearts, that we walk humble with Him. It is very logical: the key to the Kingdom is to find the paths and walk them, and the path is the Torah, the commandments of God. So the question is; who can teach us how to walk the paths today? Who can teach us everything that God has commanded us? It is a very long time since the revelation at Sinai where Moses received the commandments from God, so where can we find the knowledge and wisdom about them today? Baruch HaShem (thank God), God has organized everything very well in His Kingdom. The King Himself has entrusted the tribe of Judah, the Jews, with the very words of God. He gave them the authority and mandate to administer and take care of the law (Genesis 49:10). And He has kept the Jews alive, no one remained except the tribe of Judah in the Kingdom (2 Kings 17:18). They did not "get lost" like the other ten tribes. They have preserved the Torah very well, not even one generation has failed in protecting and keeping the wisdom and treasures of Torah and in passing it on to the next generation. Today's rabbis are the representatives for the Torah, the law, in our times. They are our connection to Moses and Mount Sinai. They are sitting in the seat of Moses. They represent the paths and roads of the Kingdom and they give us a unique chance to find the hidden paths. I believe the key to restoring this ancient and glorious Kingdom is to realize the amazing treasure the Jews have preserved for us and "take hold of the corner of the garment of a Jewish man and say: "Let us go with you, for we have heard that God is with you!" (Zechariah 8:12). I believe we need to call out and say: "Arise, let us ascend to Zion, to the LORD our God" (Jeremiah

31:5/31:6). And let us hope and pray that we will see the days speedily in our time that the prophets have spoken about when "The mountain of the Temple of the LORD will be firmly established as the head of the mountains, and it will be exalted above the hills, and all the nations will stream to it. Many peoples will go and say, 'Come, let us go to the Mountain of the LORD, to the Temple of the God of Jacob, and He will teach us of His ways and we will walk in His paths.' For from Zion will the Torah come forth, and the word of the LORD from Jerusalem" (Isaiah 2:2-3).

Someone could say; but isn't it enough that the Jews keep these commandments and live according to the Word of God? Don't forget that the Jews do not represent all of Israel. To restore the Kingdom to its fullness, I believe that all the "lost" children of Israel, those that have lost their identity and are scattered all over the world today, also need to hear the Word. For Israel to rise to its highest calling, all the twelve tribes must be reunified, Only then can we reach our ultimate goal. As Rabbi Zelig Pliskin says in his book "Growth through Torah:" "Only when there is unity among the descendants of Jacob can there be redemption." We need to strive for unity, and the Torah will be our guidance. God commanded ALL of Israel to keep the Torah; "Remember the Torah of Moses My servant, which I commanded him at Horeb for **all of Israel**—[its] decrees and [its] statutes" (Malachi 3:22/4:4). And as we mentioned earlier, the prophecies of the end of days talk about all the twelve tribes as one Kingdom (See Ezekiel 37:15-28). And since we can't know for sure who or where they are right now, we need to reach out to everyone in the world. In addition, we must not forget that the ultimate goal is to bring the light of the Torah out to all the nations in the world as it says in Isaiah 2: "For from Zion will the Torah come forth, and the word of the LORD from Jerusalem" and Isaiah 49:6: "[to] make you a light unto the nations".

My hope and prayer is that this book will be used as a tool in the "restoration of paths" (Isaiah 58:12) and to help "clear the road and remove the obstacle from the path of the Children of Israel" (Isaiah 57:14) in the Kingdom we are waiting for. I believe that when the paths and roads are restored and we walk on them—we will be able to reach the ultimate goal—the restoration of the Kingdom itself. May this book also be a tool to reunite the twelve tribes of Israel—of the Kingdom—and bringing peace to our world (Isaiah 2:4). May we all cry out to the King of this glorious Kingdom and say: "Lead me on the path of Your commandments, for that is my desire" (Psalm 119:35). And may we all hear the voice that whispers: "This is the path, walk in it" (Isaiah 30:21).

O House of Jacob: Come, let us walk by the light of the LORD! (Isaiah 2:5).

BRITT LODE,
OLJETREET (THE OLIVE TREE)
VARHAUG, NORWAY

ACKNOWLEDGMENTS

THERE ARE NO words to express the gratitude I feel in my heart towards everyone who has contributed and helped create this book. I am very grateful and humbled by the result and believe this book is filled with a lot of light, spirit and power.

First of all, I want to thank my Abba and my King who wakes me every morning and blesses me with the fullness of life; who has put this book project on my heart and has sent me wonderful people to help me complete the task. Without Him I cannot do anything, and only by His grace has He sustained me and enabled me to complete this mission. I give all my thanks to The LORD for He is good; He that open up doors that no man can open; His kindness endures forever! "Blessed is the LORD, God of Israel, from This World to the World to Come! The LORD reigns!" (Excerpts from 1 Chronicles 16:31-36).

A very special thanks to Rabbi Moshe Goldsmith, Gidon Ariel and Murray McLaren who have stood faithfully by my side the whole time. They have willingly given me their time and wisdom, and have always been available when I needed their help. You have been essential for the success of this project. I am so grateful for all your efforts, may you all be abundantly blessed in everything you do.

Again, words are not enough to describe my gratitude towards the twelve rabbis involved in this project. You are all administrators of the treasures of Heaven and appointed and trusted servants of the Almighty. You have all given from your heart, your wisdom and your knowledge. Even if you have been very busy, you have all given of your precious time to make the wisdom of Torah available and accessible for our readers. May you all be rewarded greatly by the LORD for your important contribution and willingness, in this world as well as in the world to come.

In addition, there are numerous amazing and special people that have helped in different ways to make this project a reality. I am so grateful to each and every one that has given of their time, wisdom and guidance. May The LORD reward you by opening up the windows of the heavens and pouring out upon you blessings without end.

Last, but not least, thank you to everyone that opens up this book and reads it—by this you are making this mission complete. I hope and pray that you will discover the treasures and sweet taste of the Torah. May the King of Israel let the words in this book touch your heart and bless you and your surroundings.

This mission would not be completed without the help of you all. May the King of Israel reward each and everyone with all the blessings in the Torah, and may we all be worthy of seeing the Kingdom of Israel restored speedily in our time to its proper glory and power, amen!

IMPORTANT DETAILS

THE ESSAYS YOU will find in this book are based on traditional and basic rabbinical understanding. All of the rabbis who wrote the essays in this book are educated in the same tradition, the Orthodox Jewish tradition. Yet each still speaks in his own voice, and it has been important for us to keep all of these individual voices and expressions. You will therefore find that all the essays have their own style, as each rabbi is on his own journey, has his unique background and has his special talents. This gives you a unique insight into the different work and thoughts of the rabbis and how they all complement each other.

This book project is a non-profit project and all the rabbis and the project team members have worked for free. We have all done it from our heart and because of our love for the Word of God. If there is some income from this project, it will be used to support needy children and families in Israel.

A great deal of thought has been put into the layout of this book and it is inspired by two different ideas that complement each other. The first idea is that the Word of Torah is the true nutrition for our soul. The introduction for each parasha (Torah portion) can therefore be seen as a menu: to get spiritual growth you need proper spiritual food. And the words of Torah, of the Bible, are your life (Deuteronomy 32:46,47). "Not by bread alone does man live, rather by everything that emanates from the mouth of God does man live" (Deuteronomy 8:3).

The other idea of the layout is based on the Kingdom of God. The Bible is the story of His Kingdom, and we are waiting for the restoration and redemption when there again will be a King in Jerusalem for the united twelve tribes of Israel, and there will be peace in the world. The cover design is based on the scriptures of Ezekiel 37:22, Zechariah 14:9, Micah 4:7 and Isaiah 2:2-5 among others. The final redemption is also compared to a wedding (see Isaiah 61:4,5) and the introduction to each parasha can additionally be seen as a wedding invitation. The Torah is the way to the redemption, to the final wedding. Every Shabbat is also a taste of the redemption and the World to Come, the final wedding; and the Shabbat is also called "the bride". See "The Shabbat Bride," page 35...

Please remember that this book is holy and should not be mistreated. Treat it with respect – do not read it in the bathroom or dispose of it.

29

INTRODUCTION OF TERMS

NAME OF GOD

We do not write God's name in a place where it may be discarded or erased. Treating God's name with reverence is a way to give respect to God. According to Jewish law and tradition, the various names for our Creator are all considered holy and must be treated with the utmost respect. Because of this, many Jews substitute "God" with "G-d" so that they can erase or dispose of the writing without showing disrespect to God.

The name HASHEM, which literally means *the name*, is used to refer to the Tetragrammaton (YHWH). It is often translated as *the Lord* in biblical translations.

PARASHA

Each week in synagogue, we read (or, more accurately, chant, because it is sung) a passage or portion from the Torah. This passage is referred to as a *parasha*. The first parasha, for example, is Parashat Bereishit, which covers from the beginning of Genesis to the story of Noah. There are 54 parashas (parashiyot), one for each week of a leap year, so that in the course of a year, we read the entire Torah (Genesis to Deuteronomy) in our services. During non-leap years, there are 50 weeks, so some of the shorter portions are doubled up. We reach the last portion of the Torah around a holiday called Simchat Torah (Rejoicing in the Law), which occurs in September or October, a few weeks after Rosh Hashanah (New Year). On Simchat Torah, we read the last portion of the Torah, and proceed immediately to the first paragraph of Genesis, showing that the Torah is a circle, and never ends.

TORAH

The word *Torah* can mean different things in different contexts. In its most limited sense, *Torah* refers to the Five Books of Moses: Genesis, Exodus, Leviticus, Numbers, and Deuteronomy. But the word *Torah* can also be used to refer to the entire Hebrew Bible (the body of scripture known to non-Jews as the Old Testament and to Jews as the Tanakh or Written Torah), or in its broadest sense, to the whole body of Jewish law and teachings.

TANAKH

Tanakh is an acronym of *Torah* (Law), *Nevi'im* (Prophets) and *Ketuvim* (Writings). It is the written Torah; what non-Jews call the Old Testament.

SHABBAT

Shabbat is the most important ritual observance in our faith. It is the only ritual observance instituted in the Ten Commandments. It is also the most important special day, even more important than Yom Kippur. This is suggested by the fact that more aliyoth (opportunities for congregants to be called up to the Torah) are given on Shabbat than on any other day. Leviticus 23 which lists the festivals begin by mentioning the Shabbat, thus making the Shabbat the prologue to the holy convocation.

Shabbat is primarily a day of rest and spiritual enrichment. The word *Shabbat* comes from the root Shin-Bet-Tav, meaning to cease, to end, or to rest. It is a precious gift from God, a day of great joy eagerly awaited throughout the week, a time when we can set aside all of our weekday concerns and devote ourselves to higher pursuits. In Jewish literature, poetry, and music, Shabbat is described as a bride or queen, as in the popular Shabbat hymn Lecha Dodi Likrat Kallah (come, my beloved, to meet the [Sabbath] bride).

Shabbat involves two interrelated commandments: to remember (zachor) the Shabbat, and to observe (shamor) the Shabbat. It is said "more than Israel has kept Shabbat, Shabbat has kept Israel."

MITZVOT

Mitzvot is the Hebrew word for commandments; *mitzvah* is its singular form. It refers to the 613 commandments that are found in the Torah. It can also refer to any Jewish religious obligation, or more generally to any good deed.

TALMUD

In addition to the written scriptures we have an *Oral Torah*, a tradition explaining what the Five Books of Moses mean and how to interpret them and apply the Laws. Orthodox Jews believe God taught the Oral Torah to Moses, and he taught it to others, and others taught it to others down to the present day. This tradition was maintained in oral form only until about the 2d century C.E., when much of the oral law was compiled and written down in a document called the Mishnah.

Over the next few centuries, authoritative commentaries elaborating on the Mishnah and recording the rest of the oral law were written down in Israel and Babylon. These additional commentaries are known as the Tosefta, Mekhileta, Sifra, Sifre, Jerusalem Talmud, and Babylonian Talmud. The last was completed at about 500 C.E.

The two largest works are the Jerusalem Talmud and the Babylonian Talmud. The Babylonian one is more comprehensive, and is the one most people mean when they refer to The Talmud.

MIDRASH

Midrash is an ancient commentary on part of the Hebrew scriptures that is based on Jewish methods of interpretation and attached to the biblical text.

KOSHER

Kosher means literally; fit, proper, or correct. It describes food that is permissible to eat under Jewish dietary laws. It can also describe any other ritual object that is fit for use according to Jewish law.

HASIDIC (CHASSIDIC)

A branch of Orthodox Judaism founded by Rabbi Israel Baal Shem Tov (1698-1760), stressing service of G-d through the mystical in addition to the legalistic dimension of Judaism, the power of joy, love of G-d and one's fellow, emotional involvement in prayer, finding G-dliness in every aspect of one's existence, and the elevation of the material universe.

Hasidism (Chassidism) is the teachings and philosophy of this movement.

MOSHE RABEYNU

Moshe Rabeynu is Rabbi Moses in Hebrew and refers to Moses of the Torah.

THE SHABBAT BRIDE

THE FRIDAY EVENING liturgical song *Lechah Dodi* compares the Shabbat to a bride: *"Come my friend, toward the bride; let us greet the Shabbat."* What does this metaphor teach us?

A TASTE OF THE WORLD TO COME

The Shabbat is a time of closeness to Torah and spiritual enlightenment. Through the light of our *neshamah yeteirah*, our special 'Shabbat soul,' we are able to grasp that which was distant and concealed from us during the weekdays.

This special receptiveness to Torah on the Shabbat is similar to the feelings of a bride toward her new husband. The bride does not know her husband in a deep, intimate way, the way a wife married for many years does. Yet there is an excitement and tremendous joy in the bride's love, which stems from the newness of the relationship.

The Talmud in *Berachot* 57b teaches that the Shabbat is a 'taste of the World to Come.' One day a week we can 'taste' some of the holiness and knowledge that will fill the world in the future era, a time of pure and continual Shabbat.

Our weekly Shabbat does not have the depth of enlightenment that will grace the World to Come, but there is a delight of newness, like the excitement and elation of a young bride. This bridal joy is particularly appropriate at the very start of the Shabbat, as we celebrate to greet her with *Lechah Dodi*.

The future world will also be blessed with a newlywed joy, as it says, *"God will rejoice over you as a groom rejoices over his bride."* This joy will be the product of an enlightenment that grows continually brighter, as the souls in the World to Come rejoice in their constant renewal and elevation.

From *Silver from the Land of Israel*, pp. 29-30. Adapted from *Olat Re'iyah* vol. II, p. 21

THE
FOUNDATION
OF THE FAITH

G OD, TRUSTWORTHY KING.

"Hear, O Israel: The LORD is our God, the LORD is the One and Only. You shall love the LORD, your God, with all your heart, with all your soul, and with all your resources."

DEUTERONOMY 6: 4–5

Blessed is the Name of His glorious kingdom for all eternity.

HEBREW:

אל מלך נאמן

שמע ישראל אדוני אלוהינו אדוני אחד

ואהבת את אדוני אלוהיך בכל לבבך ובכל נפשך ובכל מאודך

ברוך שם כבוד מלכותו לעולם ועד

GENESIS ✦ BERESHIT

PARASHAT
BERESHIT

In The Beginning
Genesis 1:1-6:8

בראשית

BERESHIT

TORAH LESSON BY
RABBI GEDALIA MEYER

THE CREATION

'In the beginning God created the heavens and the earth.' (Genesis 1:1)

THESE MAY BE the most famous words ever communicated in the human language. This may be the deepest, most profound and most complete thought ever expressed. This may also be the simplest answer to the ultimate question, so it is fitting that the Torah begins with these words. What could be more natural and more expected than the Bible, the ancient book whose central purpose is to tell us the relationship of God to the world, opening with the story of creation?

Let us examine these words one by one to understand what was really being conveyed with that sentence. It is only ten words in English and probably about the same in most other European languages. In Hebrew there are only seven words, and two of them are nothing more than grammatical constructs that are necessary to introduce the following word and are not really translated into western language.

The first Hebrew word is *Bereshit*, which is almost always translated as 'In the beginning'. But a question must be asked of this simple introductory phrase—in the beginning of what? Why does the Torah simply say the phrase 'in the beginning' without telling us what had begun? An easy answer to this question is to say that it was the beginning of everything. But this only begs the question—why didn't the Torah say this? Why did it leave out the word 'everything'?

Perhaps the answer to this question is contained in the second Hebrew word, *bara*, which means 'created' (in Hebrew the verb frequently comes before the noun). Creation, according to Judaism, is not to simply make some new gadget; it is the process of causing something to be. It is commonly expressed in Jewish thought as 'something from nothing'. That is what creation really is—the almost mystical concept of transforming nothing into something. We imitate this process ourselves when we think up a new idea or imagine something that wasn't there before. This is how the Bible describes the beginning of the universe. There was nothing and then there was something.

There is no real connection between these two states—the state of nothing and the state of something. There is no rational explanation as to how this miracle can happen; nothing becoming something. How does nothing become something? If one wish to look for miracles in life and has trouble believing that they actually happen, one need to look no further than the very reality of our existence. It was, and continues to be, an act of creation—something emerging from nothing. This, perhaps, is why the Torah does not start with the words; 'In the beginning *of everything*, God created (...)', but merely states; 'In the beginning God created (...)'. There was nothing on the other side of that beginning, and this is the act of creation in all its glory.

The next word in the verse is God. There are a few Hebrew names for God in the Torah. The name used throughout the creation narrative (the first chapter of Genesis) is *Elohim*. This name suggests God's image as the divine power for whom even creating the universe is the most natural of acts. This is not the most common name for God in the Torah, that honor belongs to a name made up of four Hebrew letters which Jewish tradition forbids pronouncing directly. Jews substitute the title/name *Adonai* (meaning 'my Lord') when it is used in prayer or Torah recital. At all other times they use the term *Hashem*, or 'the Name'. The combination of names is confusing for some, but Jews have long believed that they are nothing more than different images of the one divine being commonly called God. The same God, who has the image of the Creator, has a parallel and more personal image of a Lord. Belief in one God, monotheism, is the defining characteristic of Judaism. God has many names and many images, but only one essence.

The final words of the verse refer to the result of the creation. The Torah describes the byproducts as the 'heavens and the earth'. Today this may seem like a limited scope for what we now know as the infinite universe and the great complexity of all that is contained within it. The Torah, however, was written for all generations. When it was first given, this was the extent of the human conception of universe—it consisted of the heavens and the earth. The heavens contained the sun, moon, and stars, and the earth was the arena for life. We may know a great deal more about the vastness of the universe than people did thousands of years ago, but both then and now, it was/is the arena for our existence and the soil of life. How fitting a description of the very first act of creation. This simple and profound verse contains the source of our being and the seeds of life.

What did God do next? Was there any role left for God following that first moment of creation? Many people today, even among those who still acknowledge the necessity of a Creator, will claim that God has played no role in the universe since its very inception. This creation story, however, does not end with this short but immensely powerful verse The following verse takes us right to the next stage: "And the earth was desolate and empty and darkness was on the face of the depths, and the spirit of God hovered over the surface of the waters. And God said, 'Let there be light', and there was light."

Desolate and empty, darkness, the spirit of God, light—why was this the next stage after the initial act of creation? Creation, it seems, is not a one-act play. It is not a Big Bang that somehow ejects everything into existence and allows it to go its merry way, perhaps following some fixed physical laws that govern all future conditions. According to the Bible, it never ceases to involve the hidden or revealed hand of God. With this simple description the Bible tells us that creation is not an instantaneous moment but a never-ending process. God didn't disappear after the moment of creation—God hovered in the darkness until the time arrived for the next great injection of divine power. "Let there be light."

When all is dark and desolate, the spirit of God is there hovering over the void waiting to bring light. This was true at the initial stages of creation and it remains true today. We may not recognize God's spirit hovering within and around our lives but that does not mean that it is not there. Light comes in many forms, only one of which happens to be the electromagnetic waves that enable us to see. Light may be invisible to the naked eye or it may be too blinding to look at directly. It may also come in more 'spiritual' forms, which cannot be detected by any physical means, but which are just as real as their electromagnetic cousin.

Is there any more appropriate post-creation role for God the Creator than to be the Revealer of light? It may not have all the mystery of 'something-from-nothing', but it is certainly just as essential to our lives. The initial creation may have brought everything into existence, but existence can be pretty desolate and empty without God. Bringing light into the world is just as godly as bringing the world into being. God could not play one role without playing the other.

Perhaps it is appropriate that human beings—the final stage in the creation narrative of the Bible, are the single creation described as being 'in the image of God'. We therefore, perhaps uniquely, share both of these divine roles. We create in our own limited ways. We may not create a universe but we do play a significant part in creating our own world. We also have the constant challenge of bringing light into the dark, desolate and empty areas of our world. We face these moments all the time and frequently feel helpless and hopeless as we sense their depth. But we know that through it all, no matter how empty life may seem at times, there is an endless supply of light waiting our discovery. This light was revealed by God from the beginning, and we have been allowed a part in bringing its presence to our world. "Let there be light."

PARSHAT
NOACH

GENESIS 6:9–11:32

נח

NOAH (REST)

TORAH LESSON BY
RABBI TULY WEISZ

BUILDING A TOWER OF HEBREW

A N AMAZING REASON for Jews and non-Jews to study Hebrew emerges from the lesson of the Tower of Babel found in this week's Torah portion.

The whole earth was of one language and one common purpose... And they said, "Come let us build us a city, and a tower with its top in the heavens, and let us make a name for ourselves." (Genesis 11:1,4)

ויהי כל הארץ שפה אחת ודברים אחדים...

ויאמרו הבה נבנה לנו עיר ומגדל וראשו בשמים ונעשה לנו שם

בראשית יא:א,ד

Right after the famous story of Noah's flood in Genesis 11, we read about the mysterious saga of the Tower of Babel. The people of Babel join forces to build an impressive tower, but anger God in the process and are punished severely as a result. What is unclear however is what was so bad about the Tower of Babel? The people had one language and were united for a common purpose: to build a city and a tower—seemingly positive, constructive acts that sound nice. Nevertheless, the commentators say that the following sentence: "Let us build for ourselves a name" shows their desire to build a monument for humanity to prominently display the achievements of man, without acknowledging the Creator above. Jewish commentators go even further and say that the people wanted to build a tower either to hold up the heavens to prevent another flood, or to fight against God. Their misplaced purpose was to unite man against God. The punishment for the people's sin of rebellion and failure to acknowledge God as the Creator was to be scattered across the earth with their language diversified so they could no longer communicate as one.

The intriguing story of the Tower of Babel is a paradigm for Jewish history. King Solomon built the Temple in Jerusalem, a building of tremendous glory. Rabbi Yaakov Medan points out that King Solomon "did not build with the intention, heaven forbid, of using it as a base to wage war against God; on the contrary, he built a house so that God could dwell in it. Its stones did not reach the heavens, but its essence and purpose certainly ascended there." However, much later, when the Jewish people err and sin, God punishes them with the destruction of the Temple and by scattering the Jewish people to the four corners of the earth.

Rabbi Shlomo Riskin of the Center for Jewish-Christian Understanding and Cooperation explains that "unlike the people of the Tower of Babel, the Israelites will remain united as one nation with one sacred language and a universal ideal despite their far-flung Diaspora." Despite being scattered to the four corners of the earth, God will ultimately return His people to His land as it says in Deuteronomy: "If your dispersed will be at the ends of heaven, from there the Lord, your God, will gather you in and from there He will take you. The Lord, your God, will bring you to the Land that your forefathers possessed and you shall possess it." (Deuteronomy 30:4,5)

There is one final lesson that ties together the account of the Tower of Babel with the return of the people of Israel to the land of Israel, and it is found in Hebrew: The language of Israel. We know that every word of the Bible has infinite meaning; however, the true essence of the Torah can only fully be appreciated by understanding Biblical Hebrew. When you look closely at the Hebrew words used to introduce the Tower of Babel story, something incredible appears.

Chapter 11, verse 1 says that "the whole earth was of one language and one common purpose." The Hebrew word for "language," שפה (sa-FA), is a key word, like hyperlink, which reminds an astute Bible student of another time when "sa-FA" is used, much later in the Torah. In Zephaniah 3:9 the prophet describes how all the nations of the world will have "purity of speech" in the end of days: "For then I will change the nations [to speak] a language of purity so that they all will proclaim the Name of God, to worship Him with a united resolve." Jewish tradition has always maintained that the "pure language" (sa-FA beru-RA) that Zephaniah promises is the language of Hebrew.

The ultimate purpose of the return of the Jewish people to the Land is to serve God and to correct the sin of Babel, and to speak the one "language of purity," Hebrew. And in those days of redemption, not just the Jews, but all the people of the world will learn the Hebrew language. Over the last century, the Jewish people have miraculously revived Hebrew, long considered to be a dead language. The famous pedestrian mall in the center of Jerusalem,

Ben-Yehuda street is named after the father of modern Hebrew—Eliezer Ben-Yehuda (1858 – 1922).

Moreover, miracle of miracles, today there is a strong and growing Christian interest in learning Hebrew. Many non-Jews are drawn to the original language of the Bible we share, hoping to gain new insights into their faith. Perhaps the growing interest by Christian Zionists in the Hebrew language is the next step towards the time of redemption described by Zephaniah. Unlike in the generation of Babel's time, nations are now coming together to serve God through the "language of purity." With Jews and Christians reconciling for the first time in history, may our sense of unity not be for the glory of man, but may we study together the language of Hebrew to build a great tower to the One True God of Israel.

PARASHAT
LECH LECHA

Go forth, yourself!

GENESIS 12:1–17:27

LECH LECHA

TORAH LESSON BY
RABBI TULY WEISZ

WHAT REALLY MOTIVATES CHRISTIANS WHO SUPPORT ISRAEL?

AS AN ORTHODOX rabbi originally from the American Midwest, I didn't always get to meet too many Bible-belt Christian fundamentalists. However, I ran into an elderly Christian woman in Atlanta exactly two years ago whose words still ring loudly in my head. The frail but feisty lady had a bulky cast on her arm, so I told her I hoped she feels better soon and that God should bless her. Without missing a beat, "I'm already blessed," she replied, "God blesses me because I bless Israel."

The church where I met her, on a busy Atlanta street, not only proudly displayed eight enormous Israeli flags on their front lawn, but a banner broadcasting to the thousands of cars whizzing by each day: "I will bless those who bless you." (Genesis 12:3) Many Evangelical Christian Zionists consider Genesis 12:3 their main mantra, and for many Jews, it is known as the beginning of this week's Torah portion.

God's famous first words to Abraham, commands him to seek out the Promised Land, and continues by offering a Divine guarantee that, "I will bless those who bless you and curse those who curse you." (v. 3)

Millions of Christians take those words seriously and literally, doing everything they can to "bless" the State of Israel and the Jewish people in order to reap Divine reward and benefit from His blessing. In his book, *In Defense of Israel*, Pastor John Hagee, founder of *Christians United for Israel*, has a chapter called "Our Debt to the Jews." Hagee points to Genesis 12:3 as the secret to Jewish success and prosperity. "Based on the population of the Jews in proportion to the rest of the world, it's surprising that we hear about them at all beyond a brief mention in a high-school geography class."

Hagee continues with a reference that has even more meaning with this year's Nobel Prize announcements (2013) that four out of the six recipients are Jewish. He writes, "Yet throughout history, Jews have been at the center of the world's creative, scientific, and cultural achievements. They are disproportionately high as Nobel Prize recipients, they are over represented in the field of medicine, and their contributions in the area of scientific research are staggering."

Throughout history, Genesis 12:3 has been one of those Divine laws of nature. Jews have always understood this, but now Christian ministers are preaching about how countries that have welcomed Jews have been blessed with material wealth and success. Yet as soon as those very same countries turn their backs on the Jews and embrace discrimination and persecution, their days are numbered. God's blessings invariably turn into curses, and those nations are shoved off the world stage in one way or another, becoming just another footnote in history.

Some Jews don't know what to make of Christian support for Israel, and often respond with profound suspicion, if not outright hostility. "What really is their agenda?" they ask. "What is really motivating them?" they want to know. My brief conversation with that little old lady demonstrated to me that their agenda is simply trying to earn God's blessings. Sure, it's hard for many Jews to believe that after centuries of church-instigated "curses" directed towards our people, millions of Christians are suddenly so interested in becoming a source of blessing. But they truly are.

The promise to Abraham concludes, "and all the families of the earth shall bless themselves through you." We've been waiting so long for these times. Now that millions of Christians worldwide are looking to actualize Genesis 12:3 and bless the Jewish people, our response should not be one of cynicism, but of awe and appreciation.

PARASHAT
VAYERA

And He appeared

Genesis 18:1-22:24

וירא

VAYERA

TORAH LESSON BY
RABBI CHAIM RICHMAN

THE SECRET OF HOW TO FIND THE ENTRANCE TO PARADISE

"And Hashem appeared to him in the plains of Mamre while he was sitting at the entrance of the tent in the heat of the day." (Genesis 18:1)

OUR PARASHA OPENS with G-d appearing before Abraham as he is sitting at the entrance of his tent. Our sages teach that this takes place on the third day following his circumcision, and that G-d Himself was there to fulfill the mitzvah of visiting the sick. The third day after the operation is the most painful day for everyone, and let's not forget that Abraham was ninety-nine years old.

The Holy One, blessed be He, and our father Abraham were having a conversation, the contents of which are not disclosed. Then, the most amazing thing happens: Abraham looks up and sees three men, ordinary wayfarers—even idolaters, as far as he knows—and he jumps up to quickly bestow some of his famous hospitality upon them. In doing so, he leaves G-d in the lurch, so to speak, leaves the conversation dangling in the air and abruptly terminates whatever was going on between them. We never hear about that again. There is a world here, an unsaid world, that passes between verse one and verse two.

As everyone knows, Abraham was particularly dedicated to the commandment of hospitality. In fact, he was the very personification of *chesed* (kindness), so much so that his name is synonymous with that attribute. Thus he pitched his tent at a crossroads and left it open at all four sides, so that he would be able to see travelers in every direction and offer food, drink and lodging. But G-d did not want Abraham to be bothered that day, he should be recuperating from his circumcision and not waiting over every itinerant and backpacker. Knowing His friend's nature all too well, G-d miraculously changed nature—He made it exceptionally hot that day, so that nobody would be out in the streets.[1] But G-d saw Abraham's pain at not being able to have guests to care for, it was even greater than the pain he suffered over his physical operation. So, after having

---

1 The words of 18:1 are generally translated as 'he was sitting (…) in the heat of the day', the Hebrew actually reads '*like* the heat of the day, indicating that the heat was not normal, but something especially created for this occasion.

changed nature once that day by making it exceptionally hot, the Creator of the Universe had to change nature again, by providing three angels in the guise of men—just so Abraham would have recipients for his kindness.

Abraham leaves G-d so that he can attend to his guests—which he no doubt viewed as a G-dsend. He aims to prepare a banquet for them, and he tells his wife Sarah 'hurry, knead and make three cakes,' while he himself (in his condition!) goes running after the cattle.

Our sages goes on to share a remarkable tradition with us: One of the calves ran into a cave, and Abraham ran after to catch it. That cave turned out to be none other than *Ma'arat HaMachpela*, the famed Double Cave of Hebron, the Tomb of the Patriarchs. This is how Abraham discovered it—running after that little calf to prepare a feast for his three visitors!

According to the holy Zohar[2], *Ma'arat HaMachpela* is 'the entrance to *Gan Eden*' (the Garden of Eden). Whether or not this is to be taken literally, one thing is for sure: when Abraham entered the cave, he saw Adam and Eve lying there in repose, and he knew exactly who they were. He was overwhelmed with a tremendous, burning sense of yearning for this place—and from that moment on, he pined for it and wished to make it his own place of burial. He was overcome with the feeling of sheer holiness and Divine purpose in that place. It was easy enough later to purchase it from Ephron, who didn't see a thing that was particularly special or desirous about it. He just couldn't see it. But it's not a physical thing that can be seen with the naked eye, the entrance to the Garden of Eden— it's a spiritual concept.

Abraham wanted to be buried there because he wanted to be part of the legacy of *Adam HaRishon*, (the first man)—who, like himself, also had a close and personal relationship with the Creator. But even more so, Abraham was the continuation of Adam's heritage; Abraham was his guarantor that all of humanity would learn that there is only one G-d, because Abraham took responsibility to bring the light of G-d to humanity. Until Abraham came along the generations were not looking for G-d—they were running away from Him.

Abraham discovered this holy place, 'the entrance to the Garden of Eden', which was to become the Tomb of the Patriarchs, quite by accident— running

2 The Zohar is a collection of commentaries on the Torah, intended to guide people who have already achieved high spiritual degrees to the root (origin) of their souls.

after a calf which he intended to slaughter to prepare a meal for a bunch of strangers.

Open up your heart, because our sages are telling us here two of the deepest secrets in the world.

What is a true religious experience?

It's easy to pretend to be 'holy', but what does it really mean to be holy? A person can sit back and roll his eyes and make all sorts of ridiculous expressions while claiming to have 'visions' or 'prophecy.'

In the beginning of the parasha, Abraham was truly having a face to face visit with G-d, conversing with Him intimately. But when he saw what he perceived to be three ordinary men, even if they were lowly idolaters—he quickly opted to terminate his intimate meeting with G-d Himself, choosing to bestow upon these strangers an act of kindness instead. This is the true religious experience; *Imitatio Dei*, acting like G-d, not just talking about Him, or even, talking *with* Him! It's all about action and doing—that's the basis of our holy Torah and all the commandments. It's as if Abraham said to G-d: "Pardon me, but I don't have time to be with You now—I have to act like You". That's how we are measured in this world—only by our actions.

He left the conversation with G-d, and while running after a calf, stumbles upon the entrance to Paradise! Our sages are teaching us an amazing thing; the road to paradise is paved with acts of loving kindness. Abraham was simply trying to do a good deed, to catch a simple calf and prepare a meal.

Doing something for someone else is how to find the entrance to *Gan Eden*, and also the way to get in. Action is what Abraham was all about. While some might say that the road to paradise is paved with good intentions, Abraham teaches us that it's paved with good deeds.

PARASHAT
CHAYEI SARAH

Life of Sarah
Genesis 23:1-25:18

חיי שרה

CHAYEI SARAH

TORAH LESSON BY
RABBI CHANAN MORRISON

GUARDING THE INNER CHILD

THE TORAH COUNTS the years of Sarah's long life: "A hundred years and twenty years and seven years; these were the years of Sarah's life" (Gen. 23:1). Noting the verse's wordiness, the Sages commented that throughout all the years of her life—whether at age seven, twenty, or a hundred—Sarah retained the same goodness, the same purity, and the same youthful innocence.

Despite her long years of barrenness, despite twice being kidnapped as she accompanied her husband Abraham on his many journeys, Sarah did not become hard and cynical. Their son was named Isaac— יצחק, "he will laugh"— due to Abraham's feelings of wonderment and Sarah's amazed laughter. "God had given me laughter; all who hear will rejoice for me" (Gen. 21:6).

HOW TO EDUCATE

From the inspiring example of Sarah's purity and faith, we can learn an important lesson about education.

The nation's future depends upon how we educate the next generation. How should we tend to the vineyard of the House of Israel so that the saplings will prosper and grow, anchoring fast roots below and producing pleasant fruit above? How can we make sure that our children will develop into complete adults, their values firmly rooted in their heritage, living lives that are "pleasing to God and to man"?

We must take care to avoid slavish imitation of the educational methods of other nations. Our educational approach must suit the special nature and unique characteristics of our nation.

TWO VIEWS OF CHILDHOOD

The question of education revolves around an even more basic question. What is childhood? Is it just a preparatory stage leading to adulthood, or does it have intrinsic value in and of itself?

If life is all about working and earning a livelihood, then a child is simply a lump of clay to be formed into a tool to serve in the nation's workforce. Childhood is but a preparation for adulthood, when one becomes a productive member of society, a cog in the great machine of the nation's economy.

But there is another view of life, an idealistic outlook which values the qualities of purity and innocence. Such a viewpoint sees childhood as a stage of life that has value in its own right. The Sages recognized the special contribution of children to the world. "The world endures only for the sake of the breath of school children," for their Torah is learned in purity, undefiled by sin (*Shabbat* 119b).

When children are educated properly, we may discern within their pristine souls untold measures of holiness and purity. But this is only true if the grace and beauty of these delicate flowers is not crushed by the spirit-numbing reality of the factory floor and the cynical manipulations of greedy corporations.

Childhood is good and holy, but it is too weak and vulnerable to withstand the powerful forces of society. It is our duty to preserve the simplicity of childhood, to carefully allow our children to mature without losing their innate innocence. This will enable them to acquire the physical strength and spiritual resilience that they lack, while retaining the innocent exuberance of childhood.

My Anointed Ones

"'Do not harm *meshichai*, My anointed ones'—this refers to school children" (*Shabbat* 119b). Why are children called "God's anointed ones"? Anointing is not a one-time event, but an initiation ceremony which influences the years to come. Thus a king is anointed, and throughout the years of his reign he is the *melech ha-mashiach*, the anointed king.

The same is true with childhood. When it has not been debased by the pressures of an exploitative society, childhood is our anointing, our initiation, so that we may enjoy its pure fruits throughout our lives.

This is the beautiful example that Sarah provides. She lived a life of holiness and pure faith, retaining her childlike wonder and purity throughout the many vicissitudes of her long life. "All her years were equal in goodness" (Rashi (1040 – 1105)).

From *Sapphire from the Land of Israel*, pp. 50-52. Adapted from *Ma'amerei HaRe'iyah* vol. II, pp. 230-231, from a lecture that Rabbi Abraham Isaac

Kook (1865-1935, first Chief Rabbi of pre-state Israel) delivered at the opening of a Talmud Torah school in Rehovot in 1905.

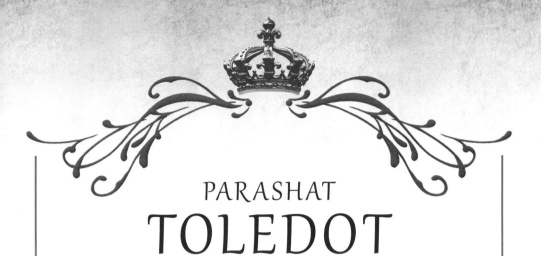

PARASHAT
TOLEDOT

Generations

Bereshit 25:19-28:9

תולדת

TOLEDOT

TORAH LESSON BY

RABBI DAVID AARON

HOW TO BE IN LOVE

FINDING THE BALANCE BETWEEN CONFIDENT ASSERTION AND HUMBLE SURRENDER

ISAAC AND REBECCA had two sons: Esau and Jacob. Although they were twins, they were far from identical. Even during Rebecca's pregnancy their character difference was visible. According to Jewish tradition, when the pregnant Rebecca stood near houses of study and prayer, Jacob struggled to come out, but when she passed temples of idolatry, Esau eagerly struggled to come out[3].

Upon birth, Esau came out reddish, as hairy as a fur coat. This is usually taken as a sign that he will be a shedder of blood[4]. They called him Esau, the Hebrew term for "made", which according to Rashi (1040-1105)[5] was "because he was made and developed with hair as one who is much older." His twin brother then emerged and his hand was grasping Esau's heal. Isaac called the second twin Jacob. If Esau was born physically complete, Jacob was born incomplete, as it says, "Jacob was born circumcised."[6] The boys grew up, and when they reached the age of thirteen, Jacob went his way to the houses of learning and Esau went his way to the house of idolatry[7].

Esau was a man who knew how to hunt; a man of the field. He ensnared people with their words, trapping them just as he would trap the animals he hunted. This is what the Midrash has to say about him:

R. Abbahu said that he was a trapper and a man of the field, trapping [i.e. deceiving] at home, trapping in the field. He deceived at home asking his father, "How do you tithe salt?" (He wanted to show that he was concerned with doing the will of G-d, although he knew full well that salt was not subject to the laws of tithes.)

He was also said to make himself "free like a field", meaning that he acted in a promiscuous way[8]. Therefore, Esau was a manipulator, liar and a cheat—not quite a good boy. He fulfilled his selfish passions without restraint.

---

3 Genesis Rabbah 63:6
4 Rashi Genesis 25:25 and Genesis Rabbah 63:8
5 Rashi Genesis 25:26
6 Avos d'Rabbi Nasson 2
7 Genesis Rabbah 63:10
8 Genesis Rabbah 63:10

Jacob, on the other hand, was a man who sat in tents, meaning that he was contented to surround himself with the study of G-d's word. He was a scholar, inclined to serving G-d, honest, straight and born already marked with the sign of the covenant with

G-d. The Torah describes him as being a "tam." Rashi explains that a tam is someone who is "not shrewd at deceiving".

ISAAC SEES THE GOOD IN ESAU.

Isaac grew old and his eyesight faded. He called his elder son Esau, and said, "I am old and have no idea when I will die. Now take up your equipment, your quiver and bow and go out to the field and hunt me game. Make it into a tasty dish, the way I like it and bring it to me to eat. My soul will then bless you before I die."[9]

The Midrash[10] comments:

"Sharpen your weapons so that you do not feed me "nevelos" and "terefos" (an animal slaughtered with a dull knife is, according to Jewish law, unfit to be eaten). Again, take your own weapons, so that you do not supply me with proceeds of robbery or violence."

If Isaac suspected Esau of this kind of misconduct and mistrusted his reliability, then why did he want to bless him?

Isaac was clearly not completely blind to Esau's selfish inclinations. However, he believed that Esau was capable of applying his incredible self-confidence and strength towards the service of G-d. Isaac hoped that Esau would transform his selfishness into maintaining a healthy sense of "self" in service to G-d rather than losing himself to G-d. Esau had great potential to achieve the ultimate in life: to be in love. He thereby indicated to him to take his skills and apply them in doing mitzvos (religious duties), in this case the mitzvah of honoring his father.

The great master of Kabbalah[11], Rabbi Isaac Luria (1534-1572), who is referred to as the Ari zt'l explains:

"He was a hunter with his mouth (Genesis 25:28): Esau's holy sparks came

---

9 Genesis 27:1-4
10 Genesis Rabbah 65:13
11 Likutei Torah, Ovadiah
Kabbalah - often referred to as the "soul" of the Torah, the Kabbalah is an ancient Jewish tradition which teaches the deepest insights into the essence of Gd, His interaction with the world, and the purpose of Creation.

from the wisdom and understanding and knowledge in his mouth and from this holiness emerged converts who were great leaders of Israel; Shemayiah, Avtalion, Rebbe Meir and Rebbe Akiva."

The Ari zt"l[12] further comments:

"It is because of this that Isaac loved him and hoped that maybe he would become rectified through this."

Isaac saw that Esau had tremendous potential, seeing in him the sparks of Rebbe Meir and Rebbe Akivah—the masters of the Talmud.

The Talmud[13] teaches that G-d did not establish His covenant with Israel except for the sake of Oral Tradition, which refers to the Mishnah[14], Talmud and the Midrash. It is through the involvement in Talmudic debate that scholars are empowered and rise to a status of godliness.[15]

These and the opinions of the disputing sages are the living words of Elohim [gods].

When people reach this level of divine significance and relationship to G-d they then fulfill the ultimate meaning of the covenant—a loving partnership.

The Torah scholar asserts himself and shares in making divine decisions through the dialectic of the Oral Tradition. He is entrusted with the responsibility for the interpretation and administration of G-d's revealed word as embodied in the five books of Moses. New situations will arise in each generation and require critical legal decisions drawn from the laws and principles recorded by the prophet Moses and applied correctly. This takes great confidence and courage. However, this also takes great commitment, devotion and service to G-d. A Torah scholar must have a balanced sense of assertive powers and yet also humility and surrender.

There are several cases in Jewish history where the sages had to have the courage and initiative to break a Torah law for the sake of G-d, as it is written in Psalms:

"It is a time to act for G-d they have dissolved Your law."[16]

Rashi[17] explains: "When the time comes to do something for the Holy One, blessed be He, it is permitted to dissolve the Torah." Rashi, therefore, reads and

---

12 Perei Eitz Chaim- Shaar 208:3
13 Talmud, Gittin 60b
14 Mishnah - the first part of the Talmud; a collection of early oral interpretations of the scriptures that was compiled about AD 200.
15 Talmud, Eruvin 30b
16 Psalms 119:126
17 Talmud Yoma 49a

interprets the verse like this: "Dissolve the law of G-d when it is a time to act for Him."

The very fact that the Oral Tradition has been put into writing is itself a violation of the Jewish law that states that the Oral Tradition must remain oral and not written down.

We find that Rabbi Yochanan and Resh Lakish were studying part of the Oral Tradition from a written text. Their behavior is justified on the basis of the fact that one can violate the law for the sake of G-d. They said: "Since it is impossible (i.e. to remember it all), it is a time to act for the sake of G-d."

Imagine what courage it takes for a Torah sage, entrusted with the preservation of G-d's Torah, to break one of its laws for the sake of G-d. Imagine also the great honesty, purity, reverence of G-d and service to G-d that is required of the sage to ensure that this violation of G-d's law is truly and only for G-d's sake without an iota of selfish motives—not even hidden in the recesses of his subconscious mind. Therefore, a Torah leader must actualize all his creative powers, courageously take initiative and assert himself while in humble service to G-d. He must be assertive in his surrender.

Isaac hoped to balance Esau's confidence and power with humbleness and surrender to G-d which would then make him a great world leader and model of true love and relationship with G-d. All he needed was the balance of Jacob's character.

Finding the Whole in One

Rebecca, however, thought that Esau was far off from making such adjustments. She saw that it was more realistic to nurture some of the qualities of Esau in Jacob—what Jacob needed was more assertion.

She said, "Now my son [Jacob] listen to me and heed my instructions. Go to the sheep and take two choice young kid-goats. I will prepare them the way your father likes. You must then bring it to your father, so that he will eat and bless you before he dies."

"But my brother Esau is hairy," replied Jacob, "I am smooth skinned."

The Midrash[18] makes a strange comment about this dialogue: when Jacob describes Esau as hairy, he uses the Hebrew term "ish sa'ir", which has the connotation of "demonic", as in the verse from Isaiah, "And satyrs (se'irim) shall

---

18 Genesis Rabbah 65:15

dance there."[19] When he describes himself as smooth, he uses the Hebrew word "chalak", having the same sense as in the verse from Deuteronomy, "For the "chelek" (portion) of G-d is His people"[20] which suggests that he was completely at one with G-d, so to speak, a part of G-d.

The Midrash compares Esau and Jacob to two men, one possessing a thick head of hair and the other bald, who stood near a threshing floor. When the chaff flew into the locks of the former, it became entangled in his hair. But when it flew on the head of the bald man he passed his hand over his head and easily removed it. In other words, hairy Esau's wild demonic desires made him susceptible to getting messed up in the chaff of life; he was not able to easily cleanse himself of his wrongdoings. However, Jacob was a simple and straight fellow and was therefore less prone to getting caught up in problems, and any mistakes he might make he could easily fix.

This Midrash seems to indicate that Jacob was reluctant to do what Rebecca suggested not only because he feared that he would get caught by Isaac, but because he saw the act as lowering himself to Esau's level. He did not want to incorporate qualities in himself that would make him vulnerable to sin, or endanger his state of purity and surrender by adopting an orientation that would generate an even greater struggle with the evil inclination. His point was: Why complicate life? Let's keep it simple.

When Jacob posed as Esau and deceived his father he actually accepted the struggles with the evil inclination implicit in the Esau-like orientation. He realized that for the sake of G-d and a true relationship of love he had to take this risk. Only a person who is capable of sinning and overcoming his personal urge can really serve G-d. Only a person who is able to violate a loving relationship can really fulfill it. Only at the risk of sin and the struggle against it can humanity develop the type of selfhood necessary for establishing the covenant and reaching the ultimate experience of being in love. It is the struggle with the evil inclination that empowers us to "be" in love—to maintain our distinct sense of self without losing ourselves in our loving service to G-d.

---

19 Isaiah 13:21
20 Deuteronomy 32:9

PARASHAT
VAYETZE

And he went out

GENESIS 28:10-32:3

ויצא

VAYETZE

TORAH LESSON BY
RABBI YEHOSHUA FRIEDMAN

TRANSFORMATIVE TORAH

PARASHAT TOLEDOT, THE previous parasha, describes the two twin sons of Yitzhak—Ya'akov and Eisav, in the following way:

And the boys grew; and Eisav was a cunning hunter, a man of the field; and Ya'akov was a quiet man (Ish tam), dwelling in tents. (Genesis 25:27)

"Ish tam" could mean a simple man, a complete man, or a plain man. Is it because he can't, because he won't, or because he doesn't need to, that he never goes out of the tent to the field? His brother, Eisav, is a cunning hunter and is said to be an entrapper not only of animals but also of men, according to the Sages. Eisav fools his father, but he doesn't fool his mother or his brother. When the time comes for Yitzhak to bless his son and pass on the family tradition to the first-born Eisav, Rivka conspires with Ya'akov to prevent the position of primacy of going to the inappropriate brother. Yitzhak doesn't seem to be aware that Eisav has sold his birthright to Ya'akov for a bowl of lentil soup, thus selling the enduring spiritual value for the satisfaction of the moment.

Rivka takes upon herself the danger of a curse which may result from deceiving Yitzhak. When Eisav realizes he has been cheated out of the primary blessing of his father, he rages and swears to kill his brother. Their mother knows that Eisav is a creature of the moment and that his rage will pass, but at the moment it is very dangerous to be around him. So she takes Ya'akov out of the house under the pretext of finding him a bride, knowing that Yitzhak is unhappy with Eisav's having married local Canaanite women. Ya'akov has so far only been reactive and somewhat passive, acting in response to initiatives by first his brother and then following the initiative of his mother. And so ends Parashat Toledot.

Vayetze picks up the story with the travels of Ya'akov. When he lies down for the night on his way north, the Sages point out that Ya'akov is sleeping in that place, which makes it the first place where he has slept for 14 years. The midrash, quoted in Rashi's (1040-1105) commentary, recounts that he spent those years in the academy of Shem and Ever in continuous study of the Torah without sleeping. As many later Torah scholars did in the ensuing millennia,

Ya'akov broadens the education acquired at home with exposure to other pre-eminent scholars. This is just what a man of the tents should be expected to do, but he decides to further challenge himself. He prepares for what he knows will be a hard life with enemies who masquerades as friends. He studies ethics with world-class ethicists to prepare himself for world-class liars and cheaters.

He is also a prophet and the divine voice speaks to him. He knows where he is going and what he will have to do there. But, nonetheless, he needed this interlude to develop himself. He was no kid when he left home, he was 63. You could figure it out, but there is a commentary by Rashi at the end of Parashat Toledot which runs the numbers. The wicked are sprinters, but the righteous are the distance runners (cf. Ps. 37 and 92 among others). Yaakov's life is a marathon.

After that night he is suddenly in a hurry, and his feet carry him with unusual speed northward. When he reaches Haran, the place of his mother's family's home, he stops. All of a sudden this self-effacing man, who does not look very physically fit after many years of sitting in tents, does something out of character. He sees some herdsmen who are apparently loitering around a well. The ethical imperative drives him to approach them. He asks why they are not going about their business, why they are wasting their own time or that of their employers? They answer that all the herdsmen have yet to arrive to unblock the well to water their flocks. Normally it is a joint project by a number of men to get the heavy stone off the top of the well. Ya'akov, a small man from the tents, stops lecturing the herdsmen and jerks the stone off the mouth of the well. How did he do it?

And that's not all. Lavan the crook cheats him time after time and Ya'akov tirelessly works and prays and deals with it. Imagine if his brother Eisav had to go through even one situation like the switching of Leah for Rachel—he would have pulled out his sword and a Shakespearean tragedy with a blood-bath would have ensued. But that is not what perpetuates a holy people—Ya'akov knows that. He has gone through years of spiritual preparation so he has both the insight and self-control to pull it off, and Hashem helps him.

Personality change and personality development are possible. But they require long, hard work which can be intensified by divine aid.

PARASHAT
VAYISHLACH

And he sent

GENESIS 32:4-36:43

וישלח

VAYISHLACH

TORAH LESSON BY
RABBI LEVI COOPER

BEING HERE, FEELING THERE

RABBI AVRAHAM DOV of Owrucz (1760-1840) was a Hasidic master during the formative years of the Hasidic movement. In 1831 he left Europe for the Land of Israel, and settled in Safed. In Safed, Rabbi Avraham Dov served as a leader of the local Hasidic community. Alas, the Hasidic master died during a plague that struck Safed in the late 1840s. Some seven years later, in 1847, a collection of Rabbi Avraham Dov's Hasidic teachings was published in Jerusalem under the title *Bat 'Ayin*. *Bat 'Ayin* literally translates as "the daughter of the eye", meaning the cherished one or the apple of the eye.

Knowing Rabbi Avraham Dov's biography, it is no wonder that we find a love for the Holy Land in his teachings. One example of Rabbi Avraham Dov's thoughts about the journey to the Land of Israel can be found in his comments on Jacob's return to the Holy Land after his years in Aram with Laban.

According to the biblical narrative, as Jacob returned, he knew that a dreaded encounter with his brother Esau awaited him. Jacob sent an advance party to Esau, bearing words of appeasement and hoping to mitigate any wrath that Esau might feel towards his brother because of past events (Genesis 32:3–5).

The Hebrew word for the members of this advance party is *mal'akhim*—a term that is generally translated as angels, but can also mean messengers. Rashi (1040-1105), the great French commentator, explained that Jacob in fact sent real angels. Whence did Jacob have spare angels that were available for this mission?

A few verses earlier in the narrative, the Bible points out that Jacob met angels of God (Genesis 32:1). There is a rabbinic tradition that distinguishes between angels that accompany a person in the Holy Land and angels that accompany a person in the Diaspora. Building on this tradition, Rashi suggested that the angels that met Jacob after he left Laban were angels of the Holy Land.

Rabbi Avraham Dov of Owrucz took note of the comings and goings of Jacob's accompanying angels, and suggested that the angels that Jacob sent to Esau were his Diaspora angels. Since Jacob now had his Holy Land angels, he could use his Diaspora angels as couriers to Esau without being left alone, unprotected by God's messengers.

However, Rabbi Avraham Dov wondered: "How could Jacob be accompanied by Holy Land angels already when he had yet to reach the Land of Israel?" This question had already vexed Nahmanides (1194-1270), who realized just how far Jacob was from the Holy Land. Nahmanides therefore rejected Rashi's idea of Holy Land angels already accompanying Jacob.

Rabbi Avraham Dov did not reject Rashi's explanation, but kept Nahmanides' objection in mind when he explained that since Jacob was on the road to the Land of Israel, Holy Land angels were already accompanying him.

This explanation recalls a tale about Rabbi Avraham Dov from before he set out from Eastern Europe, bound for the Land of Israel.

Rabbi Avraham Dov paid a visit to Rabbi Aharon of Zhitomir (d. 1816), and at the time Rabbi Aharon was ill, but he was overjoyed to see his colleague.

"For me to get better I must drink water from the Land of Israel," declared the bedridden Rabbi Aharon of Zhitomir.

Rabbi Aharon then turned to Rabbi Avraham Dov: "You intend to travel to the Land of Israel and mentally you are already there. Where a person's thoughts are, that is truly where that person is. So, please sir, put some water in your mouth and spit it into a cup. That water will be like the water from the Land of Israel! I will drink it and I will feel better."

According to the tale, Rabbi Avraham Dov was surprised because he had yet to tell anyone about his intention to move to the Holy Land.

This tale may be somewhat difficult for our modern, scientifically oriented minds to grasp—or should we say—difficult to stomach. Despite the bizarre depiction, the tale suggests an intriguing idea that has a meaningful message: the power of the focused mind to define the mental location of a person.

Jacob had set a course for the Holy Land and therefore he was already accompanied by the aura of Holy Land angels. Rabbi Avraham Dov had made a decision to move to the Land of Israel, and for medico-spiritual purposes he was therefore already there!

Of course the potential for "being here and feeling there" is a double edged sword: Just like a person can physically be in exile but mentally be in a holy space; so too can a person be in the holiest of locations but mentally be far away. With this potent force in mind, the choice of "location" appears to largely be in the hands of the individual.

PARASHAT
VAYESHEV

And he settled

GENESIS 37:1-40:23

וישב

VAYESHEV

TORAH LESSON BY

RABBI DAVID AARON

WHY IS LIFE SO DIFFICULT?

MAKING PEACE WITH OUR BATTLE

I N THIS WEEK'S portion, Jacob asks for peace and relaxation but G-d had another plan.

> **"Jacob settled (down) in the land of his father's dwellings, in the Land of Caanan."—Genesis 37:2**

The foremost commentator, Rashi (1040-1105), explains:

"Jacob wanted to settle down in tranquility but then the ordeal of his son Joseph (sale into slavery) fell upon him. The righteous seek to dwell in tranquility but G-d says, 'Is it not enough for the righteous what has been prepared for them (reward) in the World to Come, that they need to seek tranquility also in this world!'"

WHY IS LIFE SO DIFFICULT?

Some people turn to G-d and religion, hoping to find refuge from all the turbulence of life; from doubt, from inner conflicts and mental turmoil. They want instant inner peace, spiritual contentment, and tranquility for their troubled souls.

According to Kabbalah[21], that is not the purpose of life on earth, in fact, it is the complete opposite. We have been dropped right into the stormy seas of daily living. We are confronted with the problems from within and without, and we are commanded to fix problems and ourselves. The theme of life is precisely about embracing the difficulties of life and rising to the challenges.

Why did G-d create such an imperfect world filled with imperfect people?

The very first verse of the Book of Genesis tells us: "In the beginning G-d created heaven and earth, and earth was in a state of chaos." This sounds like

---

21 *Kabbalah* - often referred to as the "soul" of the Torah, the Kabbalah is an ancient Jewish tradition which teaches the deepest insights into the essence of Gd, His interaction with the world, and the purpose of Creation.

G-d did a pretty crummy job. The minute He creates the world, it's already in a state of chaos.

But the truth is that G-d did a perfect job. What's perfect about this world is the chaos! It's the perfect place for growth. It's the perfect place for challenges. It's the perfect setting for triumph. It's the perfect stage for an exciting drama about personal transformation.

This world is meant to be difficult, and your life on earth is meant to be a struggle—a struggle filled with adventure, challenges and victory. This is your divine mission if you are willing to accept it. And if you accept it, you will have the power to succeed.

ARE YOU READY TO PLAY YOUR PART?

The Torah, in the Book of Genesis, makes an outlandish claim. It says that G-d created us in His image. What's that supposed to mean? G-d created you and me in His image in the same way that an author creates all his characters in his image. Each character in the story expresses a different aspect of the author. Even the interactions between the characters are in some way an unfolding of the truth of the author.

Every good story, however, has difficulties and problem characters that create all the tension. This is because they play an essential role in bringing out the inner selves of all the other characters. That's an important factor. The difficulties help the characters in the story to reveal their deepest selves, to rise to their challenges and demonstrate extraordinary courage, tremendous fortitude and new commitment.

The Talmud refers to the evil forces in the universe as the yeast in the dough. Yeast consists of microscopic fungal organisms. Who wants to eat fungal organisms? But it's the yeast in bread dough that acts as a catalyst to make the dough rise. So, too, was evil created in the world to be a catalyst for the growth and personal enrichment of others. It, too, is serving the author within the context of the whole story.

The Zohar, the classic work of Kabbalah, metaphorically describes the power of evil in the world as a prostitute who has been hired by the king to seduce his son, the prince. Of course the king does not want her to succeed. However, he wants to create an opportunity for the prince to realize his own royal integrity by resisting this great temptation and choosing to act in the way that is befitting of his nobility. Until this test, the son's royal status was merely an inherited title and a wardrobe of regal clothing—not the genuine expression of himself, accomplished through the power of his own choices and determined efforts.

The antagonist in every story is actually providing the opportunities for the other characters to make great choices that embody great goodness. He is serving the best interest of all the other characters, and of course, the author (whom the story is really all about).

In truth, every character serves the author. However, some characters are serving the author directly as direct expressions of himself in the world he created. Others are serving the author indirectly by creating opportunities for others to be of direct service.

This is the essence of all choices made by every character. To serve or not to serve is not the question, and it is not a choice. Every character serves the author. The choice is only about how you serve—directly, playing the hero or heroine, or indirectly, playing the villain.

What difference does it make if you serve directly or indirectly? It really does not make a difference to the author—his story will be written. But it sure does make a difference to you, the character. Your choices determine not only the outcome of your final scene but also the quality of your existence throughout the whole story.

As we all know, the good guys win in the end. Sure, they might lose some battles along the way, but they always win the war. However, even when they appear to be losing, often they are actually winning, because in every moment of their struggle they achieve personal transformations and enjoy a profound sense of identification with the author.

The Talmud teaches that the *Shekhinah*—the Divine Presence, which is the feminine manifestation of G-d—desires to live in this world. But how? Through you and me when we choose to follow the commandments and directly serve G-d, the Author. This is not the case for the villain. He is not only heading for the worst ending but even his journey, the quality of his daily living, is devoid of the divine fulfillment that life in this imperfect world offers.

The villain gets clobbered in the end. He may think he is a winner, but all his apparent successes are only setting him up for his ultimate demise. Worse than the great punishment that awaits him in the final scene is the pain he suffers daily in his existential insecurity. He is not striving to grow, overcome evil, and choose goodness. He is not interested in using his imperfections as a starting point towards becoming more perfect, and thereby serving G-d and being His agent.

Therefore, the villain denies himself the greatest pleasure of all—living a life filled with G-d's Presence. His soul is alienated from its Divine Source, and his inner world has no connection with G-d's absolute reality and is therefore devoid of any lasting value or meaning.

In the world at large he may have much money, live in an elegant mansion, wear the most expensive and latest fashions, and act out all his sexual fantasies. But his inner world is hell, indeed, he creates his own hell.

"The evil ones are like the driven sea that cannot rest, and its waters throw up mire and mud. There is no peace, says G-d to the wicked." (Isaiah 57: 20-21)

Often, when people pick up the Bible and read about serving G-d, they are put off, thinking, "why would I want to *serve* G-d? Be *servile*?" It seems kind of demeaning. But if you're a character in the story, how could you not want to serve the author? It's who you are, and it's the greatest honor in the world.

What does it mean to serve the author directly? It means that I am a vehicle for the expression of the author in this story. I can't wait to serve the author, because the more I serve the author, the more the author's presence permeates my very being, and the more I discover that I am actually a spark of the author. It's not about obedience, it's about self-expression. It's about who you are, why you are, who G-d is, and why He creates.

By using this metaphor of author-character, you can start looking at your life a little differently. You can say to yourself, "I really want to serve a higher purpose. I really want to fit in the greater story. I really want to directly serve G-d, the Author, and play my part the best way possible. All the problems in my life are really opportunities to be more.

From *The Secret Life of God,* by Rabbi David Aaron, © 2005 by Rabbi David Aaron. Reprinted by arrangement with Shambhala Publications, Inc., www.shambhala.com.

PARASHAT
MIKETZ

At the end of

GENESIS 41:1-44:17

מקץ

MIKETZ

TORAH LESSON BY
RABBI ZELIG PLISKIN

WHEN YOU FEEL JOY FOR WHAT YOU HAVE YOU WILL BE FREE FROM ENVYING WHAT ANYONE ELSE HAS.

והנה מן-היאר, עלת שבע פרות, יפות מראה, ובריאת בשר; ותרעינה, באחו.

IN PHARAOH'S PROPHETIC dream:

"And behold from the Nile rose up seven cows, which looked good and healthy of flesh and they grazed in the pasture." (Genesis 41:2)

Rashi (1040-1105) comments that their looking good was a sign of the years of plenty, for then people look good to one another and are not envious of each other.

The idea that Rashi expresses is important for happiness in life. When you allow what someone else has to rob you of your own happiness, you will frequently suffer. But if you learn to appreciate what you have to its fullest, you will be so filled with good feelings yourself that you will not be disturbed by what anyone else has. The more you focus on the good in your life the less it will make a difference to you if anyone else has more than you. When you master this attribute of feeling joy for what you have, your whole life is a life of plenty.

Rabbi Yechezkail Levenstein once noticed that a *chasan* (groom) felt badly that he had just a plain watch and not a gold watch as many other people received. Rabbi Levenstein approached him and traded his own gold watch for the plain watch. When he came home, he explained, "Besides the color of the watches there is no practical difference between them. They both tell time with the same accuracy. Why should this person suffer needlessly when I can help him out?" (*Mofes Hador*, p.17)

NEVER DESPAIR, SINCE LIBERATION FROM DIFFICULTIES CAN COME AT ANY MOMENT.

וישלח פרעה ויקרא את-יוסף, ויריצהו מן-הבור; ויגלח ויחלף שמלתיו, ויבא אל-פרעה.

After Pharaoh heard that Yosef was able to interpret dreams:

> "And Pharaoh sent and he called Yosef, and they ran with him from the prison." (Genesis 41:14)

The Chofetz Chayim takes note that when the time came for Yosef's liberation, he wasn't let out of prison slowly. Rather he was rushed out of his captivity with the greatest of speed. This is the way the Almighty brings about redemption. The moment it is the proper time not even one second is lost. This is how it will be with the final redemption, said the Chofetz Chayim. As soon as the right time comes we will immediately be delivered from our exile. (*Chofetz Chayim al Hatorah*, p.49)

In every difficult life situation realize that in just one moment that entire picture can change. Yosef had no deadline by which he could count on being set free. But his imprisonment and freedom were not dependent on the whims of his mortal captors. Rather, the Almighty gave him a set time to remain in prison. As soon as the time was reached Yosef was immediately saved from his plight. This awareness can give you encouragement in difficult times. Even in those situations where you can make no change for improvement and you do not see the situation changing in the future, your liberation can still come in the next moment.

LOOK FOR EVEN MINOR VIRTUES IN OTHERS.

ויאמר פרעה אל-יוסף, אחרי הודיע אלקים אותך את-כל-זאת, אין-נבון וחכם, כמוך.

Pharaoh liked Yosef's interpretation of his dream and then appointed him to be in charge of the economy of Egypt:

> "And Pharaoh said to Yosef, after the Almighty has informed you of all this there is no one who is as understanding and wise as you." (Genesis 41:39)

How could Pharaoh have trusted Yosef to such a degree that he appointed him to be the main administrator of the plans to save Egypt from the shortages of the forthcoming famine? True, Yosef was understanding and wise, but how could Pharaoh trust someone who was just released from prison and was previously a slave?

Rabbi Chayim Shmuelevitz, the late Rosh Hayeshiva of Mir, replied that Pharaoh saw Yosef's extreme honesty in something he said before he related the interpretation of the dream. Yosef began by saying to Pharaoh that he had no power to interpret dreams on his own. It was entirely a gift from the Almighty. Yosef didn't want to take credit even for a moment. This total honesty in one minor point showed that Yosef could be completely trusted.

Note what happened here. Pharaoh saw one minor positive point in Yosef's character and extrapolated from this to see the good on the large scale. This should be our model in viewing people. Keep finding minor strengths and good qualities in others and then give the person positive feedback. This can help someone build a positive self-image. The more a person sees himself as having positive attributes the more motivated he will be to utilize those strengths for further growth.

Unfortunately there are people who have a tendency to notice minor faults and weaknesses in others and then keep telling them that they have major character problems. While it is imperative to help people overcome their faults and weaknesses, the main emphasis for most people should be on their strengths. If someone is arrogant, this is not the appropriate approach. But for anyone who has low self-esteem that's positive approach is crucial.

There are some counselors who are experts at interpreting people's behavior as problematic. For example, if someone comes late, they say he is showing passive-aggressive behavior. If he is exactly on time, they say he is an obsessive-compulsive. If he is early, they say he fears disapproval and is too concerned with what others think about him. But these same situations can be looked at quite differently. If someone is late, there is the possibility he was detained through no fault of his own. If someone is punctual, it shows that he is orderly and has good time management. If someone is early, it shows that he does not want to inconvenience another person by causing him to wait.

By choosing to focus on the positive aspects of what people do, you will look at others in a favorable light. This way you will be a source of encouragement to others. When a person views himself in a positive light, he will have the strength to deal constructively with his faults.

PEOPLE RESPECT SOMEONE WHO HAS THE COURAGE TO SAY THAT HE MADE A MISTAKE.

ויאמרו איש אל־אחיו, אבל אשמים אנחנו על־אחינו, אשר ראינו צרת נפשו
בהתחננו אלינו, ולא שמענו; על־כן באה אלינו, הצרה הזאת.

> "And they said one man to his brother, we are guilty about our brother. We saw the suffering of his soul when he pleaded to us and we did not listen to him. Therefore this misfortune has befallen us." (Genesis 42:21)

Rabbi Dovid of Zeviltov commented: If a person did something wrong and recognizes that he has done wrong, he will be forgiven. But if a person does something wrong and denies it, there is no atonement for him. When Yosef's brothers said previously that they were innocent, Yosef responded by calling them spies. When they said that they were guilty, however, Yosef was full of compassion for them and cried. (Cited in Otzer Chayim)

Many people deny their faults and the things they have done wrong because they mistakenly think that others will respect them more by their doing so. But in reality people admire someone with the honesty and courage to admit his mistakes. It takes a brave person to say, "Yes, I was wrong." This kind of integrity will not only build up your positive attribute of honesty but will also gain you the respect of others. When you apologize to someone for wronging him, he will feel more positive towards you than if you denied that you did anything wrong. This awareness will make it much easier for you to ask forgiveness from others.

PATIENCE WILL PREVENT YOU FROM PREMATURELY EVALUATING A SITUATION AS NEGATIVE.

ויאמר, ישראל, למה הרעתם, לי—להגיד לאיש, העוד לכם אח.

"And Israel said, why did you cause me bad by telling the man that you had another brother." (Genesis 43:6)

The Midrash (*Braishis Rabbah* 91:13) censures Yaakov for evaluating the situation as bad. The Almighty said, "I am involved in having his son rule in Egypt and he says, 'Why did you cause me bad.'"

There are many events in each person's life that might appear to be negative when they first happen. But if a person were to know the entire picture of the consequences of these events, he would readily see how the Almighty planned them for good. What is needed is patience. When an event that seems to be against your interests happens, ask yourself, "How can I be certain that this will turn out bad in the end?" The answer is that you never can. It is always premature to evaluate non-tragic life situations as bad. Acquire a "wait and see" attitude towards events. This will prevent you from much needless suffering in your life.

To internalize this principle make a list of events that happened in your own life that at first seemed to be negative but which you later saw were positive.

Whenever you see improvement in your character traits, feel great joy. This joy will motivate you to continue improving. Be aware of what harm your negative traits caused you in the past and feel grateful for overcoming them. Knowing that you have already been successful will give you the encouragement to work on correcting other faults.

From *Growth through Torah* by Rabbi Zelig Pliskin.

PARASHAT
VAYIGASH

And he drew near

GENESIS 44:18-47:27

ויגש

VAYIGASH

TORAH LESSON BY
RABBI MOSHE LICHTMAN

YERIDAH FOR THE SAKE OF ALIYAH[22]

THIS WEEK'S *PARASHA* marks the beginning of *galut Mitzrayim* (the Egyptian Exile). Although the servitude did not begin until *Parashat Shemot*, Ya'akov and his children were forced, in our *parasha*, to leave their homeland and settle on foreign soil. Knowing that the exile was going to be a long one, the leaders of the Children of Israel (Ya'akov and Yosef) did their best to prepare the budding nation for the centuries of exile that lay ahead.

Firstly, when Yosef revealed himself to his brothers, he said, *Hurry and* **go up** (עלו) *to my father and say to him, "So says your son Yosef, 'God has put me in charge of all of Egypt;* **come down** (רדה) *to me, do not delay'* " (Genesis 45:9). Rashi (1040-1105) comments: "AND GO UP (עלו) TO MY FATHER—**the Land of Israel is higher than all other lands.**" Why did Rashi see fit to point this out here? The verbs עלה (to go up) and רדה (to go down) have been used numerous times before in reference to the Land of Israel. In the first seventeen verses of this *parasha* alone, Yehudah uses them six times! Nonetheless, this is the first time Rashi comments on it.

I believe that Yosef was trying to teach his brothers an important lesson concerning their imminent exile. Most commentators (if not all) explain that when our Sages say that the Land of Israel is higher than all other lands, it does not mean in a physical sense. After all, many places have higher altitudes than the Land of Israel. Rather, they mean that the Holy Land is on a higher spiritual plane. Yosef wanted his family to have the right attitude when they came to Egypt. Essentially, he was saying to them: "I know what you're thinking. You think that this exile business isn't going to be that bad after all. Egypt is a nice place; there's plenty of food here; our brother is second in command; etc. Get that attitude out of your minds! No matter how good *galut (exile)* might seem, it is still a *yeridah* (descent). I have been living here for twenty-two years and I haven't lost sight of the fact that the Land of Israel is higher than all other lands." Thus, Rashi quotes this statement of *the sages* on our verse because this is the first time it is part of the Torah's message.

---

22 Yerida ("descent") is a Hebrew term referring to emigration by Israelites from the State of Israel. Yerida is the opposite of Aliyah ("ascent"), which is immigration to Israel.

Secondly, before Ya'akov left the Holy Land, HaShem appeared to him and said, *Do not be afraid to go down to Egypt, for I will make you into a great nation there* (Genesis 46:3). Rashi explains why God felt it necessary to reassure Ya'akov: "**Because [Ya'akov] was grieved that he had to leave the Land.**" *Pirkei DeRebbe Eliezer* (39) elaborates:

> Ya'akov heard that Yosef was alive, and he thought to himself: "How can I leave my fathers' Land—the Land where I was born, the Land where God's Presence is found—and go to the land of the Children of Cham, to a land whose inhabitants have no fear of Heaven?"

This is astounding! For twenty-two years Ya'akov thought that his beloved son was dead, and now he has an opportunity to see him, and all he can do is worry about leaving the Land! Perhaps he, too, wanted to teach his family an important lesson about exile. There was no denying that the Israelites had to go into exile at this point. Nevertheless, Ya'akov wanted to demonstrate how an Israelite should feel when he is forced to leave the Holy Land. He should be scared and realize that he is leaving God's presence and entering "godless" territory. Then he will surely avoid getting too comfortable in his new environment.

Two verses later the Torah states, *Ya'akov rose up from Be'er Sheva, and the sons of Yisrael carried Ya'akov their father, their children, and their wives in the wagons that Pharaoh had sent...* (Genesis 46:5). *Itturei Torah*[23] quotes a beautiful idea on this verse, which concurs with the above. It says in *Parashat Vayetze* (Genesis 29:1), *Ya'akov lifted his feet*, to which Rashi comments, "As soon as he received the good tiding that he was assured of [God's] protection, his heart carried his feet, and he walked easily." The question begs itself: In our *parasha*, as well, Ya'akov received good news—his long lost son was alive! Why, then, is there no hint of light-footedness here? On the contrary, Ya'akov had to be carried in a wagon! The answer is: In our verse, Ya'akov was going down to Egypt, to begin a lengthy and dreadful exile. He was so apprehensive about going that he could hardly get his legs to move, and he had to be carried. If only his descendants would view exile as he did!

Ya'akov did one more thing to show his disdain for foreign lands. He decided to take with him only those possessions he acquired in the Land of Canaan (v. 6), giving all that he acquired in Lavan's house to Esau for his share

---

23 Itturei Torah - a commentary upon the weekly Torah portion by Aharon-Ya'akov Greenberg.

in *Me'arat HaMachpeilah*[24] (see Rashi, ibid.). Said Ya'akov, "**Chutz-LaAretz possessions are not worthwhile to me.**" Before going down to exile, Ya'akov Avinu[25] tried to ingrain in his descendants' hearts the notion that all aspects of the Land of Israel—even mundane, material possessions—have intrinsic sanctity.

We are rapidly approaching the end of the final exile, so let us take these lessons to heart and show HaShem that we truly appreciate His Special Land. Better late than never!

From *Eretz Yisrael in the Parashah* by Rabbi Moshe Lichtman.

---

24 Me'arat HaMachpeilah - the Cave of Machpelah, the Tomb of the Patriarchs.
25 Ya'akov Avinu – Our Father Jacob.

PARASHAT
VAYECHI

And he lived

GENESIS 47:28-50:26

⬥

ויחי

VAYECHI

⬥

TORAH LESSON BY
RABBI CHANAN MORRISON

REVEALING THE END OF DAYS

"Jacob called for his sons. He said: 'Gather together, and I will
tell you what will happen at the End of Days.'" (Gen. 49:1)

I N FACT, JACOB never revealed to his sons when the final redemption would take place. According to the Midrash, this secret—the time of redemption—was hidden from Jacob. The Midrash uses the following parable to explain what transpired between Jacob and his sons at Jacob's death bed.

THE PARABLE OF THE DEVOTED SERVANT

"This is like the case of a devoted servant whom the king trusted with all that he possessed. When the servant realized his end was near, he assembled his sons in order to set them free and inform them where their will and deed were located.

The king, however, discovered [this plan] and stood over his servant. When the servant saw the king, he backtracked from what he had planned to tell his sons. He began to entreat his sons, 'Please, remain servants of the king! Honor him just as I have honored him all of my days.'

So, too, Jacob gathered his sons to reveal to them the End of Days. But the Holy One revealed Himself to Jacob. 'You summoned your sons, but not Me?'... When Jacob saw God, he began to entreat his sons, 'Please, honor the Holy One just as my fathers and I have honored Him.'

The Holy One then informed [Jacob]: 'It honors God to conceal the matter.' (Proverbs 25:2) This attribute does not belong to you.'" (*Midrash Tanchuma VaYechi* 8)

This Midrash raises many questions. Why did Jacob want to reveal to his sons when the final exile would end? Why was he prevented from doing so? Also, there are discrepancies between the parable and the referent. It was God who concealed the end of days from Jacob; thus in the parable, it should have been the king who hid the deed from the servant, not the servant who hid the deed from his sons. Furthermore, the servant wanted his sons to be free—would Jacob have wanted his sons to abandon the yoke of Heaven? And why did God reprimand Jacob for not calling Him?

THE REASON FOR THE LENGTHY EXILE

We first need to examine why the exile has lasted so long. It is written that the people of Israel "were punished twice for all their sins." (Isaiah 40:2) How could God, the compassionate Father, punish the people of Israel more severely than they deserved to be punished?

The key to understanding this matter lies in the verse:

> "I have only known you from all of the families of the earth. Therefore, I visit upon you all of your iniquities." (Amos 3:2)

If the people of Israel were like all other peoples, then the destruction of the Temple would have sufficed to atone for their sins. However, the people of Israel are destined to acquire a true, intimate love of God, permanently fixed in their hearts, as indicated by the phrase "I have only known you," which implies a unique relationship between God and the people of Israel. In order to achieve this level of unfailing, constant love, they need to undergo an intensive purification to purge all moral and spiritual failings. If not corrected, these dormant faults could be reawakened and induce moral relapses in future generations.

For this reason, the Sages wrote that the people of Israel sinned doubly, were punished doubly, and will be consoled doubly (*Pesikta deRav Kahana, Nachamu*). Their sin was twofold: besides the gravity of the sin itself, it led to their estrangement from God. They were also punished doubly: in order to cleanse them from the sin and to purify their hearts to love God. And they will also be consoled doubly: not only will their transgressions be forgiven, they will also merit a special closeness to God.

CALCULATING THE END OF DAYS

The second issue that must be clarified is: is it possible to know when the End of Days will come? The Sages interpreted the verse, "A day of retribution is in My heart" (Isaiah 63:4) as follows: "to My heart I have revealed it, but not to My limbs" (Sanhedrin 97a). The term "My limbs" is a metaphor for the angels. How could Jacob have access to information which was hidden even from the angels?

Theoretically, if we were to know the spiritual level the people of Israel need to attain, the errors that future generations will commit, and the time needed to rectify those errors, then we would be able to calculate when the End of Days will occur. However, even this complex calculation is not so straightforward. Perhaps God will not wait until the people of Israel are worthy of redemption based on their own merits? Perhaps God will not delay the redemption until their sins have been fully expiated through exile, but will hasten the end, elevating Israel even before the people have properly prepared themselves to be redeemed?

In fact, this is precisely how Daniel interpreted King Nebuchadnezzar's dream, a dream foretelling "what will be at the End of Days." In the dream, Nebuchadnezzar saw that "a stone, broken off not by [human] hands, struck the statue." (Daniel 2:34) This great statue, wrought from four different metals, symbolized the four great empires—commonly understood to be Babylon, Persia, Greece, and Rome—and the corresponding exiles of the people of Israel. The stone, the Divine instrument for destroying the statue and terminating the exile, was "broken off not by human hands," indicating that the final redemption will not be achieved solely through the efforts of the people of Israel. God desires that Israel will work toward rectifying its sins and moral deficiencies; but ultimately, it will be granted eternal spiritual greatness by God Himself (See *Zohar, Pekudei* 240).

SPIRITUAL GROWTH VERSUS SUBMISSION

The righteous who walk before God always try to attain spiritual perfection on their own, without 'burdening' Heaven and expecting Divine assistance. Jacob wanted his family to acquire the final objective of constant love for God through their own efforts. By revealing the End of Days to them, Jacob intended to indicate the objective that they should strive for, so that they could attain this level through their own actions.

God, however, had different plans. Humanity was given free will so that they should not need to rely on *nehama dekisufa*, the "bread of shame." The necessity to labor and make correct choices in life gives us the satisfaction of earning our reward. Yet there is a drawback to attaining perfection through our own efforts. While the ultimate goal is to attain love of God, we also need to feel a sense of awe and submission before God. In truth, for all of our remarkable potential, we do not deserve to be called 'God's servants.' The Midrash teaches that God held Mount Sinai over the Israelites like a bucket, forcing them to accept the Torah (Shabbat 88a). This demonstrated that the people of Israel must also acknowledge their subservience to God.

Similarly, in the end of days, God will not wait until the people of Israel have perfected themselves, for then they would only have the merit of loving God, and would lack the necessary awe and servitude to Him. God will redeem the people of Israel before they are ready; the redemption will arrive like "a stone that was not broken off by [our own] hands." It is impossible to calculate the hour of redemption, for it will not occur when the people of Israel are ready, but when God deems it time. Thus Isaiah's prophecy indicates that the date is only revealed to "My heart"—i.e., only God knows.

EXPLAINING THE PARABLE

Now we may understand the parable. The king's servant wanted to free his sons from subservience to the king so that they would be able to serve the king purely out of love. When the king stood above him, however, the servant recognized that the majesty of the king is so great, that the highest level is in fact to be the king's servant. That is why God rebuked Jacob when he summoned his sons without Him. God was questioning Jacob: Do you want the redemption to be achieved only through your own efforts? Do you want it to be exclusively based on the quality of love for God?

Complete adherence to God's will, however, could only take place after the Torah was given at Sinai. Thus the Midrash concludes with God's rejoinder to Jacob: "This matter is not for you." True subservience to God will only be possible after the revelation of the Torah and its commandments.

When the faithful servant saw the king in all his majesty standing over him, he backtracked from his original plan of freeing his sons. Similarly, after God revealed Himself, Jacob recognized God's infinitely exalted nature. He realized that, even in the End of Days, the true goal is to combine love with submission and awe. Therefore, Jacob abandoned his plan to reveal the level of pure love of God that the people of Israel need to attain in the End of Days. Instead, Jacob admonished his sons to honor and fear God, just as he and his fathers had done.

From *Sapphire from the Land of Israel*. Adapted from *Midbar Shur*, pp. 273-280.

EXODUS · SHEMOT

PARASHAT
SHEMOT

Names
Exodus 1:1–6:1

שמות

SHEMOT

TORAH LESSON BY
RABBI TULY WEISZ

THE VERY FIRST RIGHTEOUS GENTILES

I REMEMBER GOING TO the movie theatre with my entire high school to see Steven Spielberg's Holocaust film, *Schindler's List* when it came out. The epic film brought the Holocaust to the forefront of American culture through the heroic story of Oskar Schindler, a non-Jewish German businessman who saved the lives of more than a thousand Jews.

Along with Schindler, during the Holocaust there were nearly 25,000 "Righteous Among the Nations" - defined by the Yad Vashem Holocaust Museum as people who risked their lives to rescue a Jew. Certainly there were many Gentiles who were opposed to the Nazi regime, but only a person who was willing to make the ultimate sacrifice is officially recognized and honored with the "Righteous" title. This week's Torah portion contains the first example of two women who were truly righteous among the nations.

In Synagogues this week, Jews begin to read the Book of Exodus, which tells us the story of a new Pharaoh who comes to power, that does not recall the vast contributions made by Joseph in preserving Egypt during the devastating famine. Here we see the formation of a pattern that is all too well known throughout history, the original precedent for anti-Semitism. The Jews are welcomed into a country and make great contributions while there, but are ultimately forsaken. The host nation turns on its Jewish residents, using them as scapegoats, and becomes fearful and suspicious of their loyalty.

And he [Pharaoh] said unto his people: 'Behold, the people of the children of Israel are too many and too mighty for us; come, let us deal wisely with them, lest they multiply, and it come to pass, that, when there befalleth us any war, they also join themselves unto our enemies, and fight against us, and get them up out of the land.' (Exodus 1:9,10)

Pharaoh begins to make life horrific for the People of Israel. He establishes state-sponsored cruelty that could have served as Hitler's playbook. However, in the midst of this chaotic turn of events, and downward spiral of hatred, two heroines emerge:

"The king of Egypt said to the Hebrew midwives of whom the name of the first was Shifra and the name of the second was Puah. And he said "When you deliver the Hebrew women, and you see them on the birth stool: if it is a son, you are to kill him, and if it is a daughter, she shall live. But the midwives feared God and they did not do as the king of Egypt spoke to them, and they caused the boys to live." (Exodus 1:15–16)

The identity of these "Hebrew midwives" (*meyaldot haivriyot*) is debated by rabbinic commentators. Many sages have assumed the literal meaning, that they were Jewish women. Other commentators, including the Abrabanel (1437–1508), argue that the story makes much more sense if we are talking about Egyptian midwives. After all, why would Pharaoh have Jewish women do his dirty work? Moreover, the text says that it was the midwives' fear of God that guided their actions, and interestingly enough, when the Bible refers to 'fear of God,' it is often used to describe the behavior of exceptional Gentiles.

According to these interpretations, *meyaldot haivriyot*, or "Hebrew midwives," is a deliberately ambiguous phrase that actually means "midwives for the Hebrew women." Shifra and Puah were Egyptians. As such, they are the first people in history who risk their lives to rescue a Jew and incredibly, the Bible refers to these two non-Jews as Hebrews.

Throughout our history, the Jewish people have faced persecution, starting from Pharaoh and lasting till this very day. 3,500 years after Pharaoh and 70 years after Hitler, ruthless dictators still threaten Israel with extinction. Sure, there are many good people around the world who are opposed to Iran. But who are the righteous gentiles of our generation who are willing to throw their lot in together with the Jewish People?

Before moving to Israel, I went to the *Christians United for Israel* Conference in Washington DC and remember Pastor John Hagee addressing this very issue:

"I stand here as Israel is surrounded and hounded, boycotted and threatened. I stand here with a strong message of solidarity with you, my Jewish brethren, the apple of God's eye. At this difficult juncture in our history, permit me to say something to you straight from the heart. Please know that what I say now is a sentiment shared by millions of Christians across America and around the world. Today, in the world of freedom, the proudest boast is 'Ani Yisraeli - I am an Israeli'. If a line has to be drawn, then let it be drawn around both of us - Christians and Jews, Americans and Israelis."

In one of the more poignant scenes in *Schindler's List*, Oskar Schindler's workers give him a ring engraved with a quote from the Talmud, "Whoever saves one life saves the world entire." Schindler didn't save a thousand lives, he saved a thousand "entire worlds." By saving the life of baby Moses, Shifra and Puah he established the precedent that reminds us of the need for more Righteous Among the Nations. Thank God, around the world today, there are millions of Christians, not just individuals here and there, who are willing to cast their lot with the nation of Israel.

PARASHAT
VA'EIRA

And 1 appeared

EXODUS 6:2-9:35

ואַרא

VA'EIRA

TORAH LESSON BY
RABBI SHLOMO RISKIN

WHAT IS A FITTING LEGACY FOR MY CHILDREN AND GRANDCHILDREN?

And I will bring you unto the land concerning which I raised My hand to give it to Abraham, to Isaac, and to Jacob; and I will give it to you for a heritage (morasha): I am God. Exodus 6:8

EVERY PARENT WOULD like to leave an inheritance to their children and grandchildren; some even work their entire lives, denying themselves vacations and little luxuries, in order to amass some sort of nest-egg as an inheritance. And others live in disappointed frustration because they fear they will not have the wherewithal to leave behind a sizable "will and testament." What does our Torah have to say about a proper bequest for future generations?

The Bible has two cognate words which relate to bequest: *morasha* and *yerusha*. *Morasha*—which appears for the first time in the Torah in the portion of *Va'eira* with regard to the Land of Israel and only once again, with regard to Torah itself, "Moses prescribed the Torah to us, an eternal heritage (*morasha*) for the congregation of Jacob" (Deut. 33:4) —is generally translated as "heritage"; *yerusha* is translated as "inheritance" and is the frequently found form for everything except Torah and Israel. It is interesting to note that in Webster's Dictionary, the words "heritage" and "inheritance" are virtually synonymous. The lead definition for heritage is "property that is or can be inherited." The Hebrew of the Bible, however, is precise and exact. The use of different words clearly suggests a difference in meaning. The different contexts in which the two words *"morasha"* and *"yerusha"* appear can be very revealing about different kinds of bequests – and even different kinds of relationships between parents and children, different priorities handed down from generation to generation, which these bequests engender. Let us explore four different possible distinctions in meaning between *yerusha* and *morasha*, inheritance and heritage, which should provide important instruction to parents in determining their bequests to their children.

First, the Jerusalem Talmud speaks of *yerusha* as something that comes easily. A person dies, leaving an inheritance, and the heir is not required to do anything except receive the gift. But just being there is not enough when it comes to *morasha*. The added *mem* in this term, suggests the Jerusalem Talmud, is a grammatical sign of intensity, the *pi'el* form in Hebrew grammar. In order for an individual to come into possession of a *morasha* they have to work for it. An inheritance is what you get from the previous generation, without your particular input; a heritage requires your active involvement and participation. A *yerusha* is a check your father left you; a *morasha* is a business which your parents may have started, but into which you must put much sweat, blood and tears.

This will certainly explain why *morasha* is used only with regards to Torah and the Land of Israel. The sages remark that there are three gifts which God gave the people of Israel that can only be acquired through commitment and suffering: "Torah, the Land of Israel and the World to Come."[1] We understand that neither Torah nor the Land of Israel is acquired easily, passively. The Babylonian Talmud, confirming our earlier citation from the Jerusalem Talmud, specifically teaches that "Torah is not an inheritance," a *yerusha*, which comes automatically to the child of the Torah scholar. All achievement in Torah depends on an individual's own efforts. A student of Torah must be willing to suffer privation. Maimonides writes that on the path of Torah acquisition a person must be willing to eat only bread and drink only water, even snatching momentary sleep on the ground rather than in a comfortable bed.[2] Indeed, no one can merit the crown of Torah unless they are willing to destroy their desire of material blandishments while in pursuit of Torah expertise (ibid. 12). Similarly, the Land of Israel cannot be acquired without sacrifice and suffering. The final test in the life of Abraham and the source of Jewish clam to Jerusalem is the binding of Isaac on Mount Moriah; the message conveyed by the Bible is that we can only acquire our Holy Land if we are willing to place the lives of our children on the line. Nothing is more apparent in modern Israel today. A heritage comes hard, not easily, and our national heritage is Torah and Israel.

The second distinction between the terms is not how the gift is acquired but rather how it may or must be dispersed. Even the largest amount of money inherited (*yerusha*) can be squandered, or legitimately lost. In contrast, a

---

1 Berakhot 5a
2 Laws of Torah Study 3:6

morasha must be given over intact to the next generation. Its grammatical form is *hif'il*, and it literally means "to hand over to someone else." Silver is an inheritance, and can be invested, lent out, or melted down or used in whatever way the heir desires; silver Shabbat candlesticks are a heritage, meant to be passed down from parent to child and used from generation to generation.

Third, one must have the physical and objective inheritance in one's possession in order to give it to one's heir; that is not necessarily the case with regard to a heritage, or *morasha*. Jewish parents bequeathed the ideals of Torah and Israel to their children for four thousand years, even when they were living in exile far from the Promised Land and even if poverty and oppression made it impossible for them to be Torah scholars. Jewish mothers in Poland and Morocco sang their children to sleep with lullabies about the beauty of the Land of Israel and the paramount importance of Torah scholarship, singing "Torah is the best merchandise" and Jerusalem the most beautiful city. Paradoxically, one can pass on a *morasha* (heritage) even if one doesn't have it oneself!

And finally, a *yerusha* is a substantive object whereas a *morasha* may be an abstract idea or ideal. There is a charming Yiddish folk song in which the singer "laments" that while his friends' wealthy parents gave them automobiles, his parents could only give him good wishes: "Go with God." While his friends' parents gave them cash, his parents gave him aphorisms: *"Zai a mentsch*—be a good person." However, whereas the automobiles and cash were quickly dissipated, the words remained—and were passed on to the next generation.

The truth is that an inheritance pales in comparison to a heritage. The real question must be: Will you only have a transitory inheritance to leave your children, or will you merit bequeathing an eternal heritage?

From *Torah Lights: Vayikra* by Rabbi Shlomo Riskin; used with permission from Maggid Books, a division of Koren Publishers Jerusalem.

PARASHAT
BO

Enter!

Exodus 10:1-13:16

בא

BO

TORAH LESSON BY
RABBI GEDALIA MEYER

THE EXODUS

'AND I WILL pass through the land of Egypt on that night and I will strike all the firstborn in Egypt, both human and animal, and I will execute judgment upon all of Egypt, I am Hashem. And the blood shall be for you a sign upon your houses that you are there, and I shall see the blood and **pass over** you, and there will not be upon you a plague of destruction when I strike in the land of Egypt.' (Exodus 12: 12–13)

Where do we place the Exodus in the history of the world? Is it a myth or is it a fact? Did it happen in the time, place, and manner indicated in the Bible, or were the details lost in the fog of Biblical tradition that puts more emphasis on miracles and the hand of God, than on trivial details like how and when things happened? Were these Israelites the actual ancestors of the Jews or were they some ancient tribal group that the Jews somehow latched on to in order to glorify their own otherwise insignificant history?

These are questions that will be debated as long as people are interested in the Bible. Recent centuries have shown a dramatic trend of losing interest in the Bible, both among Jews and non-Jews. The Bible no longer seem that relevant to the modern mind. It is too ancient, too religious, *too Biblical*, for modern sensitivities. But there is no denying the sheer power of that dramatic period— lasting no longer than a year in its crucial stage, but still shedding its influence on humanity 3,000 years later.

Tradition has the Exodus taking place about 3,300 years ago in what is now the northern part of Egypt, mainly in the region of the Nile delta. The build-up to the Exodus took about 200 years, but actually began at least 400 years before the event. Abraham, the patriarchal ancestor of the Israelites, was prophetically told that his descendents would be oppressed in a land that was not theirs but he was also promised that they would ultimately be redeemed and brought back to the Promised Land of Israel.

The first phase of this prophecy was fulfilled when the descendents of Abraham, who were living in Egypt as a result of migration from a famine, were enslaved by a Pharaoh who selectively forgot the great benefit these migrants brought to his land. Jewish tradition holds that the period of oppression lasted a little over 200 years. It ended only through the on-the-ground guidance of Moses, the reluctant prophet/leader of what amounts to the first recorded mass slave rebellion in human history.

So far, everything could have happened according to the script. Details, such as population numbers and fitting the whole thing into the historical timeline are somewhat sketchy, but all-in-all it could very easily have taken place more or less as described. It is only when God is brought into the picture that eyebrows begin to be raised. But God is all over this story from beginning to end. Taking God out of the story is like taking the air out of a room; it loses all its life.

Moses was told about his mission during his prophetic encounter with God at the Burning Bush. It was there that he was told that his task was to bring God's people out of slavery and lead them to the land of their ancestors. Over the next year or so, he repeatedly warned Pharaoh to free the Israelites or else suffer the increasingly deadly effects of a series of natural/supernatural plagues. The famous Ten Plagues finally end with a crescendo—the plague of killing of the first born—an obvious impossibility according to the laws of nature. This plague was destined to occur on the night of Passover, the holiday Jews have celebrated ever since commemorating the birth of their nation.

Among other things, the bulk of the laws and customs of Passover are described in this parasha. The Hebrew word for Passover is *Pesach*, a word which occurs as a verb three times in our parasha. It also occurs several times as a noun, referring to the meal of lamb the Israelites were commanded to prepare for this night. It has been translated in various ways, but 'Passover' is the one that has stuck. It does not celebrate the death of the firstborn of the Egyptians, as we might be tempted to believe. Instead it celebrates the frequently overlooked fact that God 'passed over' the houses of the Israelites during this plague. This plague was an act of destruction, of death. Plagues have scourged humanity since time immemorial, but this one was different. It spared a specific group of people, a group that was singled out for a unique destiny.

Never before had such a thing happened and never would it occur again. Plagues are indiscriminate, as are hurricanes, earthquakes, and famines. But this plague was different. According to the Bible, it was different for one reason only—because God diverted its course of destruction. The plague itself may have been a perfectly normal bacteria or virus, but the immunity granted to the Israelites was anything but normal.

The first verse quoted above describes the plague itself as it unleashed its destructive force upon Egypt. The second verse describes the immunity granted to the Israelites. This immunity, it appears, was due to the fact that God would see the blood on the Israelite houses and pass over those houses. This blood, it turns out from other verses in the parasha, was the blood of the Passover lamb itself that was to be sprinkled on the doorposts of the houses. What was it that spared the Israelites from the plague? It was the simple fact that they observed the commandment to celebrate the Passover meal as the events outside were happening. The first Passover celebration took place in Egypt simultaneously with the plague. They were commemorating the very history which they were living.

Passover is not about a plague. It is not about blood and death and destruction. These are natural events that take place all the time and neither need, nor deserve, commemoration. Passover is about the hidden miracle that took place right in the midst of that plague. It is about God intervening in the natural course of events and made something happen, which cannot be explained by nature. This is really what the entire event of the Exodus represents. It was not merely an ancient slave rebellion that happened to be successful because of a series of fortuitous natural events. It really should not have succeeded at all—but it did!

It is interesting that the first of the Ten Commandments states; 'I am Hashem, your God, who took you out of the land of Egypt and the bonds of slavery.' One might have expected this commandment to emphasize a different accomplishment of God—the creation of the universe. Isn't the creation more supernatural, more miraculous, more worthy of association with God? While there is a strong argument to support such a claim, there is a counter argument that is just as strong. The creation of the universe happened when there was nobody there to witness it. We simply observe the finished product and take it for granted. The Exodus, however, was experienced by very real and very alive human beings, who witnessed its events and took part in them. The events of the Exodus demonstrate something vitally important about God that even the creation cannot show. The events show that God continues to play a role in our lives if we play our part in enabling it to happen.

PARASHAT
BESHALACH

When he let go

Exodus 13:17-17:16

בשלח

BESHALACH

TORAH LESSON BY
RABBI CHAIM RICHMAN

THE SPLITTING OF THE SEA AND THE RESURRECTION OF THE DEAD

A MAJOR COMPONENT OF Parashat Beshalach is the famed 'Song of the Sea' that was sung by Moshe and the Children of Israel during the miracle of The Parting of the Sea (Exodus 15). This seminal event was the climax of the Exodus from Egypt, and an unparalleled prophetic experience for all of Israel. All of Israel were able to directly perceive the endless love and might of the Holy One, blessed be He, witnessed by the words, "Israel saw the great hand that Hashem inflicted upon Egypt; and the people revered Hashem, and they had faith in Hashem, and in Moses, His servant" (Exodus 14:31). This was not just a matter of extraordinarily lucid perception, it was experiential; all of Israel experienced firsthand that G-d is the only reality. The event was so transcendent that our sages state that even the most ordinary person had a greater revelation at The Splitting of the Sea, than that of the prophet Ezekiel.

So what exactly did they see that was so inspiring? Our sages teach us that the entire nation walked along the sea bed the whole night. Each tribe walked along a different path, separated by walls of water that enabled them to see each other. Mothers fed their hungry children by simply reaching their arms into the water piled at their sides, and pulled out fruit for the children to eat. The event was brimming with so many miracles, no wonder our sages record that everyone sang the Song of the Sea—even the unborn babies in their mothers' womb.

In summary, the conventional understanding is that the great and overwhelming sense of joy experienced by Israel at this event came from the realization that G-d's strong hand was upon them. They also witnessed many great miracles whilst crossing the sea. However, on a deeper level, the symbolism in the Song is quite mystical and its stanzas are replete with references and allusions to cosmic themes.

In one of the Talmud's most famous lessons pertaining to these hidden references, our sages state that the Song of the Sea is itself the main "proof from the Torah" of the Resurrection. For indeed, the belief in the ultimate and eventual resurrection of the dead—one of Maimonides' Thirteen Principles of Faith—is a basic principle of our faith; it will occur, in Maimonides' words, "at the time that G-d wills it." Yet it is not mentioned explicitly in the Torah[3].

How then, does the Song of the Sea serve to prove this idea? Although Exodus 15:1 is invariably translated as "Then sang Moses and the children of Israel this song," the Hebrew words actually mean "Then Moses and the children of Israel will sing this song"—because the word yashir is future tense. The meaning is clear: Not 'then they sang' but 'then,' meaning in the future, it will be Moses and that very generation of the children of Israel, who will themselves once again sing this song...at the time of the ultimate Resurrection.

In Israel's prayer book as well as in the code of Jewish law, it is emphasized that "whoever recites the Song of the Sea daily, with intense devotion and concentration, and above all with great joy, will merit to recite it in the next world."

Given the central role that the Exodus from Egypt and The Splitting of the Sea occupies in Torah thought, why is the recital of the Song of the Sea of such paramount importance, that an assurance such as this is given? Why is it so powerful, that its proper recitation guarantees the opportunity to repeat it for all eternity? Why is it that one who joyfully utters the song in our own generation will merit to say it in the future? Is this simply an affirmation of the Talmud's idea that links this event to the final resurrection?

Could it be that as great as we understand this event to have been, as much as we think we might be grasping it intellectually, and as high as we can imagine Israel's prophetic experience to have been, that it actually meant even more than we can imagine? That we have not even begun to fathom the great lesson that the Song of the Sea is really teaching us?

The holy Arizal (1534-1572) teaches us a profound truth: in reality, the circumstances surrounding the utterance of the song by Moses and Israel at the sea, and the details pertaining to the event, are not what most people think they are. Everyone is missing it altogether.

This great Torah master explains that the true reason for Moses' and Israel's joy at The Splitting of the Sea was seeing the awesome true power of G-d, and at that moment they realized internally, on the deepest level of reality, with

---

3 This in itself is a whole mystery that the great kabbalists like the holy Arizal write about: why is that this important foundation of Torah faith is hidden in the Torah and not mentioned explicitly? That is an exquisite teaching, but we shall leave it for another time.

the perfect certain clarity of prophetic vision, that one day there really will be a resurrection of the dead. This was not a belief for them—it was knowledge. As Rabbi Abraham Isaac Kook writes, this realization is the true source of joy for the righteousness of all generations.

So open up your heart to understand what this really means for you.

When the men, women and children of Israel sang this song at the sea, it was not simply a reaction to the great prophetic revelation they experienced of G-d's love and power—as great as that revelation was. What was really happening, was that they realized deep in their souls that everything that they were seeing, which they were able to process and translate into the language of palpable, transcendent knowledge...it was just a microcosm, a preparation, a practice and forerunner for the time when it will really be sung with fullness —at the time of the Resurrection. The joy that they felt when seeing G-d's hand upon them at the sea was because they realized; if He can do this, He will certainly do that as well.

The words of the Song are indeed an allegory; the focus and intention of the singers was not about this event at all! The Splitting of the Sea was merely the catalyst that propelled the Children of Israel into an expanded state of consciousness, and every phrase of the Song of the Sea ostensibly speaking of this miraculous event, is actually an allusion to the great and magnificent future event when G-d's love and power will be displayed in the most immeasurable way—at the Resurrection. In summary, the song was never about that event at all; it was about the future!

This is the secret behind the Talmud's statement; that these verses serves as proof of the Resurrection. The common misconception is that the song will be sung at the Resurrection by all of Israel because it was sung at The Splitting of the Sea. But the opposite is true; it was only sung at the sea to a small extent. The people realized that one day the greatest moment of all will be upon us, and they experienced a shuddering twinge, a passing momentary glimpse, of how great the joy at that moment will be, when the curtains of illusion part. We will realize that life is eternal, just as G-d's love is eternal, and everything we thought was reality, was the real illusion.

The true lesson of the Song of the Sea is that the best is yet come.

PARASHA
YITRO

Jethro

Exodus 18:1-20:23

יתרו

YITRO

TORAH LESSON BY
RABBI TULY WEISZ

IS IT KOSHER FOR CHRISTIANS TO TEACH TORAH?!

WHEN MY GOOD friend, Pastor Keith Johnson approached me about sharing his video lessons on the Ten Commandments on my website *Israel365*, my first thought was, "Christians teaching Torah? That's not kosher!"

Given the major differences between Judaism and Christianity, how could a rabbi endorse a pastor's Torah lessons??

Then I noticed the irony of it all: the Ten Commandments appear in this week's Torah portion of Yitro (Jethro), who is not only a non-Jew, he was an idolatrous Midianite priest. How could it be that Jethro gets credit for, and is associated with, such a central feature of the Torah as the Ten Commandments?

The famous Rabbi Chaim ibn Attar (1696-1743) who was born in Morocco but made Aliyah (immigrated) to Israel and is buried on Jerusalem's Mount of Olives, offered an important answer to this sensitive question.

In his comments on Exodus 18:21, Attar wrote, "It appears to me that God is instructing the Children of Israel, in that generation and in every generation, that the nations of the world have giants of wisdom and understanding." He explains that God did not choose Israel to receive the Torah because of their brains or intellect, for the Jewish people do not have a monopoly on wisdom.

The "Aseret Hadibrot" (Ten Commandments in Hebrew) are the joint heritage of Jews and Bible-believing non-Jews, "in that generation and in every generation." So much so, that to this very day the Ten Commandments are the greatest symbol of our Judeo-Christian values, proudly displayed in courtrooms and public buildings throughout the United States.

Jews and non-Jews working together to further God's word might seem new and even a bit controversial, but according to the Talmud, it is the fulfillment of a prophecy from Isaiah.

Tractate Bava Batra[4] contains a story about King Herod who viciously murders the leading rabbis of his generation. The brutal monarch keeps one rabbi alive, befriends him and he ultimately becomes the King's trusted advisor.

---

4 Bava Batra is the third of the three tractates in the Talmud in the order Nezikin; it deals with a person's responsibilities and rights as the owner of property.

According to the Talmud, Herod comes to deeply regret his murderous actions and seeks atonement from the rabbi.

"What can I possibly do?" Herod sincerely asks his Jewish friend.

"The Torah is compared to light," the rabbi answers, "and by murdering so many teachers of the Torah, you extinguished God's light in the world. Therefore, in order to achieve forgiveness, you must bring more light into the world by rebuilding the Jewish Temple which is associated with light."

Isaiah 2:2 describes the Nations coming to the Mountain of the Lord in Jerusalem which housed the Temple. The prophet writes "All the nations will be drawn (*venaharu*) to it." Using an unusual Hebrew word, *venaharu* which is similar to the word for light, ohr, Isaiah is alluding to the future when the nations of the world, who for years tried to extinguish the light of the world, will ultimately seek forgiveness and commit to reigniting that light.

Based on this conversation, the non-Jewish King Herod went on to restore the Second Temple to such majestic grandeur that his name is forever associated with God's home, the Beit Hamikdash.

Perhaps Isaiah's words were not only meant for Herod, but for his generation and all generations of Jews and non-Jews.

We are seeing with our own eyes that "all the nations will be drawn" to Jerusalem. Many Christians are seeking to atone for the sins the Christian anti-Semitism committed against the Jewish people throughout history and to reignite the light by supporting Israel, the Jewish people and the Torah, like Pastor Keith Johnson.

I therefore told Pastor Johnson that it was my pleasure and responsibility to share his teachings on the Ten Commandments. This is not because I agree with everything that my good friend Pastor Keith thinks or says; after all, there are important differences between what Jews and Christians believe.

I wanted however to demonstrate my appreciation and admiration for what he is doing. I see the efforts of Christian Zionists as the miraculous fulfillment of Isaiah 2:2 where the Nations of the World will flow to Jerusalem to reignite the light of the world. I believe there is no better time to embark upon this great spiritual unity than during the week we read the Torah's portion of Jethro and we accept upon ourselves the Ten Commandments.

PARASHAT
MISHPATIM

Laws

Exodus 21:1-24:18

משפטים

MISHPATIM

TORAH LESSON BY

RABBI CHANAN MORRISON

AN EYE FOR AN EYE

AZAR'S QUESTION

URING THE YEARS that Rav Kook (1865 – 1935) served as chief rabbi of Jaffa, he met and befriended many of the Hebrew writers and intellectuals of the time. His initial contact in that circle was the "elder" of the Hebrew writers, Alexander Ziskind Rabinowitz (1854 – 1945), better known by the abbreviation "Azar." Azar was one of the leaders of Po'alei Tzion, an anti-religious, Marxist party; but over the years, Azar developed strong ties with traditional Judaism. He met with Rav Kook many times, and they became close friends.

Azar once asked Rav Kook: How can the Sages interpret the verse "an eye for an eye" (Ex. 21:24) as referring to monetary compensation? Does this explanation not contradict the *peshat*, the simple meaning of the verse?

The Talmud (*Baba Kamma* 84a) brings a number of proofs that the phrase "eye for an eye" cannot be taken literally. How, for example, could justice be served if the person who poked out his neighbor's eyes was himself blind? Or what if one of the parties had only one functioning eye before the incident? Clearly, there are many cases in which such a punishment would be neither equitable nor just.

What bothered Azar was the blatant discrepancy between the simple reading of the verse and the Talmudic interpretation. If "eye for an eye" in fact means monetary compensation, why does the Torah not state that explicitly?

THE PARABLE

Rav Kook responded by way of a parable. The Kabbalists[5], he explained, compared the Written Torah to a father and the Oral Torah to a mother. When parents discover their son has committed a grave offense, how do they react?

The father immediately raises his hand to punish his son. But the mother,

---

5 Kabbalist – a learned person in *Kabbalah* – (often referred to as the "soul" of the Torah, the Kabbalah is an ancient Jewish tradition which teaches the deepest insights into the essence of Gd, His interaction with the world, and the purpose of Creation).

full of compassion, rushes to stop him. "Please, not in anger!" she pleads, and she convinces the father to mete out a lighter punishment.

An onlooker might conclude that all this drama was superfluous. In the end, the boy did not receive corporal punishment. Why make a big show of it?

In fact, the scene provided an important educational lesson for the errant son. Even though he was only lightly disciplined, the son was made to understand that his actions deserved a much more severe punishment.

A FITTING PUNISHMENT

This is exactly the case when one individual injures another. The offender needs to understand the gravity of his actions. In practice, he only pays monetary restitution, as the Oral Law rules. But he should not think that with money alone he can repair the damage he inflicted. As Maimonides (1135 – 1204) explained, the Torah's intention is not that the court should actually injure him in the same way that he injured his neighbor, but rather "that *it is fitting* to amputate his limb or injure him, just as he did to the injured party" (*Mishneh Torah,* Laws of Personal Injuries 1:3).

Maimonides more fully developed the idea that monetary restitution alone cannot atone for physical damages in chapter 5:

> Causing bodily injury is not like causing monetary loss. One who causes monetary loss is exonerated as soon as he repays the damages. But if one injured his neighbor, even though he paid all five categories of monetary restitution—even if he offered to God all the rams of Nevayot [see Isaiah 60:7] —he is not exonerated until he has asked the injured party for forgiveness, and he agrees to forgive him. (Personal Injuries, 5:9)

Afterwards, Azar commented:

> Only Rav Kook could have given such an explanation, clarifying legal concepts in Jewish Law by way of Kabbalistic metaphors, for I once heard him say that the boundaries between *Nigleh* and *Nistar*, the exoteric and the esoteric areas of Torah, are not so rigid. For some people, Torah with Rashi's (1040-1105) commentary is an esoteric study; while for others, even a chapter in the Kabbalistic work *Eitz Chayim* belongs to the revealed part of Torah.

From *Sapphire from the Land of Israel,* pp. 151-153. Adapted from *Malachim Kivnei Adam* by R. Simcha Raz, pp. 351, 360.

PARASHAT
TERUMAH

Offering

Exodus 25:1-27:19

תרומה

TERUMAH

TORAH LESSON BY
RABBI CHAIM RICHMAN

CAN MAN CREATE SPIRITUAL REALITY THAT TRANSCENDS PHYSICAL SPACE?

THE ARK OF the Covenant is the heart and the nucleus of the Holy Temple. G-d commanded Israel to create it to serve as a receptacle for the Tablets of the Law that Moses would bring down from Mount Sinai. Thus, the Torah also refers to it as 'the Ark of the Testimony'—for the tablets are the testimony of the covenant between the Holy One, blessed be He, and Israel; a testimony of the unbreakable bond of love that exists between them.

Here, between the two golden cherubim on the Ark's cover, is the dwelling place of the *Shechina*, the Divine Presence. Even today, all of Israel throughout the world face the direction of the *Shechina* whilst doing their prayers. Located within the innermost and most sacred chamber, the Holy of Holies, the Ark is hidden from everyone—like the tree of life in the Garden of Eden. The Holy of Holies is so sacred that only the High Priest can enter, and only once a year. This happens on Yom Kippur, the awesome Day of Atonement. Indeed, our sages teach the mystical idea that the Biblical Garden of Eden comprised a very large area. But the center of the Garden of Eden is in the Land of Israel, and the heart of the Garden is the Temple Mount in Jerusalem. The altar of offerings is the location of the Tree of Knowledge, and the heart of hearts is the location of the Holy of Holies, which is the place of the Tree of Life.

With the tablets of the law and the golden cherubim as its contents, the Ark represents a perpetuation of the Sinai Revelation. The Ark is the secret of the Temple altogether: a portal, man's rendezvous with the Divine. It was here that Moshe stood, between the two poles of the Ark, to hear the voice of the *Shechina*. The Ark is *aron* in Hebrew, derived from the word *or*, light. The light that was revealed on the first day of creation and then stored away for the future rectified world, is hidden in the Ark. This is the simple meaning of the word *aron*—it's a box of light.

The Ark is the exception to every rule. It is the first vessel that was commanded to be created, and the only vessel which was commanded by G-d in plural: *"They* shall make an Ark of acacia wood..." (Exodus 25:10). The other vessels are used to perform various aspects of the Divine service: either daily (such as the kindling of the Menorah, and the offering of incense on the Golden Altar) or weekly (the placement of the loaves on the Table of the Showbread). The Ark is not used for any service. Only the High Priest enters into the Holy of Holies on the Day of Atonement to sprinkle the blood, and even that is done only in the proximity of the Ark.

The other vessels in the Sanctuary are all situated length-wise; only the Ark is to be placed by its width. This was in order to enable the two poles to extend until they slightly touched the curtain.

The poles on the Ark facilitated its transportation until it reached its permanent location. Yet, there is a special commandment to never remove the poles from the Ark. Not even in the Holy Temple, even though they were no longer needed. This was so that the protrusion of the poles would lightly touch the curtains, and could thus be slightly seen from the Sanctuary.

Numerous 'supernatural' events surrounding the Ark are recorded in the Bible, such as the plagues when the Ark was captured by the Philistines[6], and the death of Uzah[7] when the Ark was being brought to Jerusalem.

An amazing tradition testifies that the Ark 'occupies no physical space.' That is, its dimensions could not have fit within the Holy of Holies! The Ark revealed an element that was above time and space; it transcended space. The concept of transcendence, of being unbound by the limitation of space, was also manifested in the Holy Temple in the words of the Mishnah[8] as "they stood crowded, but prostrated expansively; one of the ten miracles that took place in the Second Temple" (Chapters of the Father, 5,5). This refers to the time when the people of Israel gathered together in the court of the Holy Temple; they stood packed together as a crowd, with barely room for all to stand. Yet, when the moment came for everyone to fully prostrate themselves as they heard the awesome Ineffable Name of G-d pronounced by the High Priest, there was ample room for everyone to perform their act of devotion without one person unsettling the next!

Moreover, the Ark 'lifted its bearers'. This means that despite the fact that

6 1 Samuel chap. 5 and 6
7 1 Chronicles chap. 13
8 Mishna - the first part of the Talmud; a collection of early oral interpretations of the scriptures that was compiled about AD 200.

it was very heavy, as it contained the tablets of law, not only did it not need to be carried; it lifted and bore those who carried it.

However, the greatest miracle of all, is associated with the Ark's poles. When Joshua was preparing the people to cross the Jordan to enter into the Land, he said to the Children of Israel, '*Come here* and hear the words of the Lord your G-d. *Through this* you will know that the living G-d is in your midst (. . .)' (See Joshua 3:9–10).

Citing the Midrash, Rashi (1040-1105)0 explains the meaning of the words 'come here': "(. . .) he gathered everyone in between the two poles of the Ark, and this is an example of the principal of 'a little which holds a lot' (i.e. a transcendence of space)."

Do we understand what we are reading here? "Come here," said Joshua, and he gathered the entire nation of Israel in between the two poles of the Ark! He told them: "*through this* you will know that the living G-d is in your midst (. . .)." The fact that the two poles of the Ark held all of you shows you that the *Shechina* of the Holy One, blessed be He, is amongst you. This is the revelation of Godliness which is beyond the borders of reality; the very essence of the Ark is beyond the confines of nature. Thus, through the Ark, a glimpse into the true nature of reality is revealed in this world.

When Israel was on the threshold of her entry into the land, Joshua elevated them to this level. This is the supernatural reality that was experienced in the Temple every day. In the same manner in which the Ark occupied no space within the Holy of Holies, 'lifted its bearers,' and just as 'they stood crowded but bowed down amply,' so too did Joshua reveal the spiritual root, the vortex of the dimension of holiness, between the poles of the Ark. The supernatural reality that would later be revealed through daily life in the Holy Temple, was hidden between the poles.

But let us not overlook the most amazing thing of all; the Children of Israel built this Ark out of the simple materials they brought with them from Egypt, through the harsh conditions of the desert. This portal, this box of Divine light, the dwelling place of the Divine Presence in this world, whose two poles managed to fit the entire nation of Israel. Men, women and children were able to gather between the poles, and they were not created by supernatural humans. It was created by G-d-fearing people who sought to honor and fulfill the Creator's will. This is the basis of our relationship with the Almighty: God commands and we fulfill. Man is able to activate His will through simple obedience. The building of Ark—the very heart of the Holy Temple and the resting place of the *Shechina*, from where the Creator would manifest His loving presence—was left in the hands of Israel, so that there could be a revelation of Godliness in this world. This is the beauty, the challenge and the privilege of being a human in this world: to sanctify and elevate this world and make it into a place for the Divine Presence.

PARASHAT
TETZAVEH

You shall command

EXODUS 27:20-30:10

תצוה

TETZAVEH

TORAH LESSON BY
RABBI SHLOMO RISKIN

WHEN ABSENCE PROVES LOVE

*And you shall command the children of Israel . . . And you shall bring
forth your brother Aaron and his sons together with him . . . And
you shall speak to all of the wise-hearted. Exodus 27:20–28:3*

OFTEN WHAT YOU really have is that which you give away, what you
most profoundly say is what you leave unsaid when you wisely decide
not to respond, and the most commanding presence is felt most keenly
when that presence is not around. An example of the third phenomenon is to
be found in the Torah reading of *Tetzaveh*, the only portion since the opening
of the book of Exodus wherein Moses' name does not appear even once! Why
not?

The midrashic answer suggests that Moses initiated his own absence.
When the Israelites sinned by worshiping the golden calf less than six weeks
after the divine revelation at Sinai, God's anger reaches the breaking point (as
it were) and he makes Moses the following offer:

> And now leave Me alone as my anger shall burn and I will destroy them,
> and I shall make of you a great nation. Exodus 32:10

God suggests that He wipe Israel, no longer worthy of His benevolence,
from the pages of history by starting a new nation, a new branch, from the
loins of Moses himself.

Others in his shoes might have taken up God's offer, but Moses refuses to
increase his own glory at the expense of the nation. The climax of his brilliant
argument is an emotional ultimatum: God must forgive the people.

> . . . If not [says Moses], blot me, I pray you, out of Your book which You
> have written. Exodus 32:32

God responds to Moses' pleas. But Moses' expression of identification with
the people, Moses' selfless willingness for himself to be obliterated as long as
his nation prevails, is eternalized by the fact that in one portion of the Torah,
Tetzaveh, the master prophet's name is "missing in action."

But on an even deeper level, is there a further significance to the fact that the "blotting out" of Moses' name occurs specifically in *Tetzaveh?*

Even a quick glance reveals that our portion is almost entirely devoted to the priesthood. Chapters 28 and 29 deal extensively with all the garments that the priests are commanded to wear, particularly the High Priest, as well as the sacrifices that shall be brought to "sanctify the priests." In fact, *Tetzaveh* is often called *parashat ha-kohanim*, the portion of the priests.

Without a temple, the priest's public role is severely limited. One area, though, where his presence is still felt (particularly here in Israel and among Sephardim even in the Diaspora) is the daily priestly blessing during the repetition of the morning Amida[9]: at the conclusion of the blessing for peace, the priests, attended to by Levites, stand before the congregation and invoke the biblical blessing: "May God bless you and keep you..." (Num. 6:24). Before intoning these words, they recite the following blessing:

> Blessed are You Lord, our God, king of the universe, who has sanctified
> us with the holiness of Aaron, and has commanded us to bless His people
> with love. From the siddur.[10]

The final words in the blessing— "with love" —raise certain questions, since *kohanim*, or descendants of the High Priest Aaron, are fairly typical people. Some are as sweet as cherry ices in July, and some are as cold as Alaskan ice cubes, but most change in accordance with their mood upon awakening—how can we measure the love-quotient felt by Mr. Cohen[11] when he ascends the *bimah*[12] for the blessing? How can we legislate the emotion of love which the priests are apparently expected to feel?

The first answer lies in the very nature of the priesthood, in how the Bible legislated the priestly class's means of livelihood. It's often said that if you ask a typical entrepreneur, "How's business?" if he says, "Great," it means that he is doing well and his competitor is facing bankruptcy; if he says, "Good," that means it's a good market for everyone, he's doing well and so is his competitor; and if he says, "Terrible," then that means he's facing bankruptcy but his competition is earning a lot of money. Gore Vidal (1925 – 2012) was once quoted

---

9 The *Amidah* is the central prayer of all four services: *shacharit* (morning), *mincha* (afternoon), *maariv* (evening), and *mussaf* (additional).
10 Siddur – the Jewish prayer book.
11 Mr. Cohen – the Kohen – the priest.
12 The *bimah* is the podium located in the center of the sanctuary.

by Hilma Wolitzer (1930 -) in the *New Your Times* for his poignantly honest observation: "Whenever a friend succeeds a little, something in me dies."

Enter the *kohen*. If there is one person who disagrees with Mr. Vidal, it would have to be a member of the priestly class who served in the Temple, received no portion of land to till or business to develop, and who made his living by tithes given him by the Israelites: 1/40, 1/50, 1/60 of their produce depending upon the generosity of the individual donor. And since the tithe was a percentage of the crop, the better the farmer makes out, the happier the *kohen* ends up. To modify the Vidal quote, a *kohen* would declare: "Whenever a farmer succeeds a little [and certainly a lot], something in me lives." Hence by the very nature of the economic structure set up by the Bible, the *kohen*-priest could truly give the blessing of prosperity and well-being to the congregation of Israel "with love."

And it was because the *kohanim* where freed from professional and agricultural pursuits that they were able to devote themselves entirely to God, the Holy Temple, and the religio-moral needs of the nation. Their single-minded commitment to the holy and the divine was symbolized by the words engraved upon the highly visible gold plate (*tzitz*) worn around the forehead of the High Priest: "Holy unto God" (Ex. 28:36). Indeed, so important was it deemed that the religious and moral message not be compromised by political sectarian considerations that the Bible legislates a total separation between the religious and legislative spheres. The tribe of Judah was entrusted with sovereign, legislative leadership: "The specter shall not depart from Judah..." (Gen. 49:10), whereas the tribe of Levi was entrusted with religio-moral voice which he represents, emerges in a totally independent position, above the economic interests of special-interest groups and beyond the intrigues of palace politics.

From this perspective we can offer a second interpretation of the words "with love" which conclude the introduction to the priestly benediction: "Love" does not describe the emotions of the *Kohen*, but rather defines the content of the blessing. The most important blessing that can be bestowed upon the nation is that we live together in harmony and love. And only a priestly class separated from petty self-interest and competitions, truly devoted to God, can hope to inspire such love and harmony!

Now we can understand why Moses' name is absent particularly from this portion of *Tetzaveh*. If the *kohanim* are to symbolize selfless commitment to God and to the nation, they cannot possibly have a better example than Moses, who was willing to have his name removed from the Torah for the sake of the future of his people! If any act in the Torah can be singled out for demonstrating pure love, with no stings attached, it is when Moses refuses God's offer to start a new nation from his loins; Moses would rather that he remain anonymous but let the people of Israel live. Indeed, the essence of Moses' greatness emerges most clearly from the portion of his absence and anonymity.

From *Torah Lights: Shemot* by Rabbi Shlomo Riskin; used with permission from Maggid Books, a division of Koren Publishers Jerusalem.

PARASHAT
KI TISA

When you life
Exodus 30:11-34:35

כי תשא

KI TISA

TORAH LESSON BY
RABBI GEDALIA MEYER

THE GOLDEN CALF

'And Hashem said to Moses, "Descend, for your people whom you brought
up from Egypt have become corrupt. They have quickly swerved from the
path that they were commanded to follow and made for themselves a molten
calf and bowed to it and made offerings to it and proclaimed: This is your
god, Israel, who brought you out of the land of Egypt."' (Exodus 32: 7–8)

I
F ANYONE OF us had written the Bible the last thing we would want to put
in it is the story of the Golden Calf. It takes all the heavenly glory out of
the story and brings it smashing back down to the ground with all the mud
and dirt of a Hollywood divorce. Who asked for such an outrageous fall from
grace? Why is this in the Bible?

It is in the Bible because this is the way the events occurred. Somewhat surprising to our sensitivities, the Bible is not an ancient attempt to whitewash old
tribal stories and glorify one particular group at the expense of all others. It
tells the good and the bad, the highs and the lows. The lows are just as important as the highs, as we need to understand how low we can sink in order to
see how high we can rise.

Let's get the background of this story and then lay it out in all its gory details.
The Israelites had come out of Egypt, crossed in the midst of the sea and were
being followed closely by Pharaoh's troops who drowned in the resurging
waters, before making their way into the Sinai Peninsula. The giving of the
Ten Commandments was the high point of their journey. They all heard the
voice of God in some form, resounding from the heavens through thunder and
lightning over the mountain. The details of what they experienced are subject
to great debate, but it is clear that they saw and heard something supernatural.
This event stuck with the Israelites as the defining moment of their history;
they witnessed the giving of the Torah at Mt. Sinai.

Moses remained on top of the mountain to commune with God and to
receive the tablets etched with the Ten Commandments. He was there for
40 days and 40 nights, a span of time that somehow became characteristic of
the Bible. By the end of this period the Israelites had lost patience, and they

suspected that Moses was not coming back down. They didn't know what had happened to him but whatever it was; it had left them without a leader.

At this point, two parallel dramas take place in the Bible—one on top of Mt. Sinai and the other at its base. At the base, the Israelites demands that Aaron, the brother of Moses, produce some substitute 'god' to replace Moses who had apparently abandoned them. Aaron, with what is traditionally seen as a stall tactic, tells them to give their golden jewelry as metal to melt into a statue. The statue takes the form of a calf (hence the famous name) and is declared to the Israelites as 'your god who took you up from Egypt'. How they reached this astounding conclusion after the events they personally experienced over the past year is one of the great mysteries of the Bible. The best answer to this perplexing question is that this is the spiritual nature of human beings—they can rise to the heights of heaven, but just as quickly plummet to the depths of hell.

In the meantime, Moses was up on the mountain communing with God and blissfully unaware of the calamity taking place on the ground. It was only when God informed him that he understood what had transpired. God's initial response was to destroy the Israelites and start from scratch by making a nation directly from Moses. Moses then tries to convince God (this happens a few times in the Bible) that this would only show the world that God had failed in the great project of the Exodus. God eventually relents but the situation still has to be dealt with.

It is at this point that the two dramas meet. Moses descends from the mountain with the tablets containing the Ten Commandments in his hands. These tablets are described as having been made and inscribed by the act of God. As he approaches the camp and sees first-hand what is taking place, he throws down the tablets and breaks them. He then burns the calf and grinds it into dust. He scatters the remains into water and makes the Israelites drink it. A battle ensues in which 3,000 people are killed, but the worst, it seems is over.

The rest of the story is somewhat anticlimactic. Moses ascends the mountain to intercede with God on behalf of the Israelites. Tradition ascribes another 40-day span to this period, and in the end, Moses achieves partial forgiveness for his people. Changes would have to be made, consequences would have to be born, but the Israelites survived and so did their relationship with God. A new set of tablets were made, but they didn't have quite the same divinely inscribed quality as the originals. Only the leadership qualities of Moses and his personal connection to God were the positive outcomes of this whole sequence of events. From here on in he would serve more or less as an intermediary between God and the Israelites, which perhaps was not initially intended.

What comes out of all this? What is the eternal lesson to be learned? Are we all just a bunch of fickle weaklings who cannot stomach a few difficult moments and buckle under the slightest pressure? Is spiritual enlightenment reserved for a select few—the exceedingly rare elite who have the qualities of a Moses? Perhaps this is the case, but maybe there is something else to be gleaned from this event; one of the most tragic and calamitous in the long history of the Israelites.

Our relationship with God is not an 'on-off' activity. It is not something you hold on to when it feels good and something you throw off when it is annoying. It is a permanent arrangement, a covenant that was taken by both sides to be endured forever. This is a very difficult thought for 21st century people to accept. We live in an age when fads come and go like the weather and one can change religious beliefs with the same ease as changing ones' clothing. Permanence is not a particularly praiseworthy quality any longer. If something is permanent it is bound to get old-fashioned or downright antiquated. It is not just religion that falls into this undesirable category, it is all enduring modes of life like marriage, or devotion to family, or national pride. Their very permanence makes them out-of-date.

Perhaps this is the best fate for some matters, but it was not meant to be the fate of the Torah and the covenant between God and the Israelites. It was meant to last forever. The fact that it didn't, at least in the manner originally intended, is not a reflection of God but of the Israelites. That they didn't have the patience to wait another day for Moses or weren't satisfied with a God that they could not touch, is an indication of how difficult it is to be truly dedicated to the idea of monotheism. It is a wonderful and all-encompassing form of belief, but it requires a steady supply of devotion. This, perhaps, has been the biggest reason for rejecting Judaism throughout its long history; it has always been extremely demanding. It was not just the non-Jews who saw it this way but also the Jews themselves. The Golden Calf represents that imminent temptation to be free of all religious and moral restrictions, so it is a lesson to us all. It is the lesson of sticking with one's convictions, even when the going gets tough. It is a tough lesson for a tough people.

PARASHAT
VAYAKHEL

And he assembled

Exodus 35:1-38:20

ויקהל

VAYAKHEL

TORAH LESSON BY
RABBI SHLOMO RISKIN

VANITIES AND VIRTUES

He made the copper laver and its copper base out of the mirrors of the service women [armies of women] who congregate to serve at the entrance of the Tent of Meeting. Exodus 38:8

THE SANCTUARY AND all of its furnishings are described in exquisite and sometimes seemingly repetitive detail, but the laver, the large basin within which the priests sanctified themselves by washing their hands and feet prior to each divine service, is an exception to this rule.

Several aspects distinguish this washbasin. First of all, virtually all the other items in the Sanctuary are given exact measurements, but here the Torah speaks in general terms. The precise dimensions of the laver and its base are not given. Are not these details important, and if not, why not?

Perhaps the answer to this question is found in the latter part of this same verse, where we are told that the laver was made of the "mirrors of the service women." According to R. Samson Rafael Hirsch's Torah commentary, the phrase *"ba-marot ha-tzovot"* (mirrors of the service women) suggests that the copper mirrors were not melted down at all, but that the laver was "...fitted together almost without any alteration at all, so that it would be recognizable that the basin consisted actually of mirrors" (Commentary to Ex. 38:8).

Even if this first question is answered, a second question comes in its wake. Of all contributions to the Sanctuary, why should the mirrors retain their unique identity? Does it not seem odd that the very accouterment found in every woman's possession, the very symbol of vanity, would find a new incarnation as a central piece inside the Sanctuary? Indeed, without first stopping at the laver to wash their hands and feet, the priests could not begin the Temple service.

How "vanities" could become such a significant aspect of our Sanctuary is the subject of a fascinating debate between two major commentaries.

Ibn Ezra (1089–1167) writes as follows:

> It is the custom of women to beautify themselves, to look at their faces every morning in copper or glass mirrors...And there were in Israel women who served God, and decided to turn away from all the physical

material blandishments of this would. They therefore gave their mirrors away to the Sanctuary as a gift offering because they no longer had the need to beautify themselves. From that time on they would arrive daily at the doorway of the Tent of Meeting to pray and to listen to the details of the commandments. That is the reason why the biblical text says they came in hordes [armies], *tzovot*, at the entrance to the Tent of Meeting; they were so numerous. Ibn Ezra, on Exodus 38:8.

Ibn Ezra is here describing the first women's prayer service and study hall (*bet midrash*) at the door of the Sanctuary's Tent of Meeting, a remarkable fact in itself, especially since he maintains that it was so popular that it attracted "armies" of women. But his main point is to stress an ascetic aspect of the women's relationship to God. Since mirrors represent the physical desires of this world, once the women acquired the higher spiritual plane of involvement in prayer and study, they no longer had any use for the mirrors and gave them away to the Sanctuary.

For Rashi (1040-1105), however, the inclusion of the women's mirrors inside in the Sanctuary is the story of a religious metamorphosis, not the rejection of the physical but rather the sanctification of the physical, and herein, it seems to me, lies the true message of the sanctuary. Rashi explains that when the daughters of Israel brought a gift offering of the actual mirrors, they were initially rejected by Moses

because they were made for the evil instinct. But God said to Moses: "Accept them; these are more beloved to me than anything else. Through these mirrors the women established many armies in Egypt." [A play on the word *tzovot*, service women, which literally means armies, and a reference to t he armies of children whom the women brought forth.] When the husband would come home exhausted from backbreaking work, their wives would bring them food and drink. And they would take the mirrors, and would appear together with their husbands in the reflection of the mirror. Thus they would entice their husbands and they would become pregnant. Rashi, on Exodus 38:8

According to Rashi, the mirrors represent the unswerving faith of the Israel women, their supreme confidence in an Israelite future. After all, the Israelites where enslaved and their male babies thrown into the Nile during the Egyptian subjugation. Logic certainly dictated not having any children, refusing to bring innocent babes into a life of suffering and possible death. But there was also a tradition of the Covenant of the Pieces (Gen. 15), a promise of redemption, a charge to teach the world ethical monotheism. Consider what would have happened if the Israelite women had not found a way to entice their husbands. The history of Israel would have ended almost before it began, in the very first exile of Egypt, devoid of a next generation of Israeli continuity. In effect, the transformation of these mirrors of desire into the laver of purification is the Torah's way of rewarding the women for their devotion and explaining to future generations the biblical ideal of the sanctification of the physical, the uplifting of the material. The key here is that they looked into the mirrors and saw themselves and their husbands. They looked into the mirrors and saw armies of an Israelite future. Had they seen only themselves, and not their husbands and their progeny, their place in Israel's history would hardly have been as exalted.

Which of these interpretations is easier to accept? Perhaps the following Talmudic passage can clarify matters. We read in *Nazir* an account of Shimon the Just, High Priest and one of the last Men of the Great Assembly:

> All of my life I never ate from a Nazirite's sacrificial offering, except once, when I saw a Nazirite coming towards me from the south. He was beautiful of eyes, goodly of appearance, with magnificent curly hair. I said to him, "My son, why have you decided to destroy such beautiful hair?" [because ultimately a Nazirite gives his hair as a sacrifice upon the altar]. He said to me, "I was a shepherd . . . and I once went to draw water from the well and I looked at my reflection in the water. An evil instinct began to overcome me [because I fell in love with myself]. And I said [to the evil instinct], empty one, do you not realize that ultimately you will just be worms and maggots? And I took an oath to become a Nazirite." And Shimon the Just said, "I stood and I kissed him on the forehead, and I said to him, 'May all Nazirites be like you.'" Nazir 4b

Why was this Nazirite different form all other Nazirites? Implicit in Shimon the Just's account is that all others who took this ascetic vow were in some way violating an inherent principle in the Torah by denying themselves what the Torah permits – the rationale, according to many commentaries, behind the Nazirite's sin offering. But this particular Nazirite was doing what he had to do in order to save himself from the narcissistic danger of becoming attracted to the mysterious depths of his own reflection. He was on the way to a life of egoistic self-love and self-absorption which he felt could only be put in check by his becoming a Nazirite.

How different is Rashi's brilliant description of the mirrors. The greatness of the Israel women in Egypt is that they looked at the reflection not only of themselves but of their husbands as well. And because they saw their husbands as well as themselves, they also saw, and provided for, Israelite future and Israelite destiny. They were concerned not only for their own pleasure, but also for the material pleasure of husband and wife which is only realized to its greatest degree in the creation of children, who represent personal and national continuity and future.

An amazing Talmudic text brings home this point to a striking degree:

> Rav Katina said: When the Jewish people (Israelites) would go up to Jerusalem during the festivals, the keepers of the Sanctuary would roll back the curtain covering the holy ark, and would reveal to the Jews who came up to Jerusalem, the cherubs, which were in the form of a male and female embracing each other. And they would say to them, to the Jews: 'See the love which God has for you, like the love of a male and female.'
> Yoma 54a

And the cherubs had the faces of small children, symbol of Israeli continuity. Love for another, expressed in the highest form by love of lover for beloved, husband for wife, is the greatest manifestation of sanctity, and it is precisely this male-female attraction which has the power to secure our Israeli eternity.

The Sanctuary is sanctified by the mirrors of the women in Egypt, who taught, by their example, how to turn the most physical human drive into the highest act of divine service. In a very real sense, the Sanctuary itself, replete with intricately detailed expert craftsmanship, exquisite and expensive ornamentation, and gold and silver filigreed ritual objects, was similarly an attempt to take the very basic human passion for gold and beauty, which so perverted the Israelites at the incident of the golden calf, and utilize this very materialistic drive to inspire them to divine service. "And let them make among Me a Sanctuary that I may dwell within them."

From *Torah Lights: Shemot* by Rabbi Shlomo Riskin; used with permission from Maggid Books, a division of Koren Publishers Jerusalem.

PARASHAT
PEKUDEI

Accountings of
EXODUS 38:21-40:38

פקודי

PEKUDEI

TORAH LESSON BY
RABBI ZELIG PLISKIN

LEARN TO DO THINGS IN THEIR PROPER ORDER.

ובצלאל בן-אורי בן-חור, למטה יהודה, עשה, את כל-אשר-צוה ה את-משה.

"And Betzalel the son of Chur of the tribe of Yehudah did all that the Almighty commanded Moshe." (Exodus 38:22)

RASHI (1040-1105) STATES that Betzalel realized on his own that the proper order was to make the tabernacle first and only then to make the vessels. When building a house, people need to build the house first and then they acquire the furniture to put into the house. Although at first Moshe told Betsalel what to do in the reverse order, he agreed that Betzalel was correct in changing the order.

Rabbi Yeruchem Levovitz commented that we see here the concept of the importance of having things done in their proper order. One always needs to clarify his priorities and to have the organizational skills to do things in order. (Daas Torah: Shemos, pp.350-1)

This is an important tool for accomplishing anything in life. One needs to know what he must do and then he must have an order of priorities. We will never have enough time to do everything we would like to. But by being aware of the order of importance of what you have to do, you will ensure that you will effectively accomplish the most possible within the limitations of the time allotted to you. Each day make a list of the various tasks you need to take care of. Then decide on a proper order in which to do them.

BE GRATEFUL TO PEOPLE WHO ENABLE YOU TO MAKE WORTHWHILE CONTRIBUTIONS.

וירא משה את-כל-המלאכה, והנה עשו אתה—כאשר צוה ה, כן עשו; ויברך אתם, משה.

"And Moshe saw all the work and behold they did it as the Almighty commanded, so did they do, and Moshe blessed them." (Exodus 39:43)

Rabbi Zalman Sorotzkin related that he was once at the dedication ceremony of an institution for which one Rabbi selflessly devoted an extremely large amount of time and energy. The Rabbi spoke and heaped mush praise and many blessings upon the donors whose contributions made the institution possible. Rabbi Zalman Sorotzkin was the next speaker and said, "Really the donors should be the ones to praise and bless the Rabbi. It was his efforts that enabled them to have the merit of contributing to such a worthwhile charity. But he followed in the footsteps of Moshe. After the complete report of everything that was donated to the *mishkan* (tabernacle), Moshe blessed all those who participated in the donations and contributions. They should have blessed Moshe for the opportunity he gave them."

"The same is true when a wealthy person helps a poor person. The wealthy person gains more from the poor person, since he gains spiritual merit. But what do we see in the world? The receiver expresses more thanks to the giver than the giver does to the receiver." (*Oznayim Letorah*)

When someone approaches us for a contribution for a worthy cause, we should appreciate that he is doing us a favor by giving us an opportunity to contribute. This is an important concept for fundraisers to keep in mind. They should be aware that they are doing an act of kindness for the donors.

Rabbi Yisroel Salanter once asked a wealthy person to donate money for a very worthy cause. The wealthy person, however, did not act as he should have. Rav Yisroel told him, "The truth is that you have an obligation to go around and find people who need your financial assistance. By coming to you in your home we are saving you effort. You should be grateful to us. We are doing you a favor and not you with us." (Chayai Hamussar vol.2, pp.196-7)

My late uncle, Rabbi Moshe Helfan, was a fundraiser for the Telzer Yeshiva[13] in Cleveland. There was a Jewish farmer in Pennsylvania who used to give a small yearly donation to the yeshiva. In the 1970's when the price of fuel went up, the cost of gas needed to drive to that person's farm was higher than the amount of that person's usual donation.

Rabbi Helfan said the following, "I can't not go to the person for his donation. His supporting Torah study in the yeshiva is a great merit for him and I can't deprive him of that merit. I can't make the yeshiva pay for the gas because this would cause a loss to the yeshiva. Therefore, I'll drive to his farm, but I'll pay for the gas with my own money."

---

13 Yeshiva – Institution for Torah study.

EVERYONE CAN FALL PREY TO ENVY BUT ONE CAN OVERCOME IT.

ומשחת אתם, כאשר משחת את-אביהם

After being told to anoint Aharon, Moshe was told in reference to Aharon's sons:

"And you shall anoint them as you anointed their father." (Exodus 40:15)

Rabbi Meir Simcha Hacohen explained that when Moshe was told to anoint his brother Aharon he was able to do it with a complete heart. Moshe, the younger brother, was the leader of the Israelites and was happy that his brother was the High Priest. But in reference to Aharon's sons, the situation was different. Moshe's own sons were not going to succeed him as leaders. So when it came to anointing Aharaon's sons Moshe might have felt envy. Therefore the Almighty told Moshe to anoint Aharon's sons with the same wholeheartedness and joy with which he anointed their father. (*Meshech Chochmah*)

It is amazing that Moshe would need a special command to overcome envy. We see from here that even the greatest person needs to internalize attitudes that will help him avoid envy. Moreover, we see that it is possible to feel joy and enthusiasm for another person's success even if that person has something that you do not.

FOCUS ON DOING THE WILL OF THE ALMIGHTY.

ויעש, משה: ככל אשר צוה ה אתו—כן עשה.

"And Moshe did all that the Almighty commanded him, that is what he did." (Exodus 40:16)

Moshe's motivation in all that he did for the Sanctuary was for the Almighty's honor. Even Though he personally would gain from the construction of the tabernacle, for the Almighty would communicate with him there, he was not motivated by thoughts of his own glory. Neither was he motivated by thoughts of the honor of his brother, Aharon, who was to be the High Priest. Moshe focused solely on doing the will of the Almighty. (Haamek Dover)

This is a most difficult task. To do something for which you will have great benefit yourself and still to have pure motivations. But the more sacred the work you are involved in the greater the importance of having elevated thoughts and motivations.

Rabbi Yechezkail Abramsky told Rabbi Moshe Mordechai Shulsinger, "Every time I go to deliver a Torah lecture I have in mind that I am now going to serve the Almighty with the *mitzvah* of teaching Torah. At times, to think these thoughts sincerely is even more difficult than any other aspect of giving the lecture." (Peninai Rabainu Yechezkail, p.14)

From *Growth through Torah* by Rabbi Zelig Pliskin.

LEVITICUS ✦ VAYIKRA

PARASHAT
VAYIKRA

And he called

LEVITICUS 1:1-5:26

ויקרא
VAYIKRA

TORAH LESSON BY
RABBI SHLOMO RISKIN

THE TRUEST AND THE HARDEST SACRIFICE: ADMISSION OF GUILT

When a ruler will have sinned... Leviticus 4:24

URING THEIR SOJOURN in the wilderness, the Almighty instructs Moses to inform the Israelites about the right of repentance for committing a sin:

> If anyone is guilty of transgression... he must confess the sin which he committed. Numbers 5:7

Maimonides (1135-1204) makes this commandment the hallmark of his Laws of Repentance (1:1), codifying that the command to repent must begin with a confession of guilt spoken directly and personally to the individual who was wronged (if it is an interpersonal sin), or to God if it is a ritual transgression. Above all, the person must verbalize his guilt to himself. If admission of guilt were not so difficult, it would not count as the very definition of repentance.

In biblical times, in addition to confession the individual who transgressed would also bring special sin offerings, but a sin offering without individual heartfelt repentance was not only meaningless but was considered by God an abomination (Isaiah 1:10–15).

In this portion of *Vayikra*, the Bible first sets the stage by informing us that human beings will of necessity sin, "A soul, when it will unwittingly sin..." (Lev. 4:2). And who is the very first sinner to be singled out? No lesser individual than the High Priest himself, the most exalted religious personality in Israel, the guardian of the holy Temple.

Apparently our Bible does not recognize one scintilla of "papal infallibility"; the Bible even emphasize that "if the High Priest will sin, it is a transgression upon the whole nation," a sacrilegious blotch on our national escutcheon (Lev. 4:3, Rashi (1040-1105) ad loc.). And on the great white fast of the day of forgiveness, the first individual to confess his guilt and request purification is the High Priest. Indeed, the first word to escape the mouth of our most sacred and exalted human being on the most sacred and exalted day of the year is *"Ana,"* please, oh woe, a cry of personal and human anguish.

The next in line for sinning and admission of guilt is the Sanhedrin, the highest court in the land, the keepers of the divine low. When the lawmakers sin in judgment, all of Israel automatically sins, because they—the judges—are entrusted with seeing that justice is done throughout society. The elders of the congregation as well as the High Priest must share in the guilt of the Sanhedrin, because they should have prevented the travesty of an unfit judiciary (Lev. 4:13, 15, 16).

And the third who is singled out, who must confess and atone, is the prince (*nasi*), the ruler, the president, the prime minister. Amazingly, whereas the Bible uses the word "if" (*im*) regarding the transgression of the High Priest and the Sanhedrin, it uses the word "when" (*asher*) regarding the *nasi*. Why is the number-one wielder of power most likely to fall pray to sin? Is it because he comes to believe he is above the law, that what is good for him is automatically good for the State? Is it because he must rely on popular support, so he may fell prey to giving the people not what they need but what they want, to acting not in accordance with what is right but in accordance with the latest opinion poll.[1] The Bible doesn't quite tell us, but it does say that he is most vulnerable.

King Saul didn't wait for Samuel the Judge to begin the public sacrifice, and lost the kingdom (1 Sam. 1:13). King David committed adultery and sent Bathsheba's husband to the front lines of battle to die, and remained the progenitor of the Davidic dynasty (2 Sam. 12). Why? Because Saul attempted to justify himself and blame the nation, whereas King David admitted his guilt and wept before the prophet and God.

Rashi (Lev. 4:22) links the Hebrew *"asher"* ("when" the *nasi* sins) to the Hebrew *"ashrei,"* fortunate: "fortunate is the generation whose *nasi* puts his heart and mind toward seeking forgiveness for his sins."

Apparently, the very first sacrifice the sinner must bring is his own ego, his own self-image. This sacrifice is much more difficult than any animal or meal offering; it is the admission of guilt of the individual which must be the first step in repentance and the achievement of forgiveness.

From *Torah Lights: Vayikra* by Rabbi Shlomo Riskin; used with permission of Maggid Books, a division of Koren Publishers Jerusalem.

---

1 See *Meshekh Hokhma*, ad loc.

PARASHAT
TZAV

Command!

LEVITICUS 6:1-8:36

צַו

TZAV

TORAH LESSON BY
RABBI LEVI COOPER

POST PRAYER REFRESHMENTS

PRAYER IS A central focus and one of the most challenging endeavours in Hasidism—the religious revival that began in Eastern Europe in the late eighteenth century. Hasidism flourished throughout the nineteenth century, and continues to animate contemporary Jewish discourses to this day. The story of prayer in Hasidic circles could be summed up in three salient points, each deserving of its own serious analysis.

First, Hasidic masters and their communities placed great emphasis on the enterprise of prayer. They stressed the accessibility of the prayer avenue and the efficacy of prayer as a means of communicating with the Almighty. Hasidic masters recognized that not every person was able to spend hours in the rigid intellectual pursuit of in-depth Torah study. As such, Hasidic masters taught that there were alternative, equally valid paths to God. Of the various alternatives that were touted, prayer was the path most widely favored.

Second, many innovations to the prayer ritual were introduced in a valiant attempt to overhaul the experience. Prayer rites were altered to reflect Kabbalistic lore; more hospitable and intimate places were preferred as meeting places for prayer; and times of prayer services were relaxed. Modes of prayer were revamped making it more expressive of the supplicants' feelings and emotions. This included freer physical movement during the service, expressions of joy such as dancing and clapping, using the vernacular to express heartfelt prayers rather than sticking to rigid, fossilized prayer texts alone, and being encouraged to cry out to God.

The third aspect of prayer in the Hasidic milieu, connected to the first two points, was the harsh opposition. Ringing in changes to ancient traditions greatly disturbed many traditional leaders. The Hasidic innovations transformed traditional prayer practices, and the old guard often perceived this as a threat to Jewish heritage and continuity. Polemic tracts were written, broadsides posted, and bans of ostracization were declared. In many cases, the indictments mentioned over-emphasis on prayer and wholesale changes to the traditional prayer rite practiced by most communities in Europe.

Not all changes were far-reaching; some modifications were slight and barely drew attention. One of the more trivial innovations involved a post-prayer custom. Rabbi Yisrael Friedman of Ruzhyn (1796-1850) once encountered a group of Jews living in Galicia who originally hailed from Germany. These Jews, while more open to modernity than many of their counterparts in Eastern Europe, continued to preserve *"Minhag Ashkenaz"*—the time-honored practices of German Jewry. They approached the holy Ruzhyner Rebbe and asked him: "The custom in Germany is that after the prayer service we sit down and learn *Mishna*[2]. You Hasidim have a very different practice. After the service you sit down, have a piece of cake, wash it down with a shot glass of liquor, and then bless each other with life by declaring *l'haim*[3]! Is this the appropriate behavior after prayer services?"

One of Ruzhyner Rebbe's faithful attendants, Reb Yosef the ritual slaughterer, would often offer witty remarks and quips that would bring a smile to his master's face. Reb Yosef responded without hesitation: "In memorial and for the merit of the deceased we study *Mishna* (משנה), for it has the same Hebrew letters as the word soul—*neshama* (נשמה).

"You *Yekkes*,"—continued Reb Yosef, employing the mildly derogatory term for German Jews who are legendarily known for their punctiliousness and formality—"You pray with such coldness and lack of feeling that you are effectively praying like you are dead! Thus it is eminently appropriate to study *Mishna* after the service. We Hasidim, however, pray with joy and enthusiasm. A celebrant certainly deserves to drink a *l'haim!*"

Rabbi Yisrael of Ruzhyn heard the words of his attendant-cum-jester and dismissed them: "A joke here, a joke there..."

"The real reason for drinking a *l'haim* after the service," the Ruzhyner Rebbe explained, "is that the prayer service takes the place of the Temple sacrifices and many of the laws and directives about prayer are copied from the Temple rituals."

The Torah teaches that the Temple sacrifices are disqualified and termed *"pigul"* if the supervising Kohen had the wrong intentions during the sacrifice service, namely, he intended on eating the sacrifice after the prescribed window of time. Even if the sacrifice was in fact consumed during the permitted time slot—in other words the Kohen's intent was not realized—the

---

2 Mishna - the basis of the Talmud; a collection of early oral interpretations of the scriptures that was compiled about AD 200.
3 L'haim - a Jewish salutation meaning "to life!" Generally used during toasts.

sacrifice is still void because of his intention (Leviticus 7:18; 19:5-7; Babylonian Talmud, *Zevahim* 29a).

The Holy Ruzhyner continued, explaining the relevance of the law of *pigul* to the challenge of earnest prayer: "When the Evil Inclination sees a person going to pray—that is, going to offer a sacrifice to the Almighty—the Evil Inclination does not even think to stop the person. He knows that the fortitude and commitment of the person will withstand any arguments, temptations, and attempts to be led astray."

"Instead, the Evil Inclination adopts a more cunning tack. The Evil Inclination tries to trick the person with *pigul*-like thoughts that undermine sacrifices and sacrifice-substitutes. To counter the Evil Inclination, we promise him a drink after the service, and we make a deal with him to just leave us be while we commune with the Almighty."

At first blush, thoughts appear to be merely in the mind. One might argue: as long as I act correctly, I needn't be concerned about my intentions. The original laws of *pigul* may not be applicable in Temple-less reality, yet they teach us the importance of our intent, of our frame of mind when performing God's commandments. *Pigul*-like contemplations can negate the validity and efficacy of prayers. Conversely, pure meditations and intentions can elevate an experience from being a mere robotic action to a lofty encounter.

PARASHAT
SHEMINI

Eighth

LEVITICUS 9:1-11:47

שמיני

SHEMINI

TORAH LESSON BY
RABBI MOSHE LICHTMAN

ABOVE THE REST

AFTER ENUMERATING ALL the kosher and un-kosher animals, the Torah states: *Do not make **your souls abominable** with any creeping thing that creeps, and do not defile yourselves through them, lest you become defiled through them. For I am the Lord your God: you shall sanctify yourselves and you shall be holy, for I am holy; and you shall not **defile your souls** with any creeping thing that crawls **on the earth**. For I am the Lord **Who brings you up** from the land of Egypt to be your God; you shall be holy, for I am holy* (Leviticus 11:43-45).

Many commentators are bothered by the peculiar expression *Who brings you up from the land of Egypt*, for the Torah usually says, *Who took you out of the land of Egypt.* (See Rashi (1040-1105)) Let us concentrate on the Kli Yakar's[4] answer. He first points out other peculiarities in these verses: The first verse uses the expression *"creeping thing **that creeps**,"* while the second one says, *"creeping thing **that crawls**;"* the second verse adds **on the earth**, while the first one does not; the second verse juxtaposes "defilement" to the soul, while the first one adjoins "abomination" with the soul.

The Kli Yakar explains that the closer something is to the ground, the more earthly and unholy it is. That which walks higher off the ground, however, "turns and faces its Source [of life]." This is why man stands upright, unlike the animals, which walk on all fours. Man is made up of physical and spiritual elements, and the spiritual half strives to ascend heavenward. Now to explain the differences between the verses: *"creeping thing **that crawls**"* refers to insects that crawl very low to the earth, as the verse indicates with the words **on the earth**. A *"creeping thing **that creeps**,"* however, is not as lowly. The Kli Yakar also claims that the verb *"tamei"* (to defile) is stronger that *"shaketz"* (abomination). The first implies an intrinsic defect, while the second implies only that man finds it repulsive, not that it is intrinsically defiled. Therefore, the Torah says, *"You shall not **defile** your souls"* in reference to the extremely lowly *"creeping thing **that crawls**,"* and *"Do not make your souls **abominable**"* when referring to the relatively elevated *"creeping thing **that creeps**."*

---

4 Kli Yakar – a Torah commentary written by Rabbi Shlomo Ephraim ben Aaron Luntschitz (1550-1619).

Now to return to the original question: Why does the Torah use the peculiar expression: *I am the Lord **Who brings you up** from the land of Egypt?* In line with the preceding idea, the Kli Yakar explains:

> Now [the Torah] gives a reason for this [why it is forbidden to eat insects]: *For I am the Lord **Who brings you up** from the land of Egypt*—a lowly place—to the Land of Israel which is higher than all other lands. [I did this] in order to distance you from earthiness, which dominates more in a low place, where the air is denser... Therefore, be very careful [not to defile yourselves] *with any creeping thing that crawls on the earth.*

It is evident from the Kli Yakar's comments that he takes the statement of the Sages "the Land of Israel is higher than all other lands" (*Sanhedrin* 87a) literally. He understands that the Land's geographical location affects its very nature. Others, however, disagree. They point out that since the world is round, it is difficult to say that one place is truly higher than the next. Furthermore, other places are located at higher altitudes. Therefore, they explain the statement figuratively. The Land of Israel is considered higher on a spiritual plane, for it is the place from which the rest of the world was created and from where the entire world receives its spiritual (and physical) sustenance (see *Teshuvot Chatam Sofer, Yoreh De'ah* 234; *Maharal MiPrague, Be'er HaGolah*, p. 131).

May the people of Israel in Diaspora (exile) soon recognize the physical and spiritual "ascendancy" of the Land of Israel over all other lands, so that we may all be redeemed and elevated to higher levels of sanctity.

From *Eretz Yisrael in the Parashah* by Rabbi Moshe Lichtman.

PARSHAT
TAZRIA

She bears seed
LEVITICUS 12:1-13:59

תזריע

TAZRIA

TORAH LESSON BY
RABBI MOSHE GOLDSMITH

THE POWER OF THE TONGUE

THIS WEEK, INSTEAD of reading one Torah Portion, as is usually the case, we are gifted with two, **Tazriah** and **Metzorah,** dealing mostly with the laws of leprosy—among the most complicated in the Torah. Besides the 14 chapters of the Mishnah which deal with leprosy, there are thousands of other references to it throughout the Talmud and Oral Law. This short essay will be unable to encompass all the details of our complex subject, but rather will focus on some insights garnered from the two Portions.

The Torah mentions three areas where leprosy can appear—in a person's home, on his clothes, or on his body. According to the Torah, leprosy (in Hebrew, Metzorah) comes as a result of speaking ill of others. Metzorah is an acronym for *Motzi Shem Rah*, which means giving someone a bad name (*Lashon Harah*).

The Torah tells us we can protect ourselves from this disease by *"diligently observing and doing all that the Levitical priests teach you. As I have commanded them, so you shall be careful to do. Remember what Hashem, your G-d, did to Miriam on the way as you came out of Egypt."* (Deuteronomy 24:8–9) This is a reference to Miriam's punishment for speaking disrespectfully about Moshe Rabaynu: *"Then Miriam and Aaron spoke against Moshe because of the Cushite woman whom he had married... But when the cloud had withdrawn from over the tent, behold, Miriam was leprous, as white as snow. As Aaron turned toward Miriam, behold, she was leprous."* (Numbers 12:1–16)

Even though Moshe Rabaynu, the humblest person on earth, as the Torah tells us, wouldn't have thought of punishing Miriam for gossiping about his choice of a Cushite woman, and even though Miriam was a kind of surrogate mother to Moshe and a righteous prophetess—her gossip was punished by Leprosy.

Obviously, slander is a sin that Hashem does not take lightly. Indeed, the spies who denigrated the Land of Israel caused an entire generation to perish in the desert because of their evil report. The whole nation was held in solitary confinement and forbidden to enter the Land—just as Miriam was isolated when she was afflicted by Leprosy for the sin of *Lashon Harah*, and, like any other Leper, was separated from the camp and had to remain outside it until she was healed.

Unlike our current ideas about it, the Leprosy of the Torah, which only affected the Israelites, was not an infectious disease. It began with an external attack on a person's home, and, unless the person rectified his sin, would move on to his garments and finally to his body. The lesson to be learned from this is that our ethical behavior has a direct effect on our physical well-being. If gossip can lead to such detrimental results, there should be no doubt that all serious violations of Torah values can incur severe consequences.

Therefore we should be attentive to everything that happens around us. If our home seems to be falling apart, if we're not feeling well, or if nothing seems to be going right, it may be that G-d is telling us that there are grounds for improvement somewhere. Maybe we're not acting as we should? Maybe there are deficiencies in our religious or ethical behavior?

If we could practice this kind of self-examination **honestly** and **routinely**, it might be a tremendous boon for ourselves and for everyone around us. Paying attention to the walls of our house, health, and mood are all ways of connecting with the spiritual realm that can rectify our lives.

Unfortunately our Temple is in ruins and the Laws of Leprosy in all its aspects are now moot. Nevertheless, the moral imperatives connected to those laws still apply today. Therefore, we remain responsible for being decent and G-d fearing human beings and must practice the mitzvah of *Midat HaZehirut* "(Attentiveness to How We Conduct Our Lives.) This entails paying close attention to the signs that Hashem sends us from above, as well as honest self-evaluation.

Although we may see people speaking *Lashon Harah* who appear to be in perfectly good health, they may not be so *spiritually*. The Zohar[5] teaches us that there are Spiritual Lepers who still exist today (although contemporary human lepers should not, as far as we can know, be stigmatized as spiritually defective because of their illness).

Spiritual Lepers are those who have tainted their souls by speaking evil of others and are therefore separated from the righteous when according to our tradition, their souls ascend to the upper worlds at night. In addition, their

---

5 The Zohar is a collection of commentaries on the Torah, intended to guide people who have already achieved high spiritual degrees to the root (origin) of their souls.

prayers are not accepted until they have fully repented. Although all sins cause spiritual and physical harm, the Torah singles out the sin of *Lashon Harah* because *"**Death and life are in the power of the tongue**"*. (Proverbs 18:21)

This is why contemporary Media has such a powerful grip over people and nations, rather than Presidents, Kings, and Prime Ministers, who have been eclipsed. Today it is the Media that has the *power of the tongue*, and it is the Media which is closely followed and obeyed and even worshipped, wielding its narcissistic influence over young and old alike, on nations as well as individuals. Publicity at any price is the new craving of mankind, no matter how distasteful from any religious or ethical point of view.

If only the Media were using its gargantuan power as a vessel for *Tikun Olam, rectification of the ills of the world,* rather than debasing its adherents by promoting corrupt values, such as Materialism, Self-Indulgence, Hedonism, Exhibitionism, and, perhaps ugliest of all—Mendacity, the careless or deliberate profusion of falsehoods that generally remain uncorrected, even if called to its attention.

Wouldn't it have a hugely positive influence on the world if the Media were indeed to recognize its power for good, and made an effort to use it accordingly? It might even hasten the Redemption.

Let us all at least take it upon ourselves to rectify our speech and comportment and to be constantly mindful of the effects of our behavior on others. We might find ourselves, then, in a much healthier and happier physical and spiritual state of existence.

PARASHAT
METZORA

Infected one
Leviticus 14:1-15:33

מצרע

METZORA

TORAH LESSON BY
RABBI SHLOMO RISKIN

AN OPEN HEART AND A CLOSED HAND

And his servants came near, and spoke to him, and said, "My father, if the prophet had asked you to do some great thing, would you not have done it? How much rather then when he says to you, Wash and be clean?" Then he went down and dipped himself seven times in the Jordan, according to the saying of the man of God, and his flesh was restored like the flesh of a little child, and he was clean. Haftara of Tazria, 2 Kings 5:13–14

THE TWO TORAH portions of *Tazria-Metzora* deal with a malady similar to what we know as leprosy—but it is apparent from the text (and especially from the interpretation of our sages) that the source of the disease is a spiritual rather than a physical imperfection. I believe that the two *haftara*[6] portions—or, more correctly, the unread prophetic passage—provide a fascinating insight into what that spiritual imperfection might be. Moreover, both prophetic readings teach all subsequent generations what Israeli leadership requires in order for our nation to succeed.

The *haftara* for *Tazria* is taken from the second book of Kings; it deals with the miraculous way in which Elisha, prophet of the Lord, succeeded in curing the leprosy of Na'aman, powerful general of the armies of Aram. However, the incident surrounding Na'aman's cure is the subject of the fifth chapter; the *haftara* begins, strangely enough, with the concluding three verses of the previous chapter, which tell how Elisha is able to alleviate the hunger of one hundred people with a comparatively small amount of food. This odd introduction seems to have nothing to do with the subsequent story of Na'aman or the disease which links the incident in the book of Kings to this Torah reading.

As the story unfolds, we learn that Na'aman was "general of the armies of the King of Aram, a great man before his master…a courageous soldier and—a leper" (5:1). A captive Israeli maiden suggests to Na'aman's wife that her husband seek a cure from Elisha, the prophet man-of-God of Israel. After an initial request, "Elisha sends to him (Na'aman) a messenger, who says:

---

6 Haftara - a portion of the Prophets read in the synagogue on the Sabbath and holy days immediately after the parasha.

Go and bathe [immerse yourself] seven times in the Jordan River; your
flesh will then be restored and shall be purified. 2 Kings 4:11

After the words of the prophet are proven to be efficacious, a most grateful
Na'aman exclaims: "Behold, now I know that there is no God anywhere in the
world except in Israel; and now [Na'aman requests of Elisha] please accept a
gift from your servant" (5:15). Elisha, the man of God, refuses, upon an oath to
God, to accept anything; Na'aman is so moved by what has transpired that he
asks for a small parcel of land in which he can build an alter and offer sacrifices
to the one true God of Israel and the world. And so concludes the *haftara* for the
Torah reading of *Tazria*.

The following haftara for Metzora continues with chapter seven of the second
book of Kings (note that chapter six is deleted from the public prophetic readings), and opens with a tale of four lepers outside the gate of the city. There is
apparently a bitter war going on between Israel and Aram—as well as rampant
hunger in Israel so acute that mothers are eating their own children. As a result
of Elisha's intervention, the famine ends; the four lepers bear the happy tidings
that the Aramean encampment has miraculously been evacuated, the Aramean
Army has defected, and Israel has emerged victorious. This prophetic reading
concludes by describing the death of the chief courtier of the King of Israel: he
is trampled by the hordes of Israelites rushing to pillage the Aramean encampment. Apparently he was punished for having cynically questioned Elisha's
prophecy concerning the end of the famine and the success of Israel.

A number of startling questions emerge as we read these *haftarot*. The first
reading concluded with a grateful Aramean general convinced that the God
of Israel is the only true God of the world. What has caused him, only one
chapter later in the second book of Kings, to wage war against the very people
who were responsible for the cure of his leprosy? And of what relevance to the
subject of leprosy are the opening story of Elisha's feeding of the poor and the
concluding story of the trampling to death of the Israel courtier?

I believe that we will discover the clue to our understanding by reading
the end of the fifth as well as the sixth chapter of the second book of Kings
(deleted from the public *haftara* readings, which include only the beginnings
of chapters five and seven), and by taking note of Rashi's (1040-1105) identification of the four lepers of good tidings as Gehazi and his three sons (Ibid 7:3).

Who was Gehazi? The second book of Kings records (in the passage not publicly read) that after Elisha refused to accept any gift from Na'aman for having effectuated his cure, Gehazi "the lad [go-fer] of Elisha man-of-God" ran after the Aramean general; claiming to have been sent by his master Elisha, he requests a *kikar*[7] of silver and two changes of clothes for two prophets-in-training (Elisha's *kollel*[8], as it were). Na'aman readily complies, generously given two kikars of silver in addition to the outfits of clothes. When Elisha discovers what his factotum has done, he punishes him: "The leprosy of Na'aman shall cling to you and to your children forever" (2 Kings 5:27). The next thing we learn is that Israel is suffering a grievous famine and is under siege by the armies of Aram.

Apparently Na'aman—as well as God—had turned against Israel. What caused the sudden disaffection? Clearly it was the greed of Gehazi for two kikars of silver. Elisha's storming sanctification of God's name had been turned into a devastating desecration of God's name! Na'aman had certainly been impressed with Elisha's ability to cure him—but he had known of similar acts bordering on sorcery which emanated from the pagan world. What had really impressed the general of the armies of Aram was that Elisha was a true man-of-God, an individual who did what he did purely for the sake of Heaven with no ulterior motive for personal gain. It was only at that point – when Elisha refused to take any compensation whatsoever—that Na'aman decided that he only desired to give sacrifices to God of Israel.

But when Gehazi entered the scene with his greedy desire for some silver and clothing, Na'aman understandably become disillusioned. He now sees Elisha as just another sorcerer – and if so, he is even ready to wage another war against his former enemy.

The second message of these Prophetic Readings is the necessity of the people of Israel – and especially the leaders of Israel—to believe in the future of the covenantal nation, to have faith that Israel will ultimately be saved by God. The courtier of the king cynically questioned Israel's deliverance, and he therefore deserved to die.

Perhaps both of these messages are inextricably bound together. Only when we have completely selfless leaders—who give of themselves purely for the sake of Heaven and nation without the expectation of even a scintilla of personal gain—do we have the right to expect that God will intercede on their (and

---

7 Kikars - talents or coins.
8 Kollel - is an institute for full-time, advanced study of the Talmud and rabbinic literature.

our) behalf. Such a leader was Elisha, prophetic man-of-God, in the opening verses of the *haftara* of *Tazria*. Elisha proves to be such a leader when he punishes Gehazi for his venal act of greed with the disease of leprosy—apparently a fitting punishment for the sin of inordinate materialistic desire. The courtier should have realized that Israel is guided by selfless leaders who rise above the blandishments of bribery and material compensation, God will always enable His nation not only to survive but truly to prevail.

From *Torah Lights: Vayikra* by Rabbi Shlomo Riskin; used with permission of Maggid Books, a division of Koren Publishers Jerusalem.

PARASHAT
ACHAREI MOT

After the death

LEVITICUS 16:1-18:30

אחרי מות

ACHAREI MOT

TORAH LESSON BY
RABBI ZELIG PLISKIN

USE TECHNIQUES TO OVERCOME EXCESSIVE CONCERN
ABOUT WHAT OTHERS THINK OF YOU

וכל-אדם לא-יהיה באהל מועד, בבאו לכפר בקדש...

"And there shall be no man in the Tent of Meeting when he goes
in to make atonement in the sacred place." (Leviticus 16:17)

WHEN THE HIGH Priest performed the special service on Yom Kippur,
it could have been very easy for him to feel conceited. He had been the
only one chosen from the entire nation to perform the sacred service
on this most holy of days. He might easily focus on the honor he was receiving
from others and how other people would be thinking of him with respect and
even awe. Therefore the Torah tells him, "There shall be no man," that is, the
High Priest should mentally view the world as if there were no other people in
existence. He should do this when he enters the tent of meeting to make atonement in the sacred place. By having this mental attitude, he frees himself from
any thoughts of seeking honor and approval. (*Degel Machaneh Ephraim*)

This mental technique is a very useful one for people who are overly self-
conscious and constantly worry about what other people are thinking of them.
They should imagine for a while that other people do not exist. If others do not
exist, one does not need to be concerned with what anyone thinks of him. Even
if you are only able to do this for a short while, it will enable you to decrease
your worrying about what others think of you. A large part of the concern for
the approval of others is based on illusion. In truth, others do not think about
you as much as you think they do. Even if they are thinking about you, much of
what they think makes absolutely no practical difference in your life. The illusion that there are no other people around will enable you to free yourself from
the harm and pain caused by that other illusion.

BE CAREFUL NOT TO WRONG OTHERS TO
AVOID NEEDING THEIR FORGIVENESS.

כי-ביום הזה יכפר עליכם, לטהר אתכם: מכל, חטאתיכם, לפני ה, תטהרו.

"For on this day you shall receive atonement to purify you for all your transgressions, before the Almighty you shall be purified." (Leviticus 16:30)

The Sages (Yoma 85b) comment on this that Yom Kippur atones for transgressions between man and the Almighty. But as regards transgressions between man and man Yom Kippur can only atone if a person first attains the forgiveness of those whom he has offended or harmed.

From this principle we see the importance of being careful not to cause other people harm, either financial, physical, or emotional. While it is proper to forgive those who ask for our forgiveness, not everyone is sincerely ready to forgive others. There are some people who are hypersensitive and even though they would wish to forgive others, it is very difficult for them to do so. Even though they might say that they forgive, deep down they feel resentment and have not truly forgiven. Some might say, "Well if this person is so sensitive and nonforgiving, it is his problem." Yes, it is true that he has a problem and he will suffer from this, but if you have harmed him you will still not be forgiven without his forgiveness. The best way to ensure that you will be forgiven is to be especially careful in advance not to cause pain or suffering to others. Our main reason for not hurting others should be out of compassion and caring. But at least we should be careful not to harm others out of our own self-interest.

Do something for growth every day.

את-משפטי תעשו ואת-חקתי תשמרו, ללכת בהם: אני, ה אלקיכם.

"My ordinances you shall do, and My statutes you shall observe,
to walk with them, I am the Lord, your G-d." (Leviticus 18:4)

The Ksav Sofer commented on the words, "to walk with them": a person needs to walk from one level to the next level. That is, a person should constantly keep on growing and elevating himself.

It is not enough to keep on the same level that you were on the previous day. Rather, each day should be a climb higher than the day before. When difficult tests come your way, you might not always appreciate them. But the only way to keep on elevating yourself is to keep passing more and more difficult life-tests. View every difficulty as a means of elevating yourself by applying the appropriate Torah principles. At the end of each day, ask yourself, "What did

I do today to elevate myself a little higher?" If you cannot find an answer, ask yourself, "What can I plan to do tomorrow to elevate myself?"

DO GOOD DEEDS WITH ENERGY AND ENTHUSIASM.

ושמרתם את-חקתי ואת-משפטי, אשר יעשה אתם האדם וחי בהם: אני ה.

"And you shall keep my statutes and My ordinances which a man shall do and live by them, I am the Almighty." (Leviticus 18:5)

On the words, "And live by them," the Shaloh comments: When you do good deeds they should be done with life, that is, with a lot of energy and enthusiasm. (Shnai Luchos Habris, Acharai Mos)

When you fulfill good deeds with enthusiasm, your whole being becomes alive. There is no comparison between doing a good deed with a feeling of being oppressed and forced and doing the same thing with joy and excitement. The life of a person who constantly does good deeds with joy is a life of pleasure and elevation. Not only do you gain very much yourself by this, but you will also motivate others. When others see how much enjoyment you have from doing good deeds, they too will be motivated to follow in your footsteps and their positive behavior will be a merit for you.

If you would like to experience enthusiasm but do not as yet, the *Mesilas Yeshorim*9 (ch. 7) advises you to act as if you where enthusiastic and your outer behavior will influence your inner feelings.

"The Almighty can testify that my biggest pleasure in life is praying with enthusiasm," said the Koznitzer Maggid. "This pleasure is my reward for the few good deeds that I have done." (*Niflaos Hamaggid Maikoznitz*, p.15)

From *Growth through Torah* by Rabbi Zelig Pliskin.

---

9 *Mesilas Yeshorim* - an ethical text composed by the influential Rabbi Moshe Chaim Luzzatto (1707–1746).

PARASHAT
KEDOSHIM

Holy ones
LEVITICUS 19:1-20:27

קדשים
KEDOSHIM

TORAH LESSON BY
RABBI ZELIG PLISKIN

IF SOMEONE WRONGS YOU, DON'T WASTE TIME FEELING RESENTMENT.

לא-תלין פעלת שכיר, אתך—עד-בקר לא-תקלל חרש...

"Do not leave the wages of your employee with you overnight until
the morning. You shall not curse the deaf." (Leviticus 19:13,14)

THE TORAH PUTS these two commandments one after the other to teach
us that even if your employer refuses to pay your wages, you shall not
curse him. Rather you should take him to court to receive the money
coming to you. (Baal Haturim)

When someone wrongs you in some manner, it is easy to get angry at him
and to curse him. But what do you gain from this? Absolutely nothing. All
you do is love out with your anger and resentment. Cursing him lowers you
spiritually and gives you nothing. It is an outlet for your frustration, but a very
negative outlet. Be practical. If someone wrongs you and you have a practical
means of helping yourself, do what you legally can to protect yourself from
loss. But do not needlessly focus on this person's negative behavior. Brooding
about it and indiscriminately telling others about it does not help you. Do not
waste your precious time on this earth with resentful thoughts, and do not
defile your mouth with any kind of curse. Fill your mind with elevating and
joyous thoughts and free yourself from negative thoughts about others. Take
action to help yourself when that action is appropriate. But both before and
afterwards utilize your time wisely.

Someone wrote a *sefer* (book) in which he attacked Rabbi Moshe Feinstein's
response in disrespectful and even vulgar terms. The typesetter-printer called
to ask Rav Moshe whether he should refuse to accept the job. Rav Moshe urged
him to do the assignment, explaining that both the author and the printer had
to earn a livelihood. Presumably, the author felt that he had to curry favor with
elements whose opinions he supported. As far as Rav Moshe personally was
concerned, he had no right to stand in the way. (Rabbi Nosson Scherman, The
Jewish Observer, Oct. 1986, p.25)

ONLY REBUKE OTHERS WITH A SINCERE CONCERN FOR THEIR WELFARE.

הוכח תוכיח את-עמיתך

"You shall rebuke your fellow man." (Leviticus 19:17)

When someone tries to criticize or rebuke another person, it is obligatory for those words to come from the depths of his heart. The Sages have said that only those words that come from the heart will enter the heart of the other person. Therefore, if your words of correction are not an expression of your inner feelings of care and concern for the welfare of the other person, they will not have a positive influence on the person you are speaking to. But there is yet another aspect here. If your rebuke does not come from a sincere caring for the other person, then you have personal reasons for that rebuke and your motives are not entirely pure. If that is the case, you are guilty of slighting the honor of another person and of causing him pain with words for your personal pleasure. This is a very serious offense. (Rabbi Eliyahu Eliezer Dessler; *Michtav Maieliyahu*, vol.3, p.139)

Before correcting someone, ask yourself, "What are my true motives in trying to correct this person?" Can you honestly say that your sole motivation is that you are so concerned about his welfare that you feel a need to make certain he does only good and refrains from evil? To what degree do you want to rebuke him because you feel a sense of power in telling someone off? To what degree do you want honor from others? To what degree do you derive personal pleasure from making someone else feel uncomfortable? We do have a *mitzvah* to correct others. But here motivation is an essential ingredient. Build up your inner feelings of love for others. Then your motivation will be pure and you will be able to have a positive influence on others.

In the last lecture Rabbi Nachum Perchovitz gave before *Yom Kippur* he ended by saying, "I ask forgiveness if I offended anyone or spoke harshly. Together with this I ask forgiveness from those I censured less than I should have." (Yetaid Neaman, 17 Kislaiv, 5747, p.10)

Rabbi Eliyahu Klatzkin was easily moved to tears by the suffering of any Jewish community and the mishaps which visited anyone, near or far. When he preached about the desecration of the *Shabbat* or dishonesty in business practices, he would be so choked by sobs that his voice became inaudible to the members of the audience, who would themselves be deeply stirred by his grief. (*Jewish Leaders*, p.333)

Rabbi Simcha Zissel of Kelm once found out that a student of his read his private letters. He did not censure him right away. Rather, he waited two full months until he was certain that his own anger had subsided. Then he approached that student and gave him a very stern lecture on how improper his behavior had been. (*Meoros Hagdolim*, p77)

FEEL LOVE FOR OTHER PEOPLE BECAUSE IT IS THE CREATOR'S WISHES.

ואהבת לרעך מוך: אני ה

"Love your fellow man as yourself, I am the Almighty." (Leviticus 19:18)

The Chasam Sofer commented: The commandment to love our fellow man is a concept that anyone can relate to with his own intellect. Nevertheless, the Torah tells us to love our fellow man because it is the Almighty's will. (*Toras Moshe*)

If your love of other people is based only on your own feelings, there could easily be a lack of consistency. One day you might feel positive towards someone and on the next day your feelings can change. But the Torah states that the Almighty commands us to love others. We need to develop positive attitudes towards others by focusing on their virtues whether it comes easily to us or whether it is difficult.

Very often I am asked how it is possible to feel love towards someone when you meet him for the first time. Once when I was giving a lecture to beginners in Yeshiva Aish Hatorah in the Old City of Jerusalem a cute little dog walked into the room. Everyone turned to the dog and smiled at it. I then asked, "Did anyone ever see this dog before?" No one had. I pointed out that even though this was the first time they had seen this dog, they all felt positive about it and their positive feelings were noticeable on their faces. If we would internalize the awareness that each human being is created in the image of the Almighty and the Almighty Himself wishes that we feel love for him, we would automatically have positive feelings for others.

If an extremely wealthy and generous person who was the source of your entire income would tell you to be kind and friendly to his relative, you would find it quite easy to do so. In your dealings with other people keep in mind that your Creator and the Sustainer of the universe is the Creator of this individual and He wants you to be kind and loving to him.

Before Rabbi Isser Zalman Meltzer would deliver his weekly lecture in his yeshiva[10], he would first go for a few minutes to one of the rooms of the yeshiva and close the door behind him. Once one of the students wanted to know what the Rosh Hayeshiva[11] did during those few minutes before the lecture. Very carefully, the student opened the door just a little bit and peeked inside the room. To his surprise, he saw how Rav Isser Zalman walked back and forth repeating to himself over and over again the verse, "Love your fellow man as yourself." (Bederech Aitz Hachayim, vol.1, p.249)

Anyone who interacts with other people should learn from this. By repeating this verse to yourself you will relate to other people in a much more elevated manner.

Rabbi Moshe Feinstein used to recite Psalms in his yeshiva on *Shabbat* afternoon. One *Shabbat*, as he was reciting the Psalms, a mildly retarded child stood watching him. The boy went over and turned Rav Moshe's *Tehillim* (Psalms) on an angle to the right, and Rav Moshe continued reciting. Then the boy turned the *Tehillim* to the left and Rav Moshe continued reciting. The boy took the *Tehillim* and turned it completely around and Rav Moshe continued reciting. Not satisfied, the boy turned a page, but the Rosh Hayeshiva still was not fazed. A gentleman had watched all this and, although people went out of their way to be patient with the boy, the man had seen too much. He snapped, "Stop it already! Let the Rosh Hayeshiva alone!"

Rav Moshe turned to the man and said, "He is only playing with me. I enjoy it when he plays with me. I love him like my own child!" With that, Rav Moshe embraced the boy and kissed him. (Rabbi Nosson Scherman, *The Jewish Observer*, Oct. 1986, p.29)

---

10 Yeshiva – Institution for Torah study.
11 Rosh Hayeshiva – The head of the Yeshiva.

YOUR BEHAVIOR TOWARDS OTHERS SHOULD BE MANIFESTATION OF YOUR LOVE TOWARDS THEM.

ואהבת לרעך כמוך: אני ה

"Love your fellow man as yourself, I am the Almighty." (Leviticus 19:18)

The Talmud (Shabbos 31a) relates that a non-Jew came to Hillel and said to him, "Convert me on condition that you will teach me the entire Torah while I stand on one foot." Hillel accepted his condition and told him, "What you dislike, do not do to your friend. This is the entire Torah."

Since Hillel was referring to the commandment of love your neighbor, why didn't he just mention the words of this verse? Rabbi Yeruchem Levovitz explained that this is to teach us an important principle. From the words "love your fellow man" one might think that as long as one feels the emotion of love towards others one fulfills this commandment. But the truth is that just feeling love alone is not sufficient. Rather this love must motivate us to do positive things for others and to refrain from any actions or words that could cause someone any pain or suffering. The Torah definitely requires us to feel deep love for others in our hearts. But even more than that, our behavior towards others must manifest this love. Therefore, Hillel explained to this man that a basic Torah principle is that the same commandment which requires us to have a profoundly positive feeling for others also requires us to behave in an elevated manner in our daily encounters with them. (*Daas Torah*: Vayikra, p.175)

It is very easy to just repeat the slogan that we should love others. To actually feel this in your heart is much more difficult. But even after you sincerely feel this love, your entire behavior towards others should be an expression of it. Constantly be on the lookout for acts of kindness you can do for other people. When you look for them, you will constantly find things to do and words to say. Similarly, be very careful not to do anything that will harm others or cause them any pain or suffering. This is a lifelong challenge, but it is a cornerstone of the Torah.

Rabbi Baruch Ber Leibowitz, Rosh Hayeshiva of Kamenetz, used to say, "When my time will come to stand before the Heavenly court I will be asked, 'What merits do you have?' What will I reply? If I want to say, 'With my

Torah,' do I truly have enough Torah? With my fear of Heaven? Do I really have sufficient fear? There is really only one merit that I can say for myself. I have profound *ahavas Yisroel* (love for Israel). Whenever I am walking in the street and see someone coming in my direction, I immediately say to myself, 'A blessing on his head.'" (*Marbitzai Torah Umussar*, vol.2, p.151)

The Chazon Ish would listen patiently to the problems of anyone who came to him. This was quite a feat since people would come to him at all hours of the day and night. A relative of the Chazon Ish was amazed at how he was able to listen to a certain *"nudnick"* (an annoying person) who spoke in a loud tone of voice and in a very long-winded and roundabout manner. The Chazon Ish explained, "A person who owns a mill is used to the noise of the mill. On the contrary, if the mill would stop it would give him a headache." (*P'air Hador*, vol.4, p.20)

Rabbi Chayim Koledetzky related to his family how he was a guest at the home of the Chofetz Chayim. The Chofetz Chayim personally made the bed for him and prepared the pillow and blankets. Reb Chayim was startled to see that after preparing the bed the Chofetz Chayim laid down on the bed for a few seconds to check if it would be sufficiently comfortable for his guest. (*Bederech Aitz Hachayim*, vol.1, p.61, f.n.)

From *Growth through Torah* by Rabbi Zelig Pliskin.

PARASHAT
EMOR

Say!

Leviticus 21:1-24:23

אמר

EMOR

TORAH LESSON BY
NATHAN LOPES CARDOZO

SEFIRAT HAOMER[12]: WHAT REALLY COUNTS

NUMEROUS COMMENTATORS AND philosophers have explained that the biblical commandment to count the days between Pesach[13] and Shavuot[14] (see Leviticus 23:15) is a way to encourage man to not only count these days, but to use this time to examine his thoughts and feelings and take stock of his life. The exodus from Egypt—which initiated our forefathers first encounter with liberty—as well as its culmination with the giving of the Torah—the law of moral freedom—at Mount Sinai, should both become ingrained in our personalities—inspiring constant moral elevation. The purpose of the period between the two festivals is to relive these sublime moments to ennoble ourselves.

Nothing is more dangerous for man than to remain spiritually stale, and because of this, one is required to count the 49 days of the Omer. To prepare ourselves for the upcoming celebration of Shavuot and the giving of the Torah, we are asked to climb a ladder of 49 spiritual steps where each day will add another dimension to our souls.

Commentators are therefore surprised to notice that the actual counting of the Omer begins on the second day of Pesach and not on the first (Ibid). If the purpose of the counting is indeed to re-enact the entire historical period between Pesach and Shavuot, why not start on the same day that the Exodus took place, which was also the first day that the Israelites began their journey to moral freedom?

When carefully examining the Israelites' behavior on the day of the actual Exodus, which corresponds to the first day of Pesach, we become aware of a strange phenomenon. What stands out is the astonishing passivity of the Israelites—there is no action whatsoever, no initiative. The Israelites are told to remain inside their homes and simply wait for Moshe to give the sign. There are no planned confrontations with the Egyptians; no speeches of national revival; no demonstrations, just silent waiting. They make no movements until

---

12 Sefirat HaOmer - it's Hebrew for "counting of the Omer". During *Sefirat HaOmer* we count the days from Pesach until Shavuot, when we received the Torah.
13 Pesach - Passover.
14 Shavuot - the festival of the giving of the Torah.

after Moshe gives his signal, and even then they are quiet and humble as they leave Egypt.

What becomes increasingly clear is that it is only God who acts on this day—there is no human initiative. God alone takes them out, and it is He who leads the way. It is a moment where there is no misunderstanding about who is calling the shots. It is a day where God reveals His unfathomable strength. While man remains utterly passive, God "steals the show" by displaying His absolute sovereignty. The only thing man is asked to do is to follow, as a slave follows his master. God's protection is impervious.

Once they have left the borders of Egypt, however, we see a radical change. Suddenly, the Israelites wake up from their imposed passivity and realize that they better start preparing for a long journey through the desert. It is now that they need to show courage and exercise patience. The earlier divine protection is no longer impenetrable, as only after a few days on the road the Israelites learn that Pharaoh and his army are approaching with the intent to have their revenge. He wants the Israelites back home and will use all the forces at his disposal to accomplish this goal if necessary.

The Israelites must have wondered why God didn't make sure that Pharaoh stayed home. On the previous day, the Egyptian ruler made no noise about their leaving and didn't attempt to stop them. But now, standing by the Red Sea, the Israelites ask Moshe why they have to die in the desert at the hands of Pharaoh (see Exodus 14:11). It all looked so promising on that first day of the Exodus, everything was taken care of and God's protection was complete and flawless. So why not continue this most comfortable situation?

Indeed, on the second day, God is no longer pulling the strings. It is as if He decides to fade into the background and man has to become more active. Only after many complaints and fervent prayers from the Israelites, God steps in and splits the Red Sea, providing them with basic protection. Could God not have split the sea earlier, to save the Israelites unnecessary anguish? Why not allow things to continue like the day before, when everything was under control and what prevailed was an almost messianic condition?

The message could not be clearer. It is man who must carry the responsibility for himself. The option of sitting in an armchair and passively relying on God and His benevolence does not exist. We are brought into this world to take moral action, grow spiritually and dignify ourselves through hardship and struggle. It is the desert that functions as a classroom where the Israelites learn to become "a light unto the nations" (see Isaiah 42:6; 49:6) and set a moral example. This is life's purpose and its condition.

Why, then, did God first arrange a day that resembled paradise only to plunge them into panic and feelings of insecurity the very next day? Because without knowing and actually experiencing that ultimately God possess total power, their obligation to be morally responsible would stand on shaky ground. Why be moral when there is no firm foundation on which this morality depends? First we have to learn that there is a purpose for our struggle for moral behavior, not just a utilitarian one but also an existential one. We must be convinced that there is more to life than what meets the eye. It has to become clear that God, and only God, is the ultimate source of everything. Only then will we stand in awe; overwhelmed by the grandeur of God's infinite power. We need to become completely powerless before we can take action and accept responsibility.

The real struggle for moral liberty started the day after the exodus from Egypt. The first day was a day of God, not of man. It was the day of passivity and complete surrender. The spiritual labor of man began the second day. Consequently, that was the first day of his spiritual elevation.

It is for this reason that throughout the generations we begin Pesach by learning what God's power is all about and celebrating it on the first day— specifically when reading the Haggadah[15]. Only after we are totally overpowered by God's absolute omnipotence and spend a day in contemplative awe, we are able to take moral action on the second day.

I believe this is the reason that we begin counting the Omer on the second day, as the first day doesn't count.

---

15 Haggadah - a book containing the liturgy for the Seder service on the festival of Passover.

PARASHAT
BEHAR

On the Mount
Leviticus 25:1-26:2

BEHAR

TORAH LESSON BY
RABBI DAVID AARON

BONDING OR BONDAGE
WHY SERVE THE DIVINE?

"For unto Me the children of Israel are servants; they are My servants who
I took out of the land of Egypt; I am the Lord G-d." Leviticus 25:55

THERE IS AN Eastern teaching that proclaims, "Be here and now." Torah
on the other hand would say, "Serve G-d here and now." Indeed, this is
the fullest experience of life.

The Kabbalah[16] teaches that G-d wants to be present in the here and now,
and our job is to serve G-d in that desire. Therefore, to serve G-d means to
infuse each moment with the presence of G-d. In other words, I must always
ask myself, "How can I serve G-d right now?"

If right now I am with my friend, spouse or child, I should see this moment
as an opportunity to show him/her love and thus serve G-d—who is the
source of all love. It's not my love, as I didn't invent love. I didn't create love
and I didn't give it its' power and meaning. Love didn't start with me and love
will not end with me. I am not the master of love but I am the servant of love,
and when I love someone I am serving to make G-d's love present in the here
and now.

My service to G-d (who wants to be present in this world in the here and the
now) is to channel His love, compassion, justice, wisdom or whatever divine
value the moment calls for. To live fully is to be present in this moment. The
goal of life is to serve G-d here and now, to be present in this moment.

Torah teaches that there is no greater joy in life than to serve G-d. G-d wants
to be present in this world through you and me. To live G-d's purpose is to serve.
This is our ultimate reward, accomplishment and ecstasy. This is the meaning of
our existence on earth and this is the key to happiness.

---

16 *Kabbalah* - often referred to as the "soul" of the Torah, the Kabbalah is an ancient Jewish tradition
which teaches the deepest insights into the essence of Gd, His interaction with the world, and the purpose of Creation.

SURRENDER AND SERENITY

G-d conscious people are not self-conscious. They are completely absorbed in the moment in their service to G-d; they become one with G-d and feel ecstasy.

If you are playing Frisbee and you ask yourself, "Am I having fun?" then you are definitely not having fun because it means you are not fully absorbed in the moment. If you are sitting by the sea, listening to the enchanting sound of the waves, and you ask yourself, "Am I experiencing serenity and inner peace now?" then you are definitely not because you are not fully present. You could not be fully in the moment if you could ask the question.

The highest expression of pleasure is what is described in Jewish mysticism as *Betul HaYesh*—the negation of self-consciousness. If I am self-conscious, then I am not completely absorbed in the service of the moment. When you are reading a good book, are you aware that you are reading a good book? No, you are just reading a good book. And when you are praying, how do you know that you are praying well? When you simply can't ask yourself the question, "Am I praying well?"

A story about a young yeshiva student illustrates this point well. The youngster used to pray with so much enthusiasm that he would stomp his feet without realizing it. Normally, this would pose no problem, but the boy had a lame foot. One day, his rabbi's wife said to her husband, "Please tell the youngster not to stomp his lame foot because he could really aggravate his malady."

The rabbi said to her, "If I thought he knew which foot he was stomping, I would tell him. But he's in such a state of ecstasy, so completely absorbed in his prayers and service, that he doesn't even know he's stomping on his bad foot."

TO SERVE WITH JOY

People think that serving G-d is demeaning, as servitude implies a slave-master relationship. But that is not the real meaning of serving G-d. The opportunity to serve G-d is the greatest gift we could ever imagine. It's empowering. To serve G-d means that we can do something on behalf of G-d. It's an unbelievable honor!

The Talmud teaches that if you come close to fire, you will be warm, and the servant who comes close to the king partakes in royalty.

I've been in the homes of some very, very wealthy people. I always find it so interesting that the various workers in the home—gardeners, caterers, hair-dressers, and so on—live in the mansion with their boss, eat the same food, and enjoy the use of the same facilities like the pool, sauna, and jacuzzi during their breaks.

The servants in the palace enjoy the life of royalty in many ways. They are privy to seeing the king in private moments. They even see the king in his pajamas. They come the closest and thereby enjoy the most intimate encounters with the king.

Working for G-d is not a diminishing experience. On the contrary, it's the greatest elevation of status. If I build my business for my own sake, to make money for me, it is really nothing special. But if I build my business for G-d's sake, if I look at what I do and ask myself how I can promote G-d's purpose in this world. How can I bring more love, peace, kindness, justice, and wisdom into the world? How can I be an instrument serving to reveal divine qualities and ideals in the world? This is the secret to a profoundly meaningful and fulfilling life—it's an unbelievable opportunity!

There's a striking line in a song by Bob Dylan: "You're gonna have to serve somebody." Everybody's serving somebody. There's nobody in this world that isn't serving something or somebody else. The question is not "To serve or not to serve?" The question is "*Whom* to serve?"

If my life is dedicated to gaining approval from certain people, then I am always less than what they are. But if my life is dedicated to G-d, then the sky's the limit to my self-worth. There is no greater mission waiting for me, there is nothing higher.

Our purpose on earth is not about making a lot of money. If it is, then the T-shirt slogan is right: "The one who dies with the most toys wins." But Kabbalah teaches that we have come to this world to perform the ultimate service—a mission that elevates and brings sacredness to all of life.

Life without serving a higher purpose is no life at all. A person who wakes up in the morning and has nothing sacred to do will after a while wonder: "Do I really make a difference? Does my life really matter?"

From *The God-Powered Life,* by Rabbi David Aaron, © 2010 by Rabbi David Aaron. Reprinted by arrangement with Shambhala Publications, Inc., www.shambhala.com.

PARASHAT
BECHUKOTAI

In My statutes
LEVITICUS 26:3-27:34

בחקתי

BECHUKOTAI

TORAH LESSON BY
RABBI NATHAN LOPES CARDOZO

SATISFACTION AND THE ART OF BEING

And the time of threshing shall reach until the vintage, and the vintage shall reach the sowing time. You shall eat your bread to satiety and you shall dwell in your land without worry. (Numbers 26:5)

THIS BLESSING IS promised to the people of Israel when, as a united nation, it observes the Law of the Torah and lives by its spirit. Its promise is quite surprising. Not only will the Israelites have plenty to eat, but as the verse clearly indicates, the Israelites will experience an overflow of food. The first season, when produce is brought to the threshing floor, will last until the days of the vineyard. And these days will in turn continue into the days of sowing.

Rashi (1040-1105), the great French commentator, makes an extraordinary statement when quoting Torat Cohanim[17]. He informs us that the verse is teaching us that one will "eat a little, and it will be blessed in his innards." He seems to understand this verse very differently than what one would have imagined. It appears that it is not the quantity of food that will increase, but the quality. The food consumed will be of such a high quality that eating only a small amount in a blessed year will produce the same benefit as a large amount in a year which is not specially blessed.

The explanation of the verse, as understood by Torat Cohanim and Rashi, would then indicate that people would consume very little food throughout the year so the same amount of food normally consumed in a short period of time will now last much longer. Thus, the time of threshing will hold enough food until the vintage, etc.

There is, however, a completely different way of looking at this verse that may carry great meaning for our present time. The famous thinker and teacher of Mussar[18], Rabbi Yerucham of the Mir Yeshiva in Poland (20th century), allude to an even greater miracle mentioned in our verse (see Mussarei HaTorah). This

---

17 Torat Cohanim - "instructions of the priests".
18 Arising in the 19th century, the Mussar movement is defined as the education of the individual toward strict ethical behavior in the spirit of halakhah (the totality of laws and ordinances).

time, it is not the quality of the food but the quality of Man that makes the difference.

According to Rabbi Yerucham, there will be no difference between a year that is blessed and one that is not. Both will produce the same amount and quality of food. What changes is Man's attitude to his physical possessions.

To be satisfied and happy is the greatest blessing that can ever be bestowed on Man. But such a blessing has absolutely no relation to the amount of food or possessions that Man happens to eat or own. The Torah teaches us that when the People of Israel live in accordance with the requirements of the Torah, Man will be blessed with a frame of mind where matters of possession and food will take on a completely different dimension. This attitude is not something that an individual can develop independently; it depends on one's receptiveness towards the Divine and God's response. When a person has achieved high moral and spiritual latitudes, they will see the world in a very different light. After one's basic needs are fulfilled, one will see oneself as what Erich Fromm calls a "being," i.e., one who will "be-come," and one who sees one's essence in one's spiritual growth (Erich Fromm, To Have or To Be, Abacus, 1976). It is not what a person "has," but what he "is," which is of real importance. At such a moment, satisfaction is no longer the result of possessing more, but of "being" more.

It is most remarkable that the Torah emphasizes that it is, first and foremost, our own mindset that allows for this state of "being." Judaism was the first to postulate that mental health and illness are outcomes of right and wrong living. When people are greedy or ambitious in attaining fame, we hold them in contempt because we believe that they have the wrong kind of thoughts. The Torah, however, teaches us—without denying other possible causes—that they actually suffer from a kind of mental illness that is the outcome of immoral action.

This also relates to the concept of joy. Joy is connected to productive activity. It is not a peak experience which ends suddenly, but rather a plateau which is the product of one's essential human faculties. It is not the ecstatic fire of the moment, but the glow that accompanies "being." It is only with this type of true joy where one is able to be satisfied with the minimum while experiencing the maximum.

NUMBERS ✦ BEMIDBAR

PARASHAT
BEMIDBAR

In the wilderness

Numbers 1:1-4:20

במדבר

BEMIDBAR

TORAH LESSON BY
RABBI LEVI COOPER

THE DISCIPLE AS MASTER

WHILE THE HASIDIC master is generally accepted as the leader of his charges, many Hasidic courts also employed a tiered mentoring structure. Senior disciples played an important role in educating newcomers, inculcating Hasidic values and mores, and being repositories and conduits for the community's collective memory and identity.

Thus in the court of Rabbi Naftali Zvi Horowitz of Ropczyce (1760-1827) the norm was that when a new disciple seeking to study the paths of the Almighty arrived, Rabbi Naftali would select one of his senior disciples to instruct the novice. Most of what the veteran offered would be guidance, steering the attention of the newcomer towards significant phenomena: "Pay attention to this," "this is unimportant," "this is significant," and so on. Direct spiritual counseling was still the province of the Hasidic master, who in this case was Rabbi Naftali of Ropczyce.

Such personal mentoring considered the Hasid's individual needs and talents. According to Hasidic understanding, each person has his or her own specific contribution to offer this world. No one else can do what has been assigned to that person by the Almighty. Personal mentoring was deemed necessary to assist people in identifying their own intended spiritual path and fulfill their purpose in this world. If guidance was dished out indiscriminately and impersonally, individuals might sadly not feel encouraged to walk their own particular paths.

Rabbi Hayyim Elazar Shapiro of Munkács (1871-1937), a later Hasidic master and descendant of Rabbi Naftali of Ropczyce—understood that a biblical verse suggested this pyramid structure. In relation to protecting the Kohanim (the priests) from the physical dangers of dealing with the Holy Temple artefacts, God said: "Let Aaron and his sons go in and assign each of them to his duties and to his porterage" (Numbers 4:19). The task was not entrusted to Aaron alone, as Aaron and his sons were commanded to consign each Kohen their own personal task.

Elsewhere in his writings, the rabbi of Munkács offered a different source for this structure. Before entering the Land of Israel, God urged the People of

Israel to heed the commandments, promising to assist in the conquest of the Land if the People keep the commandments, love God, walk in all the ways of God, and cleave to the Almighty (see Deuteronomy 11:22). The sages explain that one cannot physically hold on to the Omnipresent who transcends all physical manifestations, except by cleaving to the Almighty's wise people and their students. Again, seeking instruction not just from the master—in this case God—but also from the Almighty's disciples, appears to be validated and even encouraged as a necessity.

The Munkatcher Rebbe retold a well-known tale that not only exemplified this very structure but bespoke of it as a necessity. Rabbi Elimelekh of Leżajsk (1717-1786) once met a disciple, Rabbi David of Żołynia, who was making his way from Leżajsk towards nearby Łańcut. It was the eve of Shabbat and it was clear that Rabbi David was on his way to spend Shabbat in the company of Rabbi Yaakov Yitzhak Horowitz (1745-1815). Rabbi Yaakov Yitzhak—then known as "Reb Itzik'le" and later to be known as the "Hozeh (seer) of Lublin"—was a student of Rabbi Elimelekh of Leżajsk and at that time he had just set out to lead his own flock, apparently to the chagrin of his master.

Meeting the venerable Rabbi Elimelekh of Leżajsk, the student Rabbi David was worried that his teacher might interpret the journey as an affront to his honor. Rabbi David therefore decided to deal with the issue openly:

"My master, I am on my way to spend Shabbat in Łańcut, for Reb Itzik'le and I are your students and we study together. Alas, I am unable to fully fathom your exalted level of spirituality. Like a high table that requires a pedestal to reach it—the pedestal must be lower than the table, but near enough to it so that the table top can be accessed. I, too, need a pedestal to reach your holy table, a pedestal that is lower than the table but situated within close proximity. That is why I travel to Łańcut for Shabbat."

Rabbi Elimelekh of Leżajsk may not have been entirely convinced by the argument of his disciple Rabbi David of Żołynia, but the pedestal metaphor and the notion of "disciple-as-master" may be a useful frame when considering our task in this world.

We may not all be of the caliber to be great Hasidic masters. We may not all be adept at comprehending the lofty esoteric tradition. We may not all have the fortitude to lead against the tide. Even if we are students rather than teachers we still have important roles to play. If all you know is the Hebrew letter aleph—then teach aleph! For every disciple is essentially also a master.

PARASHAT
NASO

Elevate!

NUMBERS 4:21-7:89

נשא

NASO

TORAH LESSON BY
RABBI MOSHE LICHTMAN

NOT BY MIGHT NOR BY POWER

T HE FIRST TWO *mitzvot* in this week's *parasha* have to do with the pro-
hibition of entering the Temple (Beit HaMikdash) when one is ritu-
ally impure. The Torah states: *Command the Children of Israel that
they shall send away from the camp everyone with tzara'at, every zav, and
everyone contaminated by the dead... so that they not contaminate their
camps in which I dwell.* (Numbers 5:2–3) Two *mitzvot* are alluded to here:
one positive (*they shall send away*), and one negative (*so that they not contaminate*). Depending on the type of impurity a person has, he or she is prohibited
from entering one, two, or three camps – the Camp of God's Presence, the
Levite Camp, and the Camp of Israel. In the Temple, these three camps cor-
responded to the Sanctuary, the Temple Mount, and Jerusalem.

In his discussion of the underlying reasons for these *mitzvot, Sefer
HaChinuch*[1] writes: "One could compare this matter, allegorically, to **the
palace of a king** from which they distance anyone with *tzara'at*[2] or anyone
whose body or even whose clothing is loathsome. This is similar to the verse
For one is not to come to the gate of the king with sackcloth (Esther 4:2)"
(*Mitzvah* 362). In the next *mitzvah* (363), the Chinuch adds, "This *mitzvah*
applies... even nowadays... for **the sanctity of HaShem rests upon [the
site of the Temple] even today, when it is desolate,** as the Sages derive
from the verse *I will make your sanctuaries desolate (VaYikra 26:31)."*

The Chinuch is referring to a concept developed most notably by the
Rambam (Maimonides). In many places, the Talmud cites a dispute regarding
the status of the Holy Temple and the entire Land of Israel. Regarding the
Temple and Jerusalem, the Rambam rules that the sanctity generated at the
time of the First Temple took effect during that period and continues *ad infi-
nitum*; it was not abrogated when the Temple was destroyed. Regarding the
rest of the Land, however, he holds that the first sanctity was nullified by the
destruction of the First Temple; but the sanctity generated by Ezra at the time

---

1 Sefer HaChinuch (Chinuch) - is a work which systematically discusses the 613 commandments of the Torah.
2 Tzara'at – Leper.

of the Second Temple existed then and continues until this very day. The Rambam explains the reason for this difference:

> Why do I say [this]...? For the sanctity of the Temple and Jerusalem stems from the *Shechinah* [Divine Presence], and the *Shechinah* never dissolves. Behold, it says, *I will make your sanctuaries desolate*, and the Sages state, **"Even though [your sanctuaries] are desolate, they still remain holy."**
>
> The Land's obligation of *shevi'it* and *ma'asrot*[3], however, is based only on public conquest [i.e., Yehoshua's conquest[4]]. And since the Land was taken away from them [at the time of the first destruction], the conquest was annulled and [the Land] was biblically exempt from *ma'asrot* and *shivi'it*, for it was no [longer considered] the Land of Israel [in terms of these *mitzvot*].
>
> When Ezra[5] returned and sanctified [the Land], he did not sanctify it through conquest, **rather through *chazakah* – taking hold of it.** Therefore, any place that the people who ascended from Babylonia took hold of—thus sanctifying it with Ezra's second sanctification—is holy today, even though the Land was taken away from us... (*Hilchot Beit HaBechirah* 6:16)

That is, Ezra's sanctification is everlasting because it was brought about by way of settlement. *Chazakah* is a stronger mode of acquisition than conquest is, for the latter can be annulled by a subsequent conquest, while the former is immutable. In his work *"Eretz Yisrael Nachalat Am Yisrael,"* R. Yechezkel Abramsky explains the Rambam's idea thus: "Ezra's aliyah[6], which was based on a yearning for the Land where God chose to rest His name, left its mark on the Land—from a halachic[7] standpoint—for that generation and all future generations... What Yehoshua's conquest could not do with its military might, Ezra's *aliyah* accomplished with the strength of its spiritual fervor... *Not by might, nor by power, but by My spirit, said the Lord of Hosts (Zechariah 4:6)."*

The Kuzari[8] states, "If this Land had only this advantage, that the *Shechinah*

---

3 Shevi'it ("Seventh Year") is a tractate that deals with all laws of allowing the land to rest in the seventh year, the laws of shmitha produce and the remission of debts. It also discusses the 50th year, known as Jubilee.

Ma'aser ("The first tithe") is a positive commandment in the Tora requiring the giving of one tenth of agricultural produce, after the giving of the standard terumah, to the priest or Levite.

4 See the book of Joshua.

5 See the book of Ezra.

6 Aliyah – immigrate.

7 Halacha - is the collective body of Jewish religious laws derived from the Written and Oral Torah.

8 Kuzari - is one of the most famous works of the medieval Spanish Jewish philosopher and poet Rabbi Yehuda Halevi, completed around 1140.

rested there for 900 years [when the two Temples stood], it would be fitting for people to yearn to ascend there in order to purify their souls..." (*Kuzari* 2:23). It is true that nowadays the *Shechinah* rests "only" in Jerusalem, but the entire Land is holy, and this is where the *Shechinah* once dwelt and will dwell again in the very near future. Isn't this enough of an incentive for us to take possession of our historical Homeland—with spiritual fervor like Ezra did—and redeem it from those who wish to take it away from us?

From *Eretz Yisrael in the Parashah* by Rabbi Moshe Lichtman.

BEHA'ALOTECHA

When you light the lamps

NUMBERS 8:1-12:16

בהעלתך

BEHA'ALOTECHA

TORAH LESSON BY

RABBI CHANAN MORRISON

GREAT DREAMS

U NLIKE THE UNIQUE clarity of Moses' prophecy, ordinary prophecy is communicated through the medium of visions and dreams:

> If someone among you experiences Divine
> prophecy, I will make Myself known to him in a vision;
> I will speak to him in a dream. (Numbers 12:6)

WHY DREAMS?

Dreams, Rav Kook (1865 – 1935) wrote, perform a vital function in the world. Great dreams are the very foundation of the universe. Dreams exist on many levels. There are the prescient dreams of prophets, and the conscious dreaming of poets. There are the idealistic dreams of great visionaries for a better world; and there are our national dreams of redemption— "When God will return the captivity of Zion, we will be like dreamers" (Psalms 126:1).

Of course, not every dream falls under the category of a great dream. Most dreams are petty or pointless, as it says, "Dreams speak falsely" (Zechariah 10:2). What determines whether a dream is meaningless or prophetic?

TRUE DREAMS AND FALSE DREAMS

Those who are truly servants of God concentrate their aspirations and efforts on rectifying the world. When one's thoughts and actions are devoted exclusively to perfecting all of creation, then one's imagination will only be stimulated by matters that relate to the universal reality. The dreams of such individuals will naturally be of great significance. Their dreams relate to the inner truth of reality, to its past, present, and future.

But the imaginative faculties of people preoccupied with private concerns will be limited—like their waking thoughts and actions—to personal matters. What great truth could be revealed in imaginings that never succeeded in rising above the vain thoughts and desires of a self-centered individual?

The Sages expressed this idea allegorically by explaining that angels bring prophetic dreams and demons bring false dreams (*Berachot* 55b). What does this mean? Angels are constant forces in the universe, pre-arranged to perfect the world. True dreams relate to these underlying positive forces. Demons, on the other hand, are unholy forces rooted in private desires which are inconsistent with the overall universal order. False dreams are the resultant fantasies of such personal wishes.

THE TRUE REALITY OF DREAMS

What would the world be like without dreams? Life immersed solely in materialism is coarse and bleak. It lacks the inspiring grandeur of expansive horizons; like a bird with clipped wings, it cannot raise itself above the bitter harshness of the present reality. We are only able to free ourselves from these shackles through the power of dreams.

Some foolishly take pride in being 'realists.' They insist on taking into account only the present state of the world—a partial and fragmented view of reality. In fact, it is our dreams which liberate us from the limitations of the current reality. It is our dreams that accurately reveal the inner truth of the universe.

As that future reality is revealed, we merit an increasing clarity of vision. Our perception begins to approach the *aspaklaria hame'irah*, the clear vision of Moses, with whom God spoke "face to face, in a vision not containing allegory, so that he could see a true image of God" (Num. 12:8).

From *Sapphire from the Land of Israel*, pp. 265-267. Adapted from *Orot HaKodesh* vol. I, p. 226; *Ein Eyah* vol. II, p. 279.

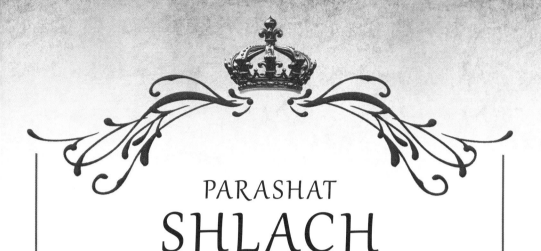

PARASHAT
SHLACH

Send for Yourself

Numbers 13:1-15:41

שלח-לך

SHLACH

TORAH LESSON BY
RABBI YEHOSHUA FRIEDMAN

THE POST-TRAUMA VICTIM

I N NUMBERS, CHAPTER 27, the daughters of Tzelofchad came before Moshe, Elazar the Kohen (who succeeded Aharon after his death) and the elders of Israel. The background was the allocation of land in Eretz Yisrael[9] which was to be conquered and given out to tribes and families. The five daughters claimed that it is not fair that their father, just because he had no son, should be done out of having an inheritance in the land for his future descendants. The reason given is that he did not participate in the rebellion of Korach[10], but died in his own sin. That is to say that although he had his own issues, he did not negatively influence others.

There is internal evidence that Tzelofchad's sin did not adversely affect others. From *pshat* (straightforward meaning of the text) we see that he had five fine, wise daughters who grew up to eloquently plead for a share in the Land. The Sages of the Talmud (Shabbat 96b) wonder what his sin really was. Rabbi Akiva (50-137 CA) claims he was the man who went out to gather straw on Shabbat and was put to death (Bam. 15:32-36). Rabbi Yehuda ben Beteira disagrees, attributing Tzelofchad's sin to joining the "presumptuous ones" who attempted to force their way into Eretz Yisrael without divine sanction and were killed (Bam. 14:39-45).

What do both of these opinions have in common? I would like to suggest that both the straw-gatherer and the presumptuous ones (Hebrew *ma'apilim*, used in modern Hebrew to refer to the illegal Jewish immigration during the British Mandate White Paper days) were two different manifestations of what we today know as Post-Stress Trauma Disorder (PSTD).

Some people who have been in mortal danger—such as soldiers in battle or firefighters—cope with their fear by recklessly charging forward into the danger without any concerns. This sometimes ends in heroism and other times in death. The Israelites accepted the evil report of the spies and expressed their wish to go back to Egypt[11]. For this G-d punished them with 40 years of wandering in the desert. None of the adult males would go into Eretz Yisrael; they all died during

---

9 Eretz Yisrael – The Land of Israel.
10 See Numbers 16.
11 See Numbers 14.

those 40 years. There were those who attempted to charge forward anyway, in spite of being told that G-d would not be with them and the enemy would destroy them; and so it was.

The other category was the straw-gatherer. The straw-gatherer was a case in which Moshe had to ask G-d specially what to do with him. This is peculiar, since it is a known fact that to transfer an object in a public domain on Shabbat is a capital offense. However, there is a principle that the actual conviction of a criminal in a capital case should be avoided at all cost to prevent the spilling of blood. Any mitigating factor is used to prevent the conviction. But apparently here the case was clear-cut; the offender was caught in the act, questioned, warned in front of at least two witnesses, and then proceeded despite being told that he would stand to be executed. Strict procedure called for stoning. But there was a wider consideration. This person was in a state of lessened volition because of the lack of a clear motive and a compulsive behavior.

Let me explain the origin of the trauma. Back in Mitzrayim[12] (Exodus Chap.5), when Moshe first came before Pharaoh and told him to release the Israelites from bondage, Pharaoh responded punitively by requiring the workers to produce the same quantity of bricks as before without being provided with straw. This forced each worker to do the additional, highly traumatic work of foraging in the sand gathering straw under threat of beating by the Egyptian taskmasters. Does this sound familiar?

The second factor was the total lack of *need* to gather straw in the Sinai desert. The people were covered with protective clouds by day and fire by night, therefore they had no need to make fires to warm themselves. None of their clothing needed to be replaced with fibers of any sort. Their food came down from heaven in an edible form. Those who felt a desire to cook it could do so, but such a desire does not seem to compel going out *davka*, purposely on Shabbat when it is forbidden, to gather straw.

It is clear from the above that the straw-gatherer is the opposite pole of PSTD, the compulsive reliving of the old stress. We may suggest that Tzelofchad, or whoever was walking along in the desert on Shabbat, just happened to look at the straw on the ground, which triggered the recurrence of the trauma from the days of slavery in Mitzrayim. The Torah puts Shabbat, the symbol of freedom from toil, in juxtaposition with this overwhelming compulsion. Moshe and the people were perplexed by this, causing Moshe

---

12 Mitzrayim – Egypt.

Rabbeinu to appeal to Hashem for an understanding of what to do. The verdict is that the individual, in principle, still has free will and is culpable, but the suffering and death of this unfortunate individual effects an atonement for his soul, since he is still a victim, has not caused others to sin and presumably received his punishment with proper confession and contrition (Yoma 85b and Rambam (1135-1204), Teshuva 1:4). Therefore, in either instance, the daughters of Tzelofchad have a case.

PARASHAT
KORACH

In The Beginning

Numbers 16:1-18:32

קרח

KORACH

TORAH LESSON BY
RABBI DAVID AARON

BEATING JEALOUSY

"Jealousy, that dragon which slays love under
the pretence of keeping it alive."

IN THIS WEEK'S Torah portion Korach, Moses' leadership and the appointment of priesthood to Moses' brother, Aaron, is challenged by a member of Moses' tribe—the Levites—and other communal leaders. Motivated by envy toward Moses and Aaron they argue for equality, "We are all holy; how can there be a hierarchy of holiness within Israel"?

They came as a group to oppose Moses and Aaron and said to them, "You have gone too far! The whole community is holy, every one of them, and the LORD is with them. Why then do you set yourselves above the LORD's assembly"?

Moses responded to Korach:

> "Now listen, you Levites! Isn't it enough for you that the G-d of Israel has separated you from the rest of the Israelite community and brought you near Himself to do the work at the Lord's tabernacle and to stand before the community and minister to them? He has brought you and all your fellow Levites near Himself, but now you are trying to get the priesthood too"! Numbers 16: 8-10

SPIRITUAL JOURNEY OR EGO TRIP

Life is a divine mission, and if Korach had understood this then he would have realized that no one has a better or more important mission.

It is ridiculous to ever be envious of another person's lot. Don't ever think that the president of the United States is any more important than a waiter in a restaurant. If G-d is with us in our mission, then one person's mission cannot be more important than another's, because everyone's mission is actually G-d's mission.

Real success does not depend on how much we accomplish on earth. And it does not have anything to do with how much attention the accomplishment gains in the public eye. What really matters is your intention and the quality of your deeds. Did you put your soul into your mission and live your life for G-d's sake, seeking to grow, striving to become better and concerned about improving yourself and the world?

The great Torah sages taught: "I am a creation and my friend (even one who is uneducated) is a creation. Just as he is not an expert in what I do, I am not an expert in what he does. Do not think that I do more and he does less, as that is incorrect. It does not matter whether he accomplishes seemingly big deeds or little deeds. What really matters is whether his intentions are for the sake of heaven."

This lesson does not make any apparent sense. These great sages made historic contributions to human spiritual and ethical development. Their names will be remembered forever. How could they have possibly compared themselves to simple people who were unlearned, whose deeds could never have earned them world recognition, and who will surely be forgotten in the annals of history? How could they say that what really matters is the purity of one's intentions and the power of one's commitment to act on behalf of G-d?

These sages understood that each and every one of us has a mission in life—a calling. You must always remember who is calling. G-d is calling you to be His agent on earth, and the mission He is asking you to fulfill is not only your mission but G-d's mission.

If we are all working for G-d, then there is no such thing as a small mission. How could one divine mission be less than another divine mission? Can either one ever be any less than the ultimate?

If we would internalize this truth, we would free ourselves of the foolish habit of comparing ourselves with others. We would heal ourselves of a debilitating disease that rots our bones—jealousy.

The Talmud tells a story about a man who got a glimpse of the afterlife. He was surprised to see that the next world was upside down. He saw some people who were very respected and famous during their lives on earth, but in the next world they were nobody. Although these people were once recognized as significant members of the upper echelons of society, they were now considered part of the lower class. He also saw people who in their lifetime were simple workers but were now prominent members of the highest order. It was a shock to him.

Imagine you are a world-renowned actor and wherever you go people look at you in great awe and admiration. Then the curtain falls on your life, and you find yourself in a new world—the afterlife. To your surprise, in this world nobody even notices you. Suddenly you see a familiar face; it is your maid surrounded by a crowd of angelic fans. In the afterlife she may be the celebrity and you the shlepper[13]. How is this possible? It all depends on the quality of your deeds and your attitude. Did you invite G-d into your work? Did you work with the intention of being G-d's agent—serving to perform a divine mission—or was it just an ego trip?

From *The Secret Life of God*, by Rabbi David Aaron, © 2005 by Rabbi David Aaron. Reprinted by arrangement with Shambhala Publications, Inc., www.shambhala.com.

---

13 Shlepper - From Yiddish, a person who sells rags, or dragging around rags. Used for a person who is ill dressed, sloppy in habits, or wears ill-fitting clothing. Also a person who is poor and shows it.

PARASHAT
CHUKAT

Ordinance of
NUMBERS 19:1-22:1

חקת
CHUKAT

TORAH LESSON BY
RABBI SHLOMO RISKIN

THE LEADER MUST RESPECT HIS
PEOPLE: KEHAL VS. EDAH

AND MOSES AND Aaron assembled the assemblage [kehal] before the rock; and he [Moses] said to them, "Listen now, rebels, from this rock shall we [be able] to extract water for you?" And Moses lifted his hand, struck the rock twice with his rod, and much water emerged to give drink to the witness community and their cattle. Numbers 20:10–11

Moses entered the stage of the history of the Israelites by striking (the Egyptian), and exited from the history of the Israelites by striking (the rock). His first act of striking out against the Egyptian taskmaster was out of love for his people and outreach to his real brethren, an act of courage and self-sacrifice which forced him to leave the house of Pharaoh; his second act of striking out against the rock, but really against the Hebrews - whom he called "rebels" right before he struck the rock—was an act of displaced anger, deep frustration with a nation which had defied his teachings and allowed rebellion after rebellion to undermine his and God's authority.

Rabbi Jacob Harlap (1883-1951), close disciple and confidante of Rabbi A.Y.H. Kook, in his multi-volume Mei Marom, describes the change in Moses' mindset towards the Hebrews by distinguishing between two descriptive nouns for the Israelite crowd which are usually taken for synonyms: "kehal" and "edah," assemblage and community. An assemblage consists of the many individuals who assemble together, the separate and disparate persons who make up a crowd; a community is guided by a specific purpose, which serves to unite (com-unity), and connotes individuals united by their commitment to historic continuity from generation to generation. Indeed, edah, really means witness, and the continued survival of the nation of Israel despite exile and persecution in accordance with the divine covenant serves as eloquent testimony to the reality and truth of God's presence and of Israel's mission: humanity perfected in a world redeemed.

With this introduction, let us take a fresh look at our biblical reading. Immediately following Miriam's death, the desert wells dried up and the

Israelites assembled as a crowd of disparate rabble (vayikahalu) in complaint against Moses and Aaron. In response, God addressed Moses,

> Take the staff, and you and Aaron assemble the witness community [hak'hel et ha'edah]. Speak to the rock in their presence and it will give forth its water. You will thus bring forth water from the rock and allow the community [ha'edah] and their beasts to drink. Numbers 20:8

Moses was thus told by God to assemble the community (edah)! However, the text records that "Moses and Aaron assembled the assemblage [vayakhilu . . . hakahal] in front of the rock" (Numbers 20:10).

What a literal reading of the text is teaching us is that God wanted Moses to look at the motley crew of complainers and see that behind the façade of rabble were to be found witnesses of the divine; Moses was supposed to appreciate the great potential of this people, the fact that standing before him were the children of Abraham, Isaac and Jacob, Sarah, Rebecca, Rachel, and Leah, and the parents of Yishai, David, and the righteous Messiah. God expected Moses to see through the angry rabble and inspiringly extract from deep within them the faith of their forebears. After all, these same people had declared their willingness to be a "kingdom of priests and a holy nation," had raised their voices and sang as one at the Reed Sea, "the Lord shall be king forever and ever." But Moses, disappointed and disgruntled, personally devastated by their "ingratitude," could only see a congregation of kvetching individuals, a mass of fearful and immature freedmen dancing before a Golden Calf, a Datan and an Aviram[14] who even refused to meet with him, a disparate crowd who allowed themselves to become paralyzed before the Canaanites. He had lost sight of the witness community of Israel and could only see the assemblage of Israel; he spoke to what was in front of him instead of to their potential, the great moments and the noble individuals who comprised historic Israel and forged the Israelites in front of him. And so he became incapable of speaking with love; he could only strike out in anger. Such an individual perforce cannot continue to lead the nation towards the fulfillment of its historical destiny.

---

14 Numbers 16:12

A Postscript about Recapturing a Sense of Community

Many years ago I had the unique pleasure and privilege of spending an unforgettable Shabbat with one of the great scholars of contemporary times, Rabbi Charles Chavel (1906-1982). I could not resist asking him how, despite the fact that he served as a rabbi of a Jewish congregation, he nevertheless found the time to be so productive in Jewish scholarship, producing special editions of and commentaries on Rashi (1040-1105) and the Nahmanides (1194-1270), as well as responses to difficult Talmudic questions asked by Rabbi Akiva Eiger (1761-1837). "I always had small congregations," he told me, "small in number and sometimes even small in soul. And after a difficult board meeting with Mrs. Goldberg and Mr. Schwartz I yearned for the company of profound minds and deep perspectives. Who could be greater antidotes to small-minded and mean-spirited individuals than the Nahmanides and Rabbi Akiva Eiger? Rabbi Chavel understood the secret; he had the capacity to look beyond the congregation and see the community. That's what every leader must aspire to do if he is to truly succeed.

From *Torah Lights: Bemidbar* by Rabbi Shlomo Riskin; used with permission from Maggid Books, a division of Koren Publishers Jerusalem.

PARASHAT
BALAK

Balak (destroyer)

Numbers 22:2-25:9

BALAK

TORAH LESSON BY
RABBI GEDALIA MEYER

THE PROPHET BALAAM

'**A**ND BALAAM SAW that it was good in the eyes of Hashem to bless Israel, so he did not use sorcery like the previous times but turned his face to the desert. And Balaam lifted up his eyes and he saw Israel dwelling in the tribal arrangement and the spirit of God came upon him. And he took up his parable and said, "Thus spoke Balaam the son of Beor and thus spoke the man of clear vision. Thus spoke the one who hears the sayings of God, who gazes upon the vision of the Almighty, the one who falls with open eyes."' (Numbers 24: 2-4)

Bilaam is not exactly a household name. Of the minority of people out there who are somewhat familiar with the Bible most will not be able to say much about him, assuming they have heard of him to begin with. He only comes up in one section of the Torah (with a few references elsewhere) at the back of the book of Numbers, and only the real devotees make it to this section. This is the particular parasha we are exploring right now. It is named 'Balak' because of the tribal king who brought Balaam into the events of the Bible.

Let's start with the background. The Israelites had spent 40 years wandering around the desert following the revolt associated with the 'Spies'. By the end of this period they were finally on the cusp of entering the Promised Land; they were on the eastern side of the Jordan River, just outside the Biblical region known as Moab.

Balak was the king of Moab, and he sensed that the Israelites were too powerful to subdue by normal means so he had to resort to the supernatural. He sent messengers to Balaam—a sorcerer from the land of Midian, a region to the south somewhere in the western area of what is now Saudi Arabia. Balaam had earned a reputation of being able to bless and curse people, an ability that was of great value in Biblical times. Balak wanted him on his side in the upcoming battle with the Israelites.

After a few rounds of negotiations, Balaam agreed to come but with the proviso that he speak only the words that God spoke to him. In other words, Balaam was a prophet who could indeed communicate with God, but would sell himself to the highest bidder. This may sound like an impossibility—how could it be that a 'man of God' could sell himself to curse the people of God? But such is the unpredictable world of the Bible—a prophet could be evil and a good person could be cursed.

While Balaam was on his way to Moab we encounter one of the strangest scenes in the Bible—even by Biblical standards this scene is downright bizarre. In the course of this routine journey Balaam's donkey starts giving him trouble. It crouches down when he should be walking, he swerves to the side of the road and he bangs into fences. The Torah explains this strange behavior with the surprising, but very Biblical, explanation of an angel being in the way. It seems that the donkey could see the angel but Balaam, the great prophet, could not.

As weird as this sounds, it gets even stranger. After the third of these hidden obstacles, Balaam finally loses his temper and hits the donkey. At this point, the donkey opens its mouth and begins to speak, rebuking Balaam for unjustly hitting him. In the course of this unlikely conversation Hashem enables Balaam to see the angel and he finally understands what has transpired. The angel, it turns out, was sent to warn Balaam to only say the words that God would put in his mouth. It was the donkey who had to drive this point home.

When Balaam finally arrives at the meeting spot with Balak he gets right to work. Twice he attempts to circumvent the restrictions God had placed upon him and twice he fails. Each time he ends up blessing the Israelites instead of cursing them. And each time, Balak rebukes him for not doing his bidding; Balaam had been hired to curse the Israelites, not to bless them. But each time, Balaam replies that he has no power to do anything without the authorization of God.

Finally, he tries it a third time and this is where the quote at the beginning of this essay comes in. He had given up on the occult methods he had tried previously, as they were unsuccessful. This time he doesn't seem to make the slightest attempt to heed the wishes of Balak, the king who hired him to curse the Israelites. This time, unlike the first two, the Torah describes his oracular statements as a result of "the spirit of God came upon him." His words include what would later become one of the best known statements of Jewish prayer, "How good are your tents Jacob, your dwelling places, Israel." Balaam was an utter failure at the mission he was hired for, but he was an unwilling success at prophesying the glorious and turbulent destiny of the nation he despised.

After the third failure Balak has had enough of Balaam, but Balaam was not finished. A fourth and final time he attains prophetic insight, and he foresees the destiny of not only Israel, but also that of the nations that surrounded it and were its principle adversaries. Balaam's prophecy is merciless in its insight and brutal in its truth: The enemies of Israel will be many, but they will perish in the end. Such is the fate of those who challenge the will of God.

One of the most perplexing questions concerning Balaam is how a person like him could have attained such great prophetic insights to begin with. Jewish tradition sees him as vain and opportunistic. He never sided with Israel, even after he himself saw the destiny accorded to both Israel and its enemies. His death comes later on in the book of Numbers, during the course of a battle between Israel and the Midianites—the land which Balaam came from. Prophecy is not something doled out to just anybody. According to Jewish tradition, prophecy is only attainable by unique individuals who are truly worthy of God's word. Prophecies that are recorded in the Bible are limited to a highly select group whose messages were deemed worthy of inclusion. Why was Balaam part of this spiritual elite?

There is no single answer to this question. Jewish sources offer many possibilities ranging from Balaam's own spiritual abilities to needing to have a prophet from the nations of the world. Perhaps the simplest answer lies right in the text itself. In the third and fourth prophecy Balaam introduces his pronouncements in almost the same way: 'the man of clear vision;' 'the one who hears the sayings of God, who gazes upon the vision of the Almighty, the one who falls with open eyes.' Before the fourth prophecy he includes another description: 'The knower of supernal knowledge'. Are these just platitudes? Is he praising himself to build confidence in the eyes of his benefactor? This explanation might work fine until the fourth prophecy, when Balak had already given up on Balaam. But the description is there, as clear as the prophecies themselves.

Perhaps these descriptions are real. Perhaps Balaam, in some manner that is hidden from us, was able to attain true prophetic insight. Perhaps, in spite of his personal shortcomings, he could see things in the spiritual world that others could not.

More than anything else, this section of the Torah gives us—the future readers of those prophecies—a clearer understanding of what prophecy truly was, and perhaps, will be again someday. It is the human mind seeing through all the haze and distractions, to what lies beyond. It is hearing the clear message of God, even if it is not necessarily what one wants to hear. It is to be 'fallen,' but nevertheless with 'open eyes.'

A Moses comes along once in human history. An Abraham or an Isaiah is unique even in the Bible. But a Balaam is not. He is like every one of us, warts and all. He is the human being with all of his or her shortcomings, but is still able to see what lies beyond. He may have fallen, but he has not closed his eyes to whatever it is that God wants him to see. Maybe this is the hidden message the Torah wants us to know from the unlikely Balaam; even though we have fallen, we can still see.

PARASHAT
PINCHAS

Phinehas (dark-skinned)

NUMBERS 25:10-30:1

פינחס

PINCHAS

TORAH LESSON BY
RABBI MOSHE GOLDSMITH

THE PERPETUITY OF ISRAEL AND THE DANGER OF ASSIMILATION

PARASHAT BALAK, LAST week's Torah portion, concludes with the execution of Zimri and Cazbi by Pinchas, whose zealotry put an end to the terrible plague that had killed twenty-four thousand Israelites.

According to our sages, the mastermind behind this plague was Bilam, [15] who was hired to curse the nation of Israel. He discovers, however, that he cannot do so because "The Nation of Israel is Blessed!" This is a law of Nature. Whether one is willing to accept it or not, Israel is G-d's Chosen People. This reality is not merely something that Balak, Bilam, the Moabites and the Midyanites had to learn—it is a lesson for all. G-d chose the nation of Israel and blessed it.

Throughout history, there have been many others who believed that, because of Israel's sins, the Israelites were no longer the Chosen People. They pointed out that the people of Israel had been exiled from their homeland; they are only a small minority of the world's population; and they have suffered endless persecution and abuse. How, then, can they be the Chosen People?

In fact, the idea that Israel is no longer the Chosen People was proven wrong time and time again as Israel outlived its oppressors. The notion completely fell apart when the Jewish people returned to their homeland after 2000 years of exile, revived their language, and restored their patrimony to a land flowing with milk and honey.

As we discussed in our last lesson, the goal of Balak and the Moabites was to prevent the nation of Israel from reaching the Land of Israel. They tried to achieve this by getting Bilam to curse the nation in order to thwart the Divine Plan. This, of course, is impossible and Bilams efforts were a classic exercise in futility.

Bilam's envy of the Nation of Israel, however, was too great to allow him to go home without a taste of victory. So his next inspiration was to cause suffering and pain to the Children of Israel by slowing down the process of their redemption. His plan was to have the Moabite women seduce the men of Israel and lure them into idol worship. This was partially successful, since,

---

15 See Numbers 24:14, and Rashi's [1040-1105] commentary.

as mentioned above, it caused the death of twenty-four thousand Israelites. Thanks to Pinchas' intervention, however, greater tragedy was averted.

After the Children of Israel begin to sin with Peor (in a particularly debased form of idol worship), G-d commands Moshe Rabeynu to assemble the Judges of Israel in order to punish the sinners. However, before the judges can do as they are told, Zimri ben Saluh, head of the tribe of Shimon, parades in front of the entire congregation of Israel, including Moshe Rabeynu, and takes a Midyanite woman of royal descent, Cazbi Bat Tzur, into his tent with the intention of sleeping with her. When Pinchas witnesses this act of brazen disrespect to G-d and the Nation, he executes both Zimri and Cazbi while they are in the act of intercourse.

Interestingly, in the description of these events there is no mention of Zimri worshiping idols, which was the only capital offence requiring the death penalty. How, then, did Pinchas have the authority to execute Zimri?

The Talmud teaches us that Zimri justifies his relationship with Cazbi to Moshe on the grounds that Moshe Rabeynu himself was married to the daughter[16] of a gentile priest of Midyan. Moshe Rabeynu is appalled by this comparison between his holy wife and Zimri's idol worshiping concubine and by the fact that Zimri is the head of a Tribe of Israel; this may account for Moshe's weeping at the entrance of the Tabernacle and for his apparent confusion, as mentioned in the Talmud, regarding the appropriate punishment for Zimri's crime. It is Pinchas who reminds him of the directive of *kanaim pogim bo*—the mitzvah of *Holy Zealotry*, and is told by Moshe to do what he thinks proper. This explains how Pinchas took the liberty of executing Zimri despite his act not having been a capital offence.

Despite the Torah law, which decrees that a priest who has blood on his hands can no longer serve in the Temple, Pinchas was granted the privilege of priesthood as a result of an act of bloodshed. Why did G-d make this exception for Pinchas?

According to Talmudic teachings, one of Pinchas' ancestors was Yitro, a former idol worshiper. The tribe of Shimon was outraged that the descendant of a gentile priest should take it on himself to kill Zimri, a Prince of Israel— but, Hashem validates Pinchas' action by rewarding him with the priesthood. Indeed, the role of the priest is to perpetuate the nation of Israel—which was Pinchas' motivation for killing Zimri and Cazbi. Pinchas saw the terrible danger

---

16 Tzippora – Exodus 2:21

of Israel's possible assimilation into the gentile world of idolatry. This is exactly what Bilam and the others wanted, as intermarriage would cause the nation of Israel to disappear, and there would be no one left in the world to carry on its special mission.

Interestingly, another act of zeal that prevented mass assimilation actually took place in the "backyard" of the community of Itamar. Shimon and Levi wiped out the city of Shechem after Jacob's daughter Dina was raped. As we may recall, Shechem Ben Chamur wanted the children of Jacob to intermarry and assimilate with them. Remarkably, Pinchas is descended from Levi and Zimri from Shimon.

It may be argued that Zimri was trying to rectify Shimon's violent act by taking a heathen woman and uplifting her. Instead of making war against the Midyanites, perhaps he thought that he could awaken them spiritually. He could even point to the precedent of Joshua, who married Rachov, a non-Israeli woman who later converted. Unfortunately, however, it was Cazbi who influenced Zimri and endangered the Nation of Israel.

(Pinchas is buried in Givat Pinchas, today know as Awarta, and is an Arab village right outside Itamar.)

PARASHAT
MATOT

Tribes

NUMBERS 30:2-32:42

מטות

MATOT

TORAH LESSON BY
RABBI NATHAN LOPES CARDOZO

THE DIMENSIONS OF PROPHECY AND THE ETERNITY OF THE TORAH

T HE TORAH USES several expressions for prophecy, and two phrases that appear frequently are *Zeh Hadavar*—"This is the word," and *Koh Amar Hashem*—"Thus says God."

We can find an example of the former in Numbers 30:2, where the Torah teaches the laws related to making vows: "And Moshe spoke to the heads of the tribes of the children of Israel and said, *'This is the word* that God has commanded: if a man makes a vow (. . .)'" An example of the latter occurs in Exodus 11:4, where Moshe informs the people that the promised redemption from the hardships of Egyptian slavery is imminent: *"Thus says the Lord,* 'about midnight I will go out into the midst of Egypt.'"

In response to this verse, Rashi (1040-1105) comments:

> "Moshe prophesied with *'Koh Amar Hashem'* (Thus says God) and the prophets prophesied with *'Koh Amar Hashem.'* Moshe, however, added [another kind of prophecy] with the words, *'Zeh Hadavar'* (This is the word)."

Rabbi Eliyahu Mizrachi (1440–1525), in his classic commentary on Rashi, explains that this subtle difference in the language hints at the unique nature of Moshe's prophecy. The Talmud observes that, with the exception of Moshe Rabeinu, the prophets of Israel experienced communication from God *be'aspaklaria she'ena me'ira*—via an obscured lens, which means that they only received prophecy while in a trance or in their dreams. Only Moshe received his prophecies at all times, even while fully conscious. He achieved a spiritual level where nothing stood between him and God. Thus, we say that Moshe's prophecy came to him *be'aspaklaria sheme'ira*—through a clear lens.

If this interpretation is correct, then the expression, *Koh amar Hashem*—"So says God," somehow implies a prophecy revealed through an "obscured lens."

Commentators point out that this kind of prophecy does not have to be transmitted as a literal word-for-word repetition of the divine communication. *Koh Amar Hashem* actually means; "this is *about* what God said," while *Zeh Hadavar* should be understood to mean; "this is the *exact* word."[17] In order to explain the Rashi commentary above (from which we learn that Moshe prophesied that both expressions would be used) one could argue that before Moshe received the Torah, he prophesied on the level of all other prophets (*Koh Amar Hashem*). But once he spoke with God "face to face" on Mt. Sinai, he and his prophecy became elevated to a higher level, at which point he started to prophesize with *Zeh Hadavar*.

The Maharal (1525-1609), however, points out that we find instances in the Torah where Moshe prophesied with *Koh Amar* even *after* the revelation at Mt. Sinai—in which case, the earlier distinction cannot be justified.[18] Consequently, the Maharal suggests another possible explanation for the two different prophetic expressions, which touches on the very nature of the Torah.

There are, in fact, two kinds of prophecies—one of a temporary nature, and the other of an eternal one. The words Moshe uttered to inform the Israelites that God would lead them out of Egypt were very much contextual. They were specific to a certain time and place, and as such, *Koh Amar Hashem* sufficed. But when God reveals His will in the form of *mitzvot*, His message takes on an *eternal* stature, and therefore requires a more forceful phraseology: *Zeh Hadavar*—"*this* is the word [forever]."

The Maharal, with his usual profundity, explains that the first kind of prophecy portends a *change*. In our case, an example is when Moshe tells the Israelites that God will effect a dramatic change by taking them out of Egypt. This was a *finite* affair belonging to the world of space and time, since change is only possible in a physical/temporal realm. The second variety of prophecy—the revelation of *mitzvot*—is, however, neither rooted in physicality nor in finitude. The *mitzvot* is the result of *eternal* spiritual realms touching the physical world without becoming a part of it. As such, *mitzvot* have no existence or role in the physical world other than as an influence. Therefore, they manifest with *Zeh Hadavar*—"*This* is the unchanging, eternal word."

Because of this explanation, the Maharal can respond to one of the fundamental questions in Judaism: Why was God unwilling to give the Torah to the

---

17 See, however, *Ha'emek Davar* of the Netziv, who rejects this interpretation (ad loc).
18 *Gur Aryeh* (ad loc).

Avot, the Fathers, Avraham, Yitzchak and Yakov? If, indeed, the Torah contains such a profound message, why hold it back for so many generations?

With the above observations in hand, the matter becomes crystal clear. One cannot put something infinite and eternal into a finite vessel—because the vessel, no matter how strong, would shatter. As long as the people of Israel were merely a collection of mortal individuals (even if those individuals possessed the towering stature and sterling character traits of Avraham, Yitzchak and Yakov), they could not receive an infinite Torah. Only after the people of Israel left Egypt and transformed into a chosen, religiously distinct Nation—only after the people of Israel became an eternal entity—did they become a vessel capable of receiving God's eternal Torah.

PARASHAT
MASEI

Journeys of
NUMBERS 33:1-36:13

מסעי

MASEI

TORAH LESSON BY

RABBI MOSHE LICHTMAN

A MATCH MADE IN HEAVEN

THE TORAH STATES in this week's *parasha*:

> Command the Children of Israel and say to them, "When you come into the Land Canaan, this is the Land **that shall fall to you** as an inheritance, the Land of Canaan according to its borders." (*BeMidbar* 34:2)

Our Sages comment on this verse:

> What does "*to you*" mean? The Land befits you. This can be compared to a king who had servants and maidservants. He used to marry off his servants to maidservants of a different family, and his maidservants to servants of a different family. The king stopped and thought, "The servants are mine and the maidservants are mine. It is preferable for me to marry my servants to my maidservants; my own to my own." So too, the Holy One blessed be He said (as it were): "The Land is Mine, as it says, *The Land is the Lord's* (*Psalms* 24:1) and, *For the Land is Mine* (*Leviticus* 25:23); and the people of Israel are Mine, as it says, *For the Children of Israel are servants to Me* (ibid. 25:55). It is preferable for Me to give My Land as an inheritance to My servants; My own to My own." Therefore it says, *This is the Land that shall fall to you as an inheritance*. (*BeMidbar Rabbah* 23:11)

Rabbi Yisachar Shlomo Teichtal, author of *Eim HaBanim Semeichah*, explains this *Midrash* beautifully:

> Why did the sages need this parable? They simply should have said, "The word 'Mine' is written about both the Land of Israel and the people of Israel etc." Furthermore, why did the *Midrash* cite the verse *For the Children of Israel are servants to Me*? They should have cited the verse from the giving of the Torah, *And you shall be to Me...* (*Shemot* 19:6) Why did they mention the verse that refers to Israel as servants?
>
> It seems that the *Midrash* was bothered by a question. Why does the verse ascribe the act of inheriting to the Land, as it says, *This is the Land that shall **fall to you** as an inheritance*? This implies that the Land itself

will "fall to you"! It should have said, "This is the Land that you shall inherit," for the act of inheriting comes from Israel, not the Land.

The *Midrash* brings its parable to answer this. For let us consider this matter. A king will certainly not entertain the thought of marrying off his children to servants or maidservants from the outside. Rather, he will marry them to people similar to them. However, he will not hesitate to marry off his servants and maidservants to servants and maidservants from the outside. Eventually, though, he realizes that it is preferable to marry even his servants and maidservants to his own. This is the meaning of the word "preferable." That is, even though this way is good, the other way is slightly better.

Now, we are familiar with our Sages' statement that when we do the will of the Omnipresent we are considered His children, and when we fail to do His will (God forbid) we are considered servants (*Bava Batra* 10a). This explains everything. When the people of Israel do the will of the Omnipresent and act properly, thereby becoming God's children, there is no doubt that they will receive the Land. For then, the match (*shidduch*) is like "grapes of the vine with grapes of the vine" (see *Pesachim* 49a). But when they fail to do His will, and are considered merely servants, one might think that perhaps the Holy One Blessed be He will "marry off" the Land to servants from the outside, meaning, the nations of the world. Therefore, the *Midrash* brings its parable to teach that even when the people of Israel are considered servants, HaShem says, "It is preferable to 'marry off' My Land to My servants."

Thus, the need for the parable is clear, for it alludes to the fact that even when the people of Israel fail to do the will of HaShem, He still wants the *shidduch* between them and the Land of Israel. This also explains why the *Midrash* specifically cites the verse *For the Children of Israel are servants to Me*. It hints to a time when the people of Israel are considered servants. The *Midrash* does not cite the verse from the giving of the Torah because that refers to a time when they listened to God, as it says, *Now, therefore, if you will hearken to My voice*. (*Shemot* 19:5)

This also explains why the verse says, *This is the Land that shall fall to you as an inheritance*, and not "that you shall inherit." "That you shall inherit" would have implied that you, by your own virtues, deserve this. Then it makes sense to ascribe the act of inheriting to Israel. It would have referred specifically to a time when the people of Israel do the will of HaShem. Therefore, the Torah says, *that shall fall to you*. This implies that you will not receive the Land because you acted properly, but because the Land desires it. The Land says, "It is preferable for me to fall to you than to other servants." (*Eim HaBanim Semeichah*, pp. 283-85)

From *Eretz Yisrael in the Parashah* by Rabbi Moshe Lichtman.

DEUTERONOMY ✦ DEVARIM

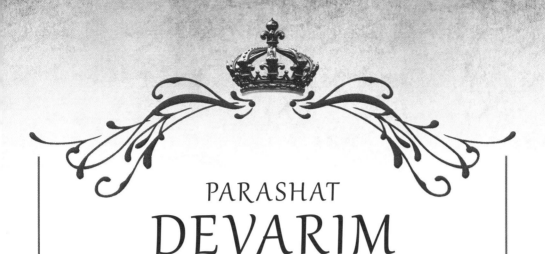

PARASHAT
DEVARIM

Words

DEUTERONOMY 1:1-3:22

דברים

DEVARIM

TORAH LESSON BY
RABBI LEVI COOPER

VIRTUAL WALLS, REAL UNITY

THE BOOK OF Deuteronomy which recounts Moses' parting speech to the Israelites, opens with the verse: "These are the words that Moses addressed to all Israel on the other side of Jordan, through the wilderness, in the Arava near Suf, between Paran and Tofel, Lavan, Hazerot, and Di-zahav" (Deuteronomy 1:1).

The introductory line is not difficult to understand, but the meaning of the second half of the verse is unclear. Why are these specific locations mentioned? Moreover, some of the places listed do not appear in parallel biblical passages that describe the journey of the Israelites through the desert (see Numbers 33:16-36). Where are these places and why are they mentioned?

One of the Hasidic masters—Hiddushei Harim—offered an innovative insight into this puzzling verse. His reading suggests an important lesson about the coveted ideal of unity.

Rabbi Yitzhak Meir Rotenberg (1799-1866) is known by the title of his writings Hiddushei Harim (the novella of HaRav Yitzhak Meir). He was the founder of the Gur Hasidic court, named after the Polish town Góra Kalwaria where the group first began. The Gur Hasidic community was politically active in Poland during the interwar period, and it still remains a major force in modern Israeli politics.

Returning to the cryptic list of places in the opening verse of Deuteronomy, commentators through the ages have grappled with this list. One approach has been to read this verse as an innuendo of various episodes of delinquent behavior during the forty-year journey in the wilderness. As Rashi (1040-1105), the great French commentator, explained: "Because of the honour of Israel" it was preferable to hint at these events rather than spell them out. Thus, Rashi explained that Hazerot—one of the places that are mentioned earlier in the biblical narrative (Numbers 11:35, 12:16, 33:17–18) refers to the Korah rebellion.

While this approach explains Hazerot, the identification is unexpected because the word Hazerot is not mentioned in the context of the Korah episode!

The Hiddushei Harim explained why Hazerot alludes to the Korah dispute.

The Talmud relates that King Solomon was responsible for two rabbinic institutions: washing hands before eating bread and Eiruv (Babylonian Talmud, Shabbat 14b). Eiruv is a legal mechanism that redefines a semi-public space as a private domain. On Shabbat it is forbidden to transfer items from a private domain to a public domain, and vice versa. It is also prohibited to move an item the distance of four cubits in a public domain. Constructing an eiruv and thereby redefining semi-public spaces as private domains, allows carrying items within that re-defined domain on Shabbat. Today, many Jewish communities—but not all—have such an eiruv that allows people to bring a siddur (prayer book) or tallit (prayer shawl) to the synagogue on Shabbat, or to carry a baby out of the house.

An eiruv can only be erected under certain conditions and by means of a number of prescribed actions. The most visible requirement is the need for a fence or virtual fence to surround the area. The string between poles that encircles many Jewish communities is exactly that—a virtual wall constructed of a series of doorways. Another lesser-known requirement is a common kitchen. In the case of an eiruv for a small number of families, each person would contribute some food to create the common kitchen. In a larger community where this is impractical, the common kitchen is set up in a different manner: community leaders legally acquire foodstuffs—generally matzot (unleavened bread traditionally eaten during the Passover) because of their extended shelf-life— on behalf of each of the community inhabitants. The joint-ownership—even if people are not aware of it—legally constructs a communal kitchen.

The Talmud tells us that when King Solomon instituted these innovations, a heavenly voice resounded: "My son, if your mind gets wisdom, my mind, too, will be gladdened. Get wisdom, my son, and gladden my heart, that I may have what to answer those who taunt me" (Proverbs 23:15, 27:11). What is the connection between wisdom and these innovations?

We can understand the link between eiruv and wisdom by considering the mechanism and result of the innovation. King Solomon demonstrated that the People of Israel have the power to join forces and be unified through food, as each person contributed a small amount. This meagre, seemingly insignificant contribution was sufficient to draw a common bond between the People and change the status of a semi-public domain. King Solomon wisely perceived the potential gains of bringing people together with an eiruv construct.

The Hiddushei Harim continued: "Korah represents the exact opposite. The opening verse of the Korah narrative begins 'And Korah took' (Numbers 16:1). The verse is strange as it does not say what Korah actually took!" Onkelos— who translated the Bible into Aramaic—rendered the Hebrew not as the standard "took," rather, Onkelos translated it as: "And Korah stirred an argument." Korah instigated a fight and thus tore down the unity that should characterize the People of Israel. Korah's actions can therefore be viewed as the opposite of the eiruv: An eiruv draws people together; Korah sought to tear people apart. Korah's intention was to disrupt unity; an eiruv is built on a legal construct of unity. An eiruv might also promote unity by assisting individuals and families in leaving the confines of their homes, allowing them to comfortably mingle with others.

With no unity-based eiruv, we have nothing more than individual courtyards, known as "hazerot" in Hebrew. Thus—explained the Hiddushei Harim— Hazerot alludes to Korah's divisive objective.

We might add that the opening verse of Deuteronomy not only refers to a historical episode, but it also alludes to the timeless challenge of unity—a lofty objective that we hope and pray will be realized in our day.

PARASHAT
VA'ETCHANAN

And I pleaded

DEUTERONOMY 3:23-7:11

ואתחנן

VA'ETCHANAN

TORAH LESSON BY
RABBI YEHOSHUA FRIEDMAN

WISDOM IN THE EYES OF THE NATIONS

MOSHE'S PARTING SPEECH to the second generation after the Exodus from Egypt is to read from the book of Deuteronomy. It was designed to prepare them for entering the Land of Israel. For this reason, I am going to tell you about a difficulty I had in understanding this portion. Appropriately enough, I attained a greater understanding of these words in the very process when I was settling the land.

The Torah tells us (Deuteronomy 4:1-8):

> And now, O Israel, hearken unto the statutes and unto the ordinances, which I teach you, to do them; that ye may live, and go in and possess the land which the LORD, the God of your fathers, giveth you. Ye shall not add unto the word which I command you, neither shall ye diminish from it, that ye may keep the commandments of the LORD your God which I command you. Your eyes have seen what the LORD did in Baal-peor; for all the men that followed the Baal of Peor, the LORD thy God hath destroyed them from the midst of thee. But ye that did cleave unto the LORD your God are alive every one of you this day. Behold, I have taught you statutes and ordinances, even as the LORD my God commanded me, that ye should do so in the midst of the land whither ye go in to possess it. Observe therefore and do them; for this is your wisdom and your understanding in the sight of the nations, that, when they hear all these statutes, shall say: 'Surely this great nation is a wise and understanding people.' For what great nation is there, that hath God so nigh unto them, as the LORD our God is whenever we call upon Him?

When I first began to read this verse with interest as a young Jew returning to Torah observance, I thought; "Wow! The other nations are going to notice how just the Torah's laws are compared to the laws of other nations. They are going to appreciate the wisdom of Jewish attitudes towards social justice, marriage and family, and other human values."

It was at a very optimistic time for me personally and for Israel. Jews were still respected in the world as the State of Israel was still basking in some of the glow of the miraculous victory of the Six-Day war of 1967. The verses of

Scripture sounded like the harbingers of a final redemption that seemed very near. A few years later, however, I saw a rabbinic statement on that verse which seemed more limited in its scope.

The Babylonian Talmud, Tractate Shabbat 75a says: "From where do we derive that a person is commanded to calculate the cycles of the calendar? As it is said, 'For it is your wisdom and your understanding in the eyes of the peoples. Which wisdom is in the sight of the peoples?' That is the calculation of the cycles of the calendar."

I was shocked! What, out of all the wisdom of the Torah—justice, morality, healthy family life, personality development—the rabbis thought that the only wisdom that non-Jews could appreciate was the calendar? I understood this to mean that although the nations hate Israel, even they must grudgingly admit that we know astronomy and our calendar works. Is that all the rabbis think the gentiles are capable of understanding? With my liberal upbringing that was hard for me to swallow. But for most of history, many groups of people have not been tremendously impressed with G-d's people and G-d's Torah—anti-Semitism has been around for a long time. I was disappointed, but I got no further answers to my questions for the next six years or so, I just held that issue in abeyance.

In Deuteronomy 1:5 the Torah tells us: "Beyond the Jordan, in the land of Moav, Moshe began to explain this Torah, saying (. . .)."

Moshe received the Torah at Sinai and taught it to the Children of Israel for 40 years in the desert. Before his death he recapitulated the teachings in a form suitable for the new generation that was about to enter the Land of Israel. The surprise is that Moshe is not merely telling it to his own people, but he passed it on to the world in all their languages. Our sages tell us that Hashem offered the Torah to the nations of the world, but it was only Israel who accepted it. Yet, Moshe still explains the Torah in all the world's tongues. Is it for the nations themselves, when they are ready to receive it? Or perhaps is it for the Israelites who will one day live in other lands in exile and will not know Hebrew well enough to read it in the original? Or is it a bit of both? Either way, what necessitated the need for the Torah to be explained in 70 tongues at that time, when no one wanted, or needed, to have it translated?

In Chapter 27 of Deuteronomy, we are told that after crossing the Jordan, the people had to write the commandments of the Torah on stones and cover the stones with plaster. It is not clear whether the writing is to be on the plaster or on the stones covered with plaster. If the words are engraved and covered over with plaster, it means that the Torah is waiting until the nations are ready to receive it. If the words are only written on plaster, they will wear away. That would mean that the Torah's current impact on the world is only a temporary result of miracles done by the Almighty through Moshe. The true impact of the Torah in the world will only become significant at the end of days. Rashi (1040-1105) also comments here that the words are to be written in 70 languages.

In the book of Yehoshua, at the end of Chapter 8, Yehoshua performs the ceremony with the twelve stones commanded to Moshe in Deuteronomy 27. There are varying opinions among commentators as to the content of the writing on the stones in verse 32. Some say it was only the Ten Commandments, others say it was all 613 commandments and lastly, some say it was the entire book of Torah that was written on those twelve stones. These different interpretations of the writing could be in accordance with the question of whether the translations were for the benefit of Israelites or other nations. Those were the texts which left me with an unanswered question.

Meanwhile our lives were moving on. In 1980 my family and I joined the new community of Kochav Hashachar. The location where we built our community was originally a Nachal outpost. Nachal is a Hebrew acronym for Fighting Pioneer Youth. The IDF set up these outposts in order to settle areas which were strategically important but not yet developed for civilian settlement. An army unit would guard the land and set up infrastructure to allow civilians to take over the area in the future. The expectation was that with the cooperation of settlement movements the outposts would become kibbutzim or moshavim[1]. But by 1980 when the time came to civilianize Kochav Hashachar, the kibbutz movements which had cooperated with the IDF in starting the Nachal outposts, were—for various reasons—no longer interested in settling Kochav Hashachar as a kibbutz. In contrast, religious settlers of the Gush Emunim movement, who considered it a duty and a privilege to settle the Biblical heartland of Israel, were happy to build a community in this beautiful location.

And there we were, a handful of young couples and a few singles who wanted a spiritual leader, a rabbi, but we didn't have one yet. We traveled to work or studies daily, tended to our families, and did guard duty; we were pretty exhausted. On Shabbat we often hosted rabbis and other mentors to provide guidance.

---

1 Kibbutzim or moshavim are types of cooperative villages in Israel.

When Kochav Hashachar planned to host the illustrious Rabbi Yehoshua Zuckerman our neighbors—all young, newlywed couples—expressed concern over who could host the rabbi who was coming with his family that included 12 children and his elderly mother. We were living in pretty small quarters. None of these young Israelis had ever hosted large numbers of people in their own homes. We lived in fairly primitive conditions, occasionally getting warnings to boil the tap water, electricity was received through a noisy generator, no phone lines (1980 – no cell phones, remember?). Some women who had recently given birth just went home to their mothers for a month afterward. My wife, whose mother was in the US, didn't think in terms of going "home". This was home. We had previously held parties for our yeshiva friends and knew how to entertain in cramped conditions. Our years spent half a world away from our parents gave us perhaps exaggerated confidence in our ability to host. Our neighbors could contribute food.

Suddenly I found myself sitting elbow to elbow with an esteemed rabbi, and I realized that I had a golden opportunity to ask the rabbi my six-year-old unanswered question. "Rabbi, why does the Gemara[2] trivialize this verse by reducing wisdom to astronomy? Can't the nations of the world recognize any higher values in the Torah?"

Rav Zuckerman's answer was astounding. "What do you mean, trivial? Timing is of vital importance! Ancient pagans were sacrificing their virgin daughters in desperate efforts to get the planting time right. And along comes this little Hebrew who just looks at the sun, the moon and some astronomical tables, and knows straight away when to sow and when to reap. This was revolutionary in both thought and practice. Timing is vital. The Hebrew calendar is a gift and a commandment from G-d, perfectly suited to the people of Israel and the land of Israel—we didn't figure it out ourselves. Even today, people are still concerned with timing in business, in war, in whatever they consider vital to their success."

Rabbi Zuckerman made me appreciate the importance of the calendar and timing in the development of civilization. Maybe I had previously failed to appreciate the importance of timing since I am a confirmed procrastinator. But now it all made sense. Prophecy teaches us that in the future the nations

---

2 Gemara - the second part of the *Talmud*, consisting primarily of commentary on the Mishnah. (Mishna - the first part of the Talmud; a collection of early oral interpretations of the scriptures that was compiled about AD 200.)

of the world will value Israel and the rest of the Torah, too, as it is written (Zechariah 8:22-23):

> Yea, many peoples and mighty nations shall come to seek the LORD of hosts in Jerusalem, and to entreat the favor of the LORD. Thus saith the LORD of hosts: In those days it shall come to pass, that ten men shall take hold, out of all the languages of the nations, shall even take hold of the skirt of him that is a Jew, saying: 'We will go with you, for we have heard that God is with you.'

PARASHAT
EIKEV

As a result

DEUTERONOMY 7:12-11:25

עקב

EIKEV

TORAH LESSON BY
RABBI SHLOMO RISKIN

WHAT IS UP TO GOD AND WHAT IS UP TO HUMANS?

And when your herds and flocks multiply, and your silver and gold are multiplied, and all that you have is multiplied; then your heart may grow haughty, and you may forget God your Lord. Deuteronomy 8:13–14

ONE OF THE thorniest questions theologians deal with is the issue of free will. It's clear that if we are to assign meaning and significance to the actions of humans in a universe created by God, then there must be free will for individuals to do as they please. Without it, how can we possibly reward good and punish evil, praise the saint and revile the sinner?

On the other hand, free will flies in the face of the omniscience of God who, by definition, must know everything in advance. But if God knows what will happen to a person's life, doesn't that mean that the choices we make have already been determined in some computer in the sky, and that there really is no free will to begin with?

Turning to this week's portion of *Eikev*, I'd like to suggest two interpretations of a key biblical verse. The first leans toward a view of the universe wherein God is the only One who makes things happen, and so human choices are hardly central to God's role in history. However, with a slightly different stress, the very same verse can be shown to yield the opposite idea: not only is God's role central, but our human role is central as well. My own view, as you have probably garnered from many past commentaries, is more closely identified with the second view.

In the verses under scrutiny (Deut. 8:11–18), the Torah confronts those who attribute their success and riches to their own efforts. The issue is a classical one. The day will come when the Israelites shall live in stately homes, adorned with gold and silver, surrounded by vineyards and flocks, and they will glory in the power of their might an in the cleverness of their mind. So self-impressed will they be that they will forget that had it not been for God's miraculous gifts of manna, the protective clouds, and the directional fire, they would never have survived in the dry, snake-infested, scorpion-ridden desert. Blindly, they will make the arrogant claim: "My power and the might of my hand has gotten me this wealth" (8:17). But what God warns the people is to "remember the Lord your God, for it is He who has given you power to get wealth, that He may establish His covenant which He swore unto your fathers" (8:18).

Nahmanides (1194-1270) understands this verse to mean that whatever the individual may think he accomplished was in reality accomplished by God. Indeed, this great Jewish commentary and philosopher obviates and distinction between the supernatural and the natural.

In an earlier passage (Ex. 13:16), Nahmanides writes that a person must come to recognize the existence of the hidden miracles that are commonplace in the world, but that we generally overlook: "No one can have a part in the Torah of Moses our teacher unless he believes that all our actions and all our happenings are miraculous [that is, God induces] and that there is no nature or the usual order of the world."

What Nahmanides is saying is that most people are quick to acknowledge the divine role in the overwhelming and seemingly supernatural miracles of the Torah, in the grand design of the escape from Egypt, the ten plagues, and the splitting of the Reed Sea. They are not ready to realize, however, that everything in life as well as in the Torah is a miracle. When Nahmanides says that "there is no nature or the usual order of the world," I believe he is saying that even natural events should be called supernatural (miraculous), brought about by the One who is above nature, and that what we think of as the usual order of the world is really quite unusual and even miraculous. Everything happens as a result of the divine will, from sunset to plant growth, to childbirth, to human reason, to individual creativity. God makes things happen—not us. Witness the *Asher Yatzar* blessing we recite after exercising natural bodily functions, concluding with the words, "Blessed are you, O God, the healer of all flesh, who does wondrous things!"

This is the divine message to the power-brokers, the self-appointed human Masters of the Universe we cited earlier. Each of us must understand that all we think we have achieved is in reality a product of the divine will. Had God not wanted it to have happened, it would never have taken place. *"A mentch tut, der Aibishter tut uff"* (a human being does, but God accomplishes), goes the Yiddish proverb.

Given all that we've said until now regarding the idea of a universe where the prime mover is God and only God, it certainly seems to chip away at whatever hope we might still harbor for free will. But there is another position, that of Maimonides (1135-1204), and we may find in his words a source for the recognition of the significance of choice even in a world whose reality bears the signature of God on every level of existence.

In the last mishna[3] in the fourth chapter of Tractate Pesahim, we read an account of six actions taken by King Hizkiya, three of which evoked praise from the sages, the three of which evoked criticism. Among those for which he was praised was concealing a work called the *Book of Healings*. Why this was worthy of praise is addressed by Rashi (1040-1105), who suggests that the sages saw in the king's action the desire to prevent people from ignoring God in their pursuit of health; had there remained access to the *Book of Healings*, people would rely on its formulas rather than on the Creator of the universe in times of illness.

Maimonides profoundly disagrees, assailing the view that a book of legitimate cures was to be removed from circulation in order to rouse more people to depend solely on God in times of illness as "nonsensical and insane." Instead, this great sage insists that the *Book of Healings* was both ineffective and idolatrous. Imagine a starving individual who cures his malady of hunger by baking bread; does he then desist from thanking the Almighty in the Grace after Meals? Indeed, it is precisely the blessing of the Grace after Meals that the Bible ordains us to recite! The Grace after Meals is the mother of all blessings!

To the contrary, the one who recites the blessings after bread is giving his gratitude to God for providing the agricultural, physical, and intellectual wherewithal to turn wheat into bread. After all, God created the world, with the raw grains and herbs, and He created the human being with physical and intellectual potential. However, it is up to us to realize the potential and produce the proper results. God lays the groundwork; we must actualize the product. (Maimonides, *Commentary to the Mishna*, Pesahim, chapter 4, last mishna.)

Nahmanides sees the human being as the agent through whom the Divine operates; Maimonides sees the human being as a full partner with God in order to improve and eventually perfect the world.

Interestingly, the verse, "But you shall remember the Lord your God for it is He that gives you power to get wealth, that He may establish His covenant which He swore to your fathers, as it is this day" (Deut. 8:18), may be taken either way. When seen through a Nahmanidean perspective, it stresses human frailty

---

3 Mishna - the first part of the Talmud; a collection of early oral interpretations of the scriptures that was compiled about AD 200

and divine accomplishment; but is can also be read with a Maimonidean filter, which merely reminds us that the source of our energy and talents is, after all, the Creator of the universe. And it would seem to me that the very usage of the term "covenant" implies a mutual endeavor, a partnership. God will not enable Israel to prosper unless we take proper action and responsibility. God provides the strength, the knowledge, the ability, and the potential—but whether it happens or not depends on our performance.

And this certainly includes our giving God His due, our recognizing His participation in our potential and in the potential of His world, as well as our own individual ethical, moral, and religious commitment to carry out His will.

From *Torah Lights: Devarim* by Rabbi Shlomo Riskin; used with permission of Maggid Books, a division of Koren Publishers Jerusalem.

PARASHAT
RE'EH

See!

DEUTERONOMY 11:26-16:17

ראה

RE'EH

TORAH LESSON BY

RABBI MOSHE GOLDSMITH

EXPERIENCE THE WORLD TO COME TODAY.

THE RENOWNED RABBI Yehudah Halevi (1075-1141), in his *magnum opus*, the Kuzari, discusses the difference between Judaism and other religions. He asks: "Why doesn't the Torah stress the reward awaiting the righteous in the World to Come?" Instead, the Torah describes at length the reward one receives in this physical world. According to the Pshat (a straightforward understanding of the verses), the World to Come is ignored, though the subject is discussed at length in our Oral and Rabbinic traditions.

Below are a few examples from the Torah of the rewards that can be gained in *this* world.

"I will give to you and to your descendants after you, the land of your sojourns, all the land of Canaan, for an everlasting possession; and I will be their God." (Genesis 17:8)

"If you walk in my statutes and observe my commandments and do them—then I shall give you rains in their season, so that the land will yield its produce and the trees of the field will bear their fruit. Indeed, your threshing will last for you until grape gathering, and grape gathering will last until sowing time. You will thus eat your food to the full and live securely in your land. I shall also grant peace in the land, so that you may lie down with no one to fear. I shall also eliminate harmful beasts from the land, and no sword will pass through your land." (Leviticus 26:3–6)

"… He will give the rain for your land in its season, the early and late rain, that you may gather in your grain and your new wine and your oil. He will give grass in your fields for your cattle, and you will eat and be satisfied." (Deuteronomy 11:14)

The Torah stresses in the above verses that when following the right path, your reward comes in *this* world, and that it is a *material* reward, realized in the Land of Israel. Rabbi Yehudah Halevi goes on to explain that a person who maintains a life of true spiritual connection to Hashem can achieve a closeness to the world to come *while living in this world*. Through the true Prophets, the people of Israel were in constant connection with the upper world while living a physical life in this world, even as angels were walking amongst them.

The Temple was meant to be the center of Divine Prophecy and Worship here, in *this* world, where the *lower world* and the *upper world* would be combined. This is what Jacob's dream, involving the ladders, was all about. (See Genesis 28:12)

Rabbi Kook (1865-1935) explains that during the First Temple period, there was no emphasis on *the world to come* because miracles and prophecy took place every day. It was natural at that time for the nation to feel a spiritual connection with Hashem in *this* world. Therefore, there was no need to focus on *life after death*.

However, during the Second Temple period and throughout the 2000-year exile, when prophecy ceased and miracles were no longer manifest, the nation began to focus on the World to Come; a spiritual vacuum needed to be filled. When the sun shines there is no need for a candle—it is only when darkness prevails that one feels the need for a candle to give light.

The famous Rabbi Meir Leibush Weiser (1809-1879), known as the Malbim, opens his commentary by explaining that up to this week's Portion, Re'eh (Deuteronomy 11:26), the Torah describes at length the reward for those who follow the Mitzvoth, and the punishment for those who do not. The reward is the inheritance of the land and, living a successful and peaceful life both materially and spiritually. The punishment, on the other hand, is to be banished from the land, and persecuted in exile by the gentile nations.

The Malbim then refers to the words of Rav Yehudah Halevi and explains that they represent the precise meaning of the opening words of this week's portion:

> "Behold, I am setting before you **today** a blessing and a curse—the blessing, if you listen to the commandments of Hashem your God, which I am commanding you **today**; and the curse, if you do not listen to the commandments of Hashem your God, but turn aside from the way which I am commanding you **today**, by following other gods which you have not known." (Deuteronomy 11:26–27)

If we look carefully at the above verse, we see that the word "today" is mentioned three times, when the Torah, which does not use words idly, could have mentioned it only once. The reason for emphasizing this word, the Malbim explains, is to stress that by following the Torah, we can merit the blessings of Hashem in this world **today** and will not have to leave it in order to experience the Divine. Here on Itamar, the exact location where this week's Torah portion takes place, its message resonates more than anywhere else on earth.

> "It shall come about, when Hashem your God brings you into the land to possess it, that you shall place the blessing on Mount Gerizim and the curse on Mount Eval,"(The *blessing* on Mt. Gerizim refers to the acceptance of the Covenant, and the *curse* on Mt. Aval pertains to the rejection of the covenant) "... these mountains lie across the Jordan, west of the way toward the sunset, in the land of the Canaanites who live in the Aravah, opposite Gilgal, beside the oaks of Moreh." (Deuteronomy 11:29–30)

These verses describe my backyard view here on Itamar. It was to this place first that Hashem sent Abraham, and later, Joshua. How privileged we are, I feel—myself, and those like me, who have chosen to settle here, where we can receive the blessing **today**, by leading a spiritual life through building and defending the land of Israel.

A defining moment for the people of Israel was the renewal of the Covenant by receiving the Torah on the Land. Unlike at Mt. Sinai, where Moses was atop the mountain and the Nation below, at this time, all Twelve Tribes of Israel were on top of the mountain. Six tribes stood on Gerizim and six tribes stood on Eval, while the leaders were in the valley. below. By this placement, G-d was perhaps showing us that not only the Prophets and Spiritual Leaders can reach the upper worlds here in the Land, but all of Israel can rise to the top of the mountain and touch the heavens by living a spiritual life and continuing to develop the precious Land of Israel, our birthright.

PARASHAT
SHOFTIM

Judges

DEUTERONOMY 16:18-21:9

שפטים

SHOFTIM

TORAH LESSON BY
RABBI CHANAN MORRISON

THE KING'S TORAH SCROLL

WHILE THE TORAH commands every Israelite to write a Torah scroll, there is one individual who is obligated to write an additional Torah scroll.[4] Surprisingly, it is neither the high priest, nor the head of Sanhedrin[5]. It is the *king* who is commanded to write a second Torah scroll during his reign and keep it with him at all times (Deut. 17:18–19, *Sanhedrin* 2:4).

What is the significance of these two Torah scrolls, that of the individual and that of the king?

PERSONAL TORAH AND COMMUNAL TORAH

The people of Israel accepted the Torah at Sinai on two levels. Each individual consented to follow the Torah's laws as a member of the people of Israel. And the people of Israel as a nation also accepted the Torah, so that its moral instructions are binding on its national institutions—the judiciary, the government, the army, and so on.

Observing the Torah on the national level is, however, far more complex than the individual's observance of the Torah. The Torah and its mitzvot were given to refine and elevate humanity. The process of uplifting an entire nation, with its political exigencies and security needs, is far more complicated than the process of elevating the individual.

As individuals, we approach issues of interpersonal morality informed by an innate sense of justice. Mankind, however, has yet to attain a consensus on the ethical issues connected to affairs of state. Furthermore, the propensity for moral lapse—and the severity of such lapses—is far greater on the national level. As a result, all notions of good and evil, propriety and injustice, are frequently lost amidst the raging turmoil of political issues and national concerns.

The greatness of the messianic king lies in his potential to fulfill the Torah's ethical ideals also in the political realm. We read about the foundation of the

---

4 *Sanhedrin* 91b, based on Deut. 31:19. However, the *Shulchan Aruch* (*Yoreh Dei'ah* 270:2) quotes the opinion of Rabbeinu Asher (the *Rosh*), that "nowadays it is a mitzvah to write books of the Pentateuch, Mishnah, Talmud, and their commentaries," since we no longer study directly from Torah scrolls. (The authorities debate whether there is still a mitzvah to write a Torah scroll, see *Shach* and *Taz* ad loc.)
5 *Sanhedrin* was the Jewish supreme court, based in Jerusalem.

messianic dynasty in the book of Ruth, which concludes with the lineage of David, king of Israel. Why is it customary to read the book of Ruth on the holiday of Shavuot? Because the account of the origins of the Davidic dynasty reminds us of the second level of Torah law that we accepted at Sinai, that of the nation as a whole.

Rav Kook (1865 – 1935) cautioned regarding the moral and spiritual dangers inherent in political life:

> We must not allow the tendency toward factionalism, which threatens most strongly at the inception of a political movement, to deter us from seeking justice and truth, from loving all of humanity, both the collective and the individual, from love for the people of Israel, and from the holy obligations that are unique to Israel. We are commanded not only to be holy individuals, but also, and especially, to be "a kingdom of priests and a holy nation."

From *Silver from the Land of Israel*, pp. 221-222. Adapted from *Ma'amarei HaRe'iyah*, pp. 173-174.

PARASHAT
KI TEITZEI

When you go out
DEUTERONOMY 21:10-25:19

כי-תצא

KI TEITZEI

TORAH LESSON BY
RABBI NATHAN LOPES CARDOZO

THE FIGHT FOR A 4,000-YEAR OLD MARRIAGE

A MARRIAGE HAS MUCH in common with the merit of living in the Land of Israel. After Sarah's death, Avraham buys a portion in the Land of Israel, including the Cave of Machpelah, for the purpose of burying her there. Speaking to Ephron, the owner, Avraham says, "I am giving you the money for the field. Take it from me (*kach mimeni*) and I will bury my dead there" (Genesis 23:13). Ephron takes the money, and Avraham becomes the official owner of this field, making him the legal landlord of a portion in the Land of Israel.

The Talmud connects this incident with the institution of marriage[6]. In Deuteronomy we read: *Ki yikach ish ishah*— "When a man takes (*yikach*) a woman [to be his wife] ..." (Deuteronomy 22:13). Since the same root word— "to take" (*kach/yikach*)—is used in both Genesis and Deuteronomy, the talmudic sages draw the conclusion that one should marry one's wife in the same way that one buys a portion in the Land of Israel. That is, with money, or an object of value such as a ring. This is an application of the hermeneutic rule called *gezerah shavah*, which can be described as an argument by analogy. It infers from two identical words found in different passages where, even if they are used in completely different contexts, the legal decision given for one applies to the other as well.

This Talmudic ruling has obviously drawn a lot of criticism. How can one compare both of these cases? Is marrying one's wife similar to buying a piece of land? This seems offensive and in complete opposition to what a marriage is all about. Nowhere do we find that Jewish law allows a man to treat his wife as his possession. In fact, if he does, the woman is allowed to demand an immediate divorce. Jewish law objects to any such comparison, so why make this analogy?

Many excellent explanations have been given, and without denying their great importance and truth, we would like to suggest a new approach. It may quite well be that the Sages wanted to emphasize the holiness of the Land of Israel by comparing it to a marriage. Buying a portion of land in the Holy Land is not like buying a piece of land anywhere else in the world. In the case of Israel,

---

6 *Kiddushin* 2a.

one *marries* the land! The land becomes a loving partner, and one's love for it is of a singular nature. Israelites treat the Land of Israel as they would a living person with whom they have a deep and emotional connection. We do not relate it to a possession, but rather as a living entity with a *neshama*[7]. Our love for the Land of Israel is not like the love described by natives of other lands. Like a marriage, it is a covenant; and a covenant is founded on the basis of duties, not rights. It is a pledge, and one does not betray a pledge. Just as one gives his bride an object of value, as a symbolic expression of his willingness to make sacrifices for her sake during the marriage ceremony, so one pays for the land by making a financial offering. Just as in matrimony one marries for high and noble goals, so one betroths the Holy Land to achieve *kedushah* (holiness) to transform oneself into a more dignified person, and to make the world a better place. The many laws related to the land indicate that one must care for it almost as one tends to the needs of his wife. The Israelites' relationship with the Land of Israel is a love story, and that is why we were unable to divorce ourselves from this land even while spending thousands of years in exile. One does not abandon one's wife! For other nations, this may be difficult to fathom; for the Israelite, it is the air he breathes.

Rabbi Moshe Avigdor Amiel (1883-1946), former Chief Rabbi of Tel Aviv, gave this idea yet another important dimension[8]. Just as giving a valued object to one's wife at the time of the marriage ceremony is only the first payment, so is buying the land only a first installment. No one should ever believe that Israel is an intrinsic inheritance simply because the people of Israel once bought it. One needs to merit and inherit it anew every moment. Just as no marriage will endure unless one continues to toil for its success, so does the Land of Israel demand one's constant spiritual labor to merit possessing it as well as living in it. Anything less will lead to divorce.

That is what our soldiers are fighting for: a 4,000-year old marriage.

---

7 Neshama - "soul" or "spirit".
8 See *Drashot El Ami*, published in Hebrew by Hotzaat Shem, Jerusalem, 1936.

PARASHAT
KI TAVO

When you enter in

Deuteronomy 26:1-29:8

כִּי-תָבוֹא

KI TAVO

TORAH LESSON BY
RABBI MOSHE GOLDSMITH

"THERE ARE HEARTS OF STONE, BUT THERE ARE STONES THAT ARE HEARTS" (RAV KOOK)

BLESSED WITH LIVING on Itamar in the Shomron[9] Mountain Range, I have the glorious privilege of seeing every day the mountains mentioned in the Torah—*Har Grizim* and *Har Eval*, the famed Mountains of the Blessing and the Curse which rise above the city of Shechem.

This week's Portion describes Joshua leading the people of Israel into the Promised Land. This essay will focus on two of three, events that took place on the mountains mentioned above. These events have been overshadowed by the establishment of the *Covenant of Mutual Responsibility*, which is incumbent on all members of the house of Israel. The two events referred to above are the construction of the Altar on Mt. Eval and the Inscription of the Torah on the Stones (See Deuteronomy chapter 27).

When the Israelites crossed the Jordan River and entered the land of Israel, they were commanded to take stones from the River and erect a monument in their encampment at Gilgal. These stones were meant to serve as a memorial for generations to come, a milestone in the history of Israel, commemorating the longed-for event of crossing the Jordan River into the Promised Land. In addition to these stones, Joshua had also placed stones along the temporarily-split riverbed, where the feet of the Cohanim[10] had stood, while watching the nation crossover.

Immediately upon entering the land, Joshua began following the instructions in our Portion, commanding the writing of the entire Torah on stone, and the building of an altar on Mt. Eval. According to our tradition, the stones which were taken out of the Jordan River were the ones used for the inscription of the Torah and the building of the Altar. These stones were later brought to the Israeli encampment at Gilgal and used for the monument mentioned earlier.

The idea of Writing the Torah on stone did not originate with Joshua—the Ten Commandments were written in stone, and—a fact not as well known-Moshe Rabeynu wrote the Torah on stone in the land of Moav before he passed

---

9 Shomron - Samaria
10 Cohanim – the priests.

away. Our sages add that the entire Torah was written by Moshe in Hebrew as well as in the seventy languages of the Nations. Similarly, Joshua wrote the Torah on Mt. Eval in seventy languages for the Seventy Nations.

A small passage of the Talmud, in the tractate Sotah 35B, involves a discussion between Rabbi Shimon and Rabbi Yehudah. The Rabbis discuss two possibilities for understanding how the Torah was written on the stones. According to Rabbi Yehudah, the Torah was written on the stones and then covered over with plaster. Rabbi Shimon asks Rabbi Yehudah, "If this is the case, how did the nations learn the Torah?" Rabbi Yehudah answers, "G-d gave them the insight to call on their professional scribes who peeled off the plaster and took the Torah with them (thus giving all the Nations access to the written Torah). "For this reason," according to Rabbi Yehudah,"they were punished, because they should have studied the Torah instead of transgressing it."

Rabbi Shimon holds that the Torah was written on top of the plaster so that all the nations could see it clearly. On the lower part of the huge stones on which the Torah was written, the following verse was written again for emphasis—*"so that they may not teach you to do according to all their detestable things which they have done for their gods, so that you would sin against Hashem your God."* (Deuteronomy 20:18) This verse explains Israel's legitimate and moral right to go to war against the Seventy Nations. If the Nations do not accept Israel's call for peace (see verse (ibid 20:11)), which includes taking upon themselves the moral code of Noach, Israel will wage war against them. We derive from this that had the Nations given up their barbaric practices, they would not have been driven from the land.

It is important to emphasize that before Joshua began the wars against the 31 kings to capture the land of Israel, the Torah was put on display before the Nations. Hashem wanted them to be inspired by the Light of Torah and to abandon their idolatrous ways. For the same reason, as mentioned before, Moshe wrote the Torah in 70 languages before he passed away. Moshe had begun the process of reaching out to the nations and later, on the other side of the Jordan, Joshua was told to do the same on Mt. Eval.

It should be noted that this is not the first time the nations had been given the opportunity to accept the Torah. On Mt. Sinai, we learned, Hashem offered the Torah to every nation on earth but each refused to accept it. Clearly, it was Hashem's Divine Plan that the conduct of the nations would be rectified by their eventual acceptance of the Torah.

Indeed, the spiritual light of the Torah, which descends from the highest places above, has the power to unify all realms of creation, including the Inanimate, the Plant, and the Animal Kingdoms. This unity is symbolized by the inscription of the Torah in stone (Inanimate), as was done by G-d on Sinai, and by the writing of the Torah by Moshe on stone, as well as on parchment (animal) before his death; and by Joshua, who continued Moshe's tradition, upon entering the Land of Israel. The plant kingdom is represented in the ink which derives from plants and is used for the writing of the Torah.

Despite great advancements in science and in our knowledge of the universe, what we know and understand is dwarfed by our ignorance of the true nature of the cosmos. As religious belief declines, man's arrogance climbs, imagining that he knows all there is to know. Yet there is a vast spiritual treasure, which remains hidden from him because he chooses to remain ignorant.

The Hebrew word for stone is *"Even"* (אבן) and it contains the first two letters of the Hebrew alphabet. The word *alphabet* comes from Aleph (א) Beit (ב). The letter Nun (ן) has the numerical value of fifty. This represents the fifty gates to understanding the Torah which is communicated through the *Aleph Beit*.

Stones are referred to as letters in our esoteric teachings. *"Even"* also stands for the relationship between parent and child. *Aleph* is the first letter of the word for Mother and Father in Hebrew, and *Beit Nun*, "Ben", is the child.

Jacobs departure from the land of Israel is described as follows: *"He came to a certain place and spent the night there, because the sun had set; and he took one of the stones of the place and put it under his head, and lay down in that place."* (Genesis 28:11)

Before going into exile, Jacob needed to connect with the stones of the land of Israel, which represent the everlasting spiritual and physical bond connecting him to his ancestors, his family and the land of Israel.

"For thy servants take pleasure in her stones, and favor its dust."
(Psalms 102:15)

According to Rabbi Yehudah, as mentioned earlier, although the Torah was displayed to the nations, it was still covered with plaster. Possibly, we were being given to understand that one must work hard and diligently when studying Torah: it is endlessly deep and we must peel away the layers that could block us from its deepest truths.

Rabbi Shimon, on the other hand, holds that the Torah was written clearly, and he presents us with another approach—one must bring people to the Torah slowly by first teaching them the basic concepts that are easy to comprehend. Meanwhile, unfortunately, both approaches failed to bring the Nations to repent and rectify themselves.

In conclusion, the events on the Mountains of Grizim and Eval involved the weaving together of three fundamental cords: the Torah, the Land, and the People. The intertwining of these threads created a powerful rope that was meant to pull the Nations out of the mud of idolatry.

Although, our prophet's vision of the end of days did not materialize in the periods of the first and second commonwealths, we are today beginning to see clear signs of its fruition. Never before in our long history have we seen such a growing wave of interest in Israel, its people, and its Torah.

As described by our prophets:

> *"Now it will come about that in the end of days the mountain of the house of the Hashem will be established as the chief of the mountains, and will be raised above the hills; And all the nations will stream to it. And many people will come and say, "Come, let us go up to the mountain of the Hashem, to the house of the God of Jacob; That He may teach us concerning His ways And that we may walk in His paths." For the Torah will go forth from Zion and the word of the Hashem from Jerusalem.*" (Isaiah 2:2–3)

> *"Thus says G-d of hosts, 'In those days, ten men from all the nations will grasp the garment of a Jew, saying, "Let us go with you, for we have heard that G-d is with you."* (Zachariah 8:23)

PARASHAT
NITZAVIM

You are standing
Deuteronomy 29:9-30:20

נצבים

NITZAVIM

TORAH LESSON BY
RABBI GEDALIA MEYER

FREE WILL

See, I have given you today life and good, and death and evil . . .
I call the heavens and the earth today to testify upon you that I have given
you life and death, blessing and curse; and you should choose life in order
that you and your descendents live. To love Hashem your God, to listen
to His voice and to cling to Him, for He is your life and the length of
your days to dwell in the land that Hashem swore to your forefathers, to
Abraham, to Isaac, and to Jacob, to give to you" (Deuteronomy 30: 19-20).

NITZAVIM IS AN extremely short parasha consisting of only 40 verses.
It is not the shortest in the Torah as the next parasha contains a mere
30 verses. But within those 40 verses a treasure trove of Torah ideas
can be found. It tells us about the forging of a new covenant between God
and the Israelites; the warning of future failure to keep that covenant; the dire
consequences of that failure—exile and curse; but also the promise of ultimate redemption, including the return from exile and the renewing of God's
covenant. The seemingly miraculous destiny of the people of Israel—the
incredibly long Diaspora and the equally incredible ingathering in the distant
future—are written into a couple of dozen verses with such simplicity and
such straightforwardness that it reads like an article in the newspaper.

There is also more to it than that, as the final six verses of this parasha deal
with a topic that has never been hinted at in the Torah before. It is a topic that
was never broached again in the rest of the Bible. On the one hand, it is a topic
that is so obvious, one wonders why the Torah mentioned it at all. On the
other hand, it is also a topic that is so important for the essence of what it is to
be a human being that one wonders why it only gets mentioned once. What is
this unusual but vital topic?

It is the topic of free will. You read that correctly, free will is discussed in
the Torah. It is discussed once and only once. It is discussed in a manner that
is both profoundly serious and disturbingly simply. The verses quoted above
are the core of the Torah's discussion of free will. The phrase, "choose life" is
the core of those two verses.

This topic deserves to be examined in detail. Free will is something that most of us take for granted. It is so blatantly obvious to the human mind that there is almost no room to think otherwise. Yet, at the same time, it has always been one of the most hotly debated aspects of human existence. Do we really have free will? The ancient and medieval problem with free will centered on the glaring contradiction it presented to the power of God. If God is all-powerful and all-knowing, how could something as mundane and as mortal as a human being possibly have the ability to do something independent of God. If God controls nature, life, death and the destiny of the word, how could an ordinary human being have the power to choose what God has not chosen? This was the original problem that vexed the greatest minds of monotheistic religion—from Judaism to Christianity to Islam. Because of this problem, some were forced to abandon the idea of free will, despite its undeniable reality in the human experience. Others were forced to admit that there was a flaw to God's absolute power and perfection, despite the theological implications of such a radical step.

In modern times, the problem has taken a different form as God is no longer an important part of the scientific and philosophical understanding of reality. We are here by accident with no creator, and no ultimate purpose. Our entire reality is explainable within the workings of natural and physical forces. There is simply no room for anything as unnatural and unphysical as free will. What natural explanation could possibly account for such an unnatural thing? Calling it 'spiritual' does not help, this simply associates a word with an otherwise inexplicable phenomenon. Because of this, free will must not exist. It cannot be explained through the known physical laws so it must be nothing more than an illusion.

On top of this, the latest findings in neuroscience claim to confirm this seemingly obvious conclusion of free will made by modern thought. Brain scans attempting to trace actual moments of decision appear to show that choices are made by the physical properties of the brain and not by some mysterious 'soul' or 'spirit'. These findings come as no surprise to the scientific world that is bent on proving that human beings are nothing more than complicated rocks. They do however strike everyone, including the scientists themselves, as profoundly at odds with human experience. We think that we have choices, and we sense that our choices matter and that we matter. We believe that life itself is precious and of great significance, perhaps even with some ultimate consequences. Claiming otherwise strikes us as both inhumane and wrong.

To all of these problems the Torah states a simple truth, "I have given you life and death, blessing and curse; and you should choose life in order that you and your descendants live". The absolute and undeniable nature of human free will is contained in that sentence. It is the ability to choose life over death, blessing over curse, and good over evil. This ability to choose, first and foremost, is described as a gift. It is a gift from God, not a 'natural' ability. The scientists got it right on that point; there is nothing natural about free will, however natural it may seem to us. It is a gift from God.

We can choose to use it or to decline that choice. The Torah describes the high stakes that follow this choice in the most serious of terms: life or death; blessing or curse; good or evil. The divine gift of free will was not meant to be squandered on mundane things like food or comfort. It was meant for the really big things, the things that matter in life. But free will is used even for the mundane things. It covers everything from the choice between Coke and Sprite to the most profound moral struggle. Every time we make a true choice based on our free will, we are choosing between life and death, and good and evil. It may not seem all that important to us at the time of making a choice, but if it truly uses the power of free will it will always contain an element of vital importance to our lives.

As far as the ancient and modern problems of free will, the Torah seems to dismiss the issues with a simple statement: we have free will. We can use it if we choose to. It comes from God. Our moral and spiritual fate lies in our own hands and not in the hands of God or the forces of nature. Whether or not theologians of the past or scientists of the present are able to encompass this truth within their system is not a concern of the Torah. The theologians and scientists will have to work that problem out for themselves, the Torah only states the truth.

We have free will. We have the ability to choose. Choose life.

PARASHAT
VAYELECH

And he went
DEUTERONOMY 31:1-31:30

וַיֵּלֶךְ

VAYELECH

TORAH LESSON BY
RABBI NATHAN LOPES CARDOZO

SONG AND ECSTASY IN THE RELIGIOUS EXPERIENCE[11]

"Now, Write This Song for Yourselves and Teach it to
the Children of Israel." (Deuteronomy 31:19)

IN THIS VERSE God commands Moshe to write down the words of the Torah
and teach the Children of Israel how to contemplate them and use them
as their guide. Commentators and philosophers throughout the ages have
wondered why it was called a *song*?

Just after Moshe's death and before the battle at Jericho, a heavenly being
with the appearance of a man confronts Yehoshua, Israel's new leader, with a
sword in his hand.

"Yehoshua asks him, *'HaLanu Ata?* Are you with us [or against us]?' The
divine being responds: 'No, I am the commander of God's legion. Now I have
come!' Yehoshua prostrated himself before him." (Joshua 5:13—15)

The Talmud interprets this rather strange and incomprehensible interaction as an allegory whereby Yehoshua understood the threatening sword in
the creature's hand as a symbol of God's displeasure with him and the whole
Nation of Israel.[12] He therefore questioned whether their commitment to
God's Torah was wanting.

"Did God send you to us because we are not fulfilling the Torah 'that Moshe
commanded *us (lanu)?*' Yehoshua asks him.[13] *'No'*, answered the heavenly man,
'I have not come to criticize your commitment to the Torah but I *did* come to
criticize the People of Israel for their failure to fulfill the intention behind the
command, *Now!* as it says in the verse, *Now*, write this song for yourselves and
teach it to the children of Israel.'"

What does this all mean? Indeed, one of the major questions of religious
Jewish life is whether one commits oneself to Torah because it is an inheritance (i.e. tradition), or because it is truly the song of one's life. Judaism as
inheritance functions as a comfortable lifestyle, a heritage that one is happy to

---

11 Based on an oral interpretation in the name of the late Ponevezher Rav, Rabbi Yosef Kahaneman *z"l*.
12 Megilla 7a.
13 The Gemara understands this statement as a reference to a verse that continues, "...is the heritage of
the Congregation of Yakov" (Deuteronomy 33:4).

continue because of history and values, but not because one's whole life's mission is interwoven in it.

A song however, is something entirely different. A song comes from within when a person feels overwhelmed and touched in the deepest levels of his soul. A song expresses meaning beyond the logic of words. An authentic song reveals the ineffable as it protests against the rigidness of a purely verbal mindset.

Such a song never comes about simply from a commitment to a lifestyle. True song bursts forth when a person's whole being becomes absorbed in its deep inner dimensions. Only when one experiences the blur of boundaries between doer and deed, singer and song, can one speak of an authentic religious experience. One must achieve a state of ecstasy in which one no longer sings the song but *is* the song.

This is the reason why the Torah is called a Song. "Now write for yourselves this song," means that an Israelite must strive with passion to make his relationship with the Almighty his ongoing "raison d'être"—his song of life. This verse calls on man to do no less than turn his life into a work of art in which every moment expresses holiness, dignity, and the ultimate beauty.

A young admirer once asked the renowned poet, Rainer Maria Rilke, whether he should become a poet. Rilke responded, "only when you cannot live without being a poet." And so it is with a life of Torah—only when one cannot imagine a life without it, the Torah truly becomes a song.

PARASHAT
HAAZINU

Give ear!

DEUTERONOMY 32:1-32:52

האזינו

HAAZINU

TORAH LESSON BY
RABBI ZELIG PLISKIN

YOUR CHARACTER TRAITS ARE THE KEY TO HOW YOU WILL GROW WHEN YOU STUDY TORAH.

יערף כמטר לקחי

"My teachings should come down to you as rain." (Deuteronomy 32:2)

RABBI CHAYIM SHMUELEVITZ used to cite the Vilna Gaon on this verse that rain helps things grow. But what grows? Only what is there from before. If someone has vegetables and fruits that are healthy and delicious, rain will help them develop. But if there are poisonous mushrooms, rain will help them grow too. Similarly, Torah study makes one grow. But it depends on one's character traits what one will become. A person who has elevated traits will become a greatly elevated person. But if a person has faulty character traits, the more Torah he studies the greater menace he will become.

An arrogant person is likely to become more arrogant when he becomes more knowledgeable. Such a person is likely to use his Torah knowledge for one-upmanship. He will try to show others that they are inferior to him. If a person is cruel, the more he knows the more pain he will try to inflict on others. When a person who is power-hungry gains more knowledge, he will feel more justified in manipulating others. A selfish person will utilize his knowledge to become even more selfish. On the other hand, a person with positive character traits will use his Torah knowledge to help as many people as he can. He will readily share his knowledge with others. The more Torah he studies the more elevated he will become. His entire behavior towards others will be a *kidush Hashem*, a sanctification of the Almighty's name.

A Rabbi told the Chazon Ish about the positive intellectual qualities of a young man whom his sister-in-law considered marrying. The Chazon Ish interrupted him with the question, "Will he also be a good husband?" (*P'air Hador*, vol.4, p.85)

A newly married yeshiva[14] student's wife requested that he take out the garbage, but he felt that it was not fitting for someone who studies Torah to have

14 Yeshiva – Torah school.

to deal with the garbage. He approached his Rosh Hayeshiva[15] and asked him for his opinion. "Yes it is not fitting for someone like yourself to take out the garbage," the distinguished Rosh Hayeshiva replied. The next day there was a knock on the door of the young man's house. To his surprise it was his Rosh Hayeshiva. "Could you please show me where you keep your garbage?" the Rosh Hayeshiva asked him. "I came to take it out for you."

THE ALMIGHTY ALWAYS DOES FOR YOU
WHAT IS IN YOUR BEST INTERESTS.

הצור תמים פעלו, כי כל-דרכיו משפט

"The Rock His acts are perfect, all of His ways are just." (Deuteronomy 32:4)

The Chofetz Chayim once asked someone about how things were going for him. "It wouldn't hurt if things were a bit better," the man replied.

"How can you possibly know that it wouldn't hurt?" replied the Chofetz Chayim. "The Almighty knows better than you. He is merciful and compassionate. If He felt it would be good for you for things to be better. He definitely would have made them better. Certainly thing are good for you the way they are." (*Chofetz Chayim al Hatorah*, p.284)

Things are not always the way we wish them to be, but they are always for our good. This awareness will give you an elevated feeling in your life. You have every right to try to improve your situation. But whenever you do all you can to try, and the situation is still not the way you would wish, work on internalizing the consciousness that the Almighty is doing for you what is in your best interests.

BE CAREFUL TO USE ALL YOUR ATTRIBUTES
AND TRAITS IN ONLY POSITIVE WAYS.

צור ילדך, תשי; ותשכח, אל מחללך.

"You were unmindful of the Almighty who begot you, and
you forgot G-d who bore you." (Deuteronomy 32:18)

---

15 Rosh Hayeshiva – Head of the Torah school.

The Dubner Maggid explained this verse with the following parable: Reuven owed Shimon a large sum of money and lacked the necessary funds to repay his debt. His creditor was pestering him very much and he didn't know what to do. He therefore approached his close friend Levi and asked for advice. Levi told him that when Shimon approached him again he should act as if he were totally insane and then Shimon would have to leave him alone. Following this suggestion, he made all kinds of crazy sounds and movements when he was in the presence of Shimon and it worked well. Shimon left him alone. The next day Reuven asked Levi to lend him a sizable sum of money for a few days. A week later Levi asked Shimon to repay him but Shimon just acted crazy again. Levi was furious at him and shouted, "I'm the one who gave you the idea to use this method. It's a real *chutzpah* (insolence) for you to use that against me."

The Almighty created forgetfulness as a benefit for people who have suffered in the past. If someone would always remember clearly every bit of suffering that occurred to him in his life, he would find it very difficult to cope with life. He would not enjoy the positive things in his life because of the remembrance of the pain of the past. By forgetting the misfortunes of one's life one can live a happy life even though one has suffered in the past. But forgetfulness can also be a very negative trait if one forgets the Almighty and his obligations to Him. This, said the Dubner Maggid, is the message of our verse. The Almighty created forgetfulness (*teshi* as Rashi explains is forgetfulness). He did so for your benefit. But unfortunately you used this to forget him. (*Ohel Yaakov*)

Every trait and attribute can be used for good and can be used for bad. It is up to you to utilize all that you were given in positive ways.

IF YOU ARE TEMPTED TO DO SOMETHING IMPROPER, THINK OF THE POSITIVE THINGS YOU CAN DO INSTEAD.

על אשר מעלתם בי, בתוך בני ישראל, במי-מריבת קדש, מדברצן—
על אשר לא-קדשתם אותי, בתוך בני ישראל.

The Almighty told Moshe he would not enter the land of Israel:

"Because you trespassed against Me in the midst of the Children of Israel at the waters of Merivat-Kadesh, in the Wilderness of Tzin, because you did not sanctify Me in the midst of the Children of Israel." (Deuteronomy 32:51)

Rabbi Meir Simcha Hacohen explains that the concept of *din* and *cheshbon* is being referred to in this verse. *Din* is the judgment for what one has done wrong. Therefore the first part of the verse mentions that Moshe trespassed against the Almighty. The second part of the verse is the *cheshbon*, that is, the calculation of what one could accomplish if one would have done what was proper. Therefore the verse states, "because you did not sanctify Me." This means that if Moshe would have done what was proper by speaking to the rock instead of hitting it, he would have had the merit of a major *kidush Hashem*. (*Meshech Chochmah*)

Before doing something that is improper, think in these terms. First, "What is the harm of the negative thing I am about to do?" Then ask yourself: "What positive things could I do in this time or with this energy?" Some people are more motivated by fear of doing something wrong, while others are more motivated when they think in terms of what they can gain by positive accomplishments. By keeping both thoughts in mind you will be doubly motivated to do good and keep away from wrong. Similarly, when you try to motivate others to refrain from doing something wrong, help them focus on both the harm of doing wrong and on how they could gain by positive accomplishments.

From *Growth through Torah* by Rabbi Zelig Pliskin.

PARASHAT
V'ZOT HABERACHAH

And this the blessing
DEUTERONOMY 33:1-34:12

וזאת הברכה

V'ZOT HABERACHAH

TORAH LESSON BY
RABBI CHAIM RICHMAN

"Before the Eyes of All of Israel" - The Blessing of Starting All Over Again

THE FIVE BOOKS of Moses are divided into weekly portions. When we read each portion, we are not studying ancient history. This weekly study is nothing less than the story of our own unfolding lives thus far. Each year when we finish the cycle of Torah portions on the festival of *Simchat Torah*, and read the last parasha in the book of Deuteronomy, *V'Zot HaBerachah*, we experience a restart. We immediately begin to read the Torah anew that very day, starting from Parashat *Bereshit*, the beginning of Genesis.

We never get tired of this cycle. It's an amazing experience. Each year we uncover more of the Torah's mysteries, delving deeper and deeper into its secrets. As we mature, we can see deeper, and our constantly changing understanding and appreciation of the lessons of Torah helps us to serve G-d better, first and foremost, by helping us to become better people.

Yet this restart is also quite elusive, and the passage from Deuteronomy back to Genesis can seem jolting and disquieting. After all, we have been so thoroughly immersed in study throughout this cycle. The last four Torah portions in Deuteronomy alone takes place on the day of Moshe's passing, after he reiterated his concern for the people of Israel so many times, and the pitfalls that were waiting for them in the future. He spoke many times of the challenges they will constantly face, most of them, as a result of their own insubordination. Now, in *Genesis,* we are back at the beginning of creation, the beginning of everything. This transition can leave us dazed.

Parashat *V'Zot HaBerachah* is Moshe's blessing to the Children of Israel. It is a prophetic vision in which he alludes to what will befall his cherished people. The beloved leader, who lived for his people and loved them so much, is about to leave them. Before he departs this world he must leave them with a powerful message. How shall he be remembered? What is the succinct statement of his life's work on behalf of Israel?

The relationship that all of Israel had with Moses, who is universally acknowledged as *Moshe Rabbeinu* (Moses our master, our teacher), is unparalleled. The Torah itself testifies to the great compassion he possessed for his people, to the point of ultimate self-sacrifice. When following the debacle of the Golden Calf he said, "And now if You would but forgive their sin! But if not, erase me now from Your book that You have written" (Exodus 32:32). He was ready to die, to never have existed in the first place, in order to save his people. He was completely without ego, to the point where the Almighty Himself bears witness and states, "And Moshe was the humblest man upon the face of the earth" (Numbers 12:3).

This is the Moshe who brought his people out of Egypt. This is the Moshe who ascended to Mount Sinai and brought down the Torah; who on two separate occasions did not eat or drink for forty days; who faced down the spies and their wicked intentions against the Land, and Korach and his co-conspirators, and the kings of Ammon and Moab. After all those adventures, all that travail, all that spiritual hope and longing and accomplishment—the last words of the Torah, the last verses of parashat *V'Zot HaBerachah* serve to sum up his life as he should be remembered by Israel. What is the main thing the Nation should remember about Moshe, which he would like to be remembered for? What did he do for the people of Israel that will remain with them forever? That he delivered them from the house of bondage, or that he ascended to Heaven and received the Torah? The surprising answer can be found in the last verses of the Torah:

> "Never again has there arisen in Israel a prophet like Moses, whom Hashem had known face to face, as evidenced by all the signs and wonders that Hashem sent him to perform in the land of Egypt, against Pharaoh and all his courtiers and all his land, (. . .) and by all the strong hand and awesome power that Moses performed **before the eyes of all Israel**." (Deuteronomy 34:10–12)

The holy Rashi (1040-1105) explains that the words 'before the eyes of all Israel' refer to Moshe's inspiration to break the tablets before their eyes as the verse states, "and I broke them before your eyes" (Deuteronomy 9:17), "and the Holy One, blessed be He, agreed with Moses that this was the right thing to do" (BT Shabbat 87: a).

Was breaking the tablets the ultimate thing that Moshe did before the eyes of all of Israel? Was this really the single most important thing he had done, and how he should be remembered?

This is certainly difficult to understand. The question becomes even stronger when we begin to study the deep teachings of our sages regarding the difference between the first and the second tablets.

The original two tablets were written by the finger of G-d. The tablets represent the potential for living on a much higher spiritual plane. According to our sages, if the original tablets had not been broken, Israel would have remained on an exalted level of Torah knowledge. Our sages famously state that no one would ever forget anything they learned! The knowledge of Torah would have been anchored in such a deep way in their souls, that it would never be forgotten. But when Moshe descended and witnessed how Israel, under the influence and at the instigation of the mixed multitude, were reveling around the golden calf, the holy letters on the tablets, written by G-d Himself, flew off the tablets and back up to Heaven. The stones then became unbearably heavy in his hands, thus we read, "It happened as he drew near the camp and saw the calf and the dances, that Moshe's anger flared up. He threw down the tablets from his hands and shattered them at the foot of the mountain" (Exodus 32:19).

Was Moses indeed angry? The verse certainly implies that Moses' action was caused by a fit of rage. However, the simple reading of these words hides a great secret. Moshe did not break the tablets in a momentary act of anger. He did not lose his self-control, even for an instant. Rather, the breaking of the tablets was a calculated, well thought-out plan for the benefit of his beloved Israel. And G-d agreed with his plan. This was therefore not a momentary loss of composure, but quite the opposite. It was a deed of unparalleled importance and, as the Torah testifies in this last verse, "before the eyes of all Israel", it was possibly the single most important thing that Moshe ever did, and that which he and the Torah wishes us to remember. For through this act, Moshe bequeathed to Israel the Divine ability to forget and begin anew, shedding off all previous knowledge and preconceived notions and ideas.

If the original tablets had not been broken things would have been different— even higher—but not better. True, not a letter of Torah would have been forgotten; the potential for ultimate rectification would have been very great; but Moshe realized that such an expectation would not have been realistic. When he came down and saw the debauchery of the golden calf, he realized with great compassion and deep insight, that things can't be rushed. The accumulation of the knowledge and life experience needs time. Knowledge can't be forced. We need to fix ourselves a little at a time, bit by bit, every year. Everything that transpires in the life of a human being, all the things we go through, are all necessary stations along our road to awareness. Disappointments along the way are inevitable but a person must never become despondent. Every time one falls he must get up. If we obsess about past mistakes and failures, we would be so overwhelmed that we would not be able to get up!

Thus, the ability to gain perspective, forget the past and move forward, is a great blessing. This is the secret our sages refer to as *the holiness of forgetting*, and that ability comes from Moshe breaking the tablets. This was the single greatest legacy he bequeathed to his people. Had the first tablets remained intact, Israel would have been permanently 'stuck', albeit on a rarified level, but it would not have served the purpose of striving to become better. The new era of the breaking of the tablets and the following second set, brought with it the very human ability to strive to fix, to strive for improvement and knowledge. The work is harder than if the original tablets had remained intact—but the personal acquisition of true Torah is more real, more anchored, more lasting, more internal.

This is exactly the secret of why we conclude reading Deuteronomy during the High Holy Days of judgment, and immediately begin again with Genesis. Because just as the year is brand new, so is all of creation renewed, and every person is renewed and able to start again, no matter what we have been through! We are always able to start again, realizing: I really don't know anything. I am just starting now. How do I start reading about creation all over again? Haven' t I read this before?

It is because I am just now being created anew, the year is being created anew, the whole world is being created anew. I forget everything I knew, because it is a new year, and whatever I knew, is no longer relevant. I am a new person. And we never, ever fall into despair.

Moshe's wisdom foresaw all this and so he broke the tablets; enabling each of us to start again and forget the mistakes of the past. Whatever happened and whatever I knew before does not matter. So the last thing we read when we conclude the Torah is that Moshe broke the tablets before the eyes of all Israel, and then immediately we start reading the Torah from the beginning. This is exactly what the *teshuva,* the repentance of *Rosh HaShana* and *Yom Kippur,* and the joy of *Sukkot* is all about! It is precisely why every year at this time, we conclude the Torah and start again, because in G-d's great kindness everything is reset.

The Torah is concluded and begun again; the year concludes and the New

Year begins. Whatever happened in the past, stays in the past. Now is a time to go forward, the tablets were broken so we can—we must—begin again. We strive with all our being to become real people, to work at it relentlessly and not give up, just as G-d constantly renews creation. We need to believe and know in our hearts that everything is constantly new, no day is like the previous one, no year is like the previous one, whatever we thought we knew, we are starting over again.

Thus the yearly cycle of reading the Torah is a never-ending Mobius strip of ever-increasing self-knowledge and exploration. Moshe's laser-sharp response to a gathering spiritual crisis changed everything in life since then. It enables us to begin the adventure of Torah anew each year, with new eyes and pure hearts.

THE HOLIDAYS

HOLIDAY LESSON
FOR

ROSH HASHANA

BY
RABBI LEVI COOPER

BROKEN WATCHES, BROKEN SOULS

THE ROSH HASHANA experience is punctuated by the *shofar* blasts: the sounding of the ram's horn in the synagogue as a part of the prayer service. The sages explained that this act reminds the Almighty of the Binding of Isaac, invoking ancestral merit and the dedicated fidelity of our forebears. The sages also explained that the *shofar* acts like an alarm clock, waking our slumbering souls and acting as a call for renewed commitment to God. Historically, clock metaphors abound in Jewish tradition.

When Rabbi Shlomo Shapiro (1831-1893) reached marriageable age, he travelled with his father, Rabbi Elazar of Łancut (1808-1865), to meet the prospective bride, Haya Frima Rivka (d. 1887), daughter of Rabbi Yekutiel Shmelke of Sasów (1800-1861). After marriage arrangements were agreed upon, the young groom and his father began the journey back to their home town. Along the way they made a detour to visit the well-respected Hasidic master, Rabbi Meir'l of Przemyślany (1783-1850).

Rabbi Meir'l welcomed the visitors and in the course of the conversation he noticed the new pocket watch that the young groom was wearing. To this day, in many traditional Jewish communities, a groom receives a watch as a gift from his prospective in-laws—though there is no requirement in Jewish law to give such a gift. Observing the glistening new timepiece, Rabbi Meir'l took the opportunity to comment on its symbolism:

"A watch is like a human being: When it is new, it keeps time faithfully, just as the watchmaker intended. As the years pass, it may break—not the hands or the face, but the delicate balance wheel or the hairspring may become worn or specks of dirt may disrupt the fragile mechanism. Maintenance and adjustment might be necessary. The only solution is to take the timepiece to a watchmaker, who opens the watch and dissembles it into a myriad of tiny pieces until he locates the problem. After he has identified the issue, fixed whatever needs to be fixed and cleaned the insides, the watchmaker puts the timepiece back together again. Once again, the watch keeps time faithfully."

Rabbi Meir'l unpacked the parable:

"This is the nature of a person: God creates people to live their lives faithfully. Alas, specks of dirt enter into our delicate souls and disrupt our spiritual mechanism. The only solution is to break down our egos, identify our failings, cleanse our souls, and then reconstruct ourselves."

Rabbi Meir'l took the parable a step further by drawing a parallel between the watch/human image and the *shofar* blasts on Rosh Hashana:

"This process"—referring to the deconstruction and subsequent reconstruction of the watch/soul—"Is indicated by the way we sound the *shofar*." When we blow the *shofar* on Rosh Hashana, there are different types of sounds: *teki'ah*, *shevarim*, and *teru'ah*. A set of shofar blasts is bracketed by a *teki'ah* at the beginning and a *teki'ah* at the end. Rabbi Meir'l explained: "We begin with a *teki'ah*—a single, pure, unbroken blast. As we deal with the vagaries of life we become a *shevarim*—a broken blast that bespeaks fragmentation and loss of purity and wholeness. At that time, we must become a *teru'ah*—a sound broken into innumerable, tiny pieces. It is only after we have truly become a *teru'ah, that* we can reconstruct the pieces and sound the *teki'ah* once again, indicating that we have returned to the original, pure, unified, and divine self."

With that, Rabbi Meir'l concluded the parable and its explanation, leaving a lesson in the minds of all present as they pondered the symbolism of the watch.

Rabbi Meir'l then leaned over to the father of the groom, Rabbi Elazar of Łancut—also a Hasidic leader and a scion of a famous Hasidic family—and he added in a still, silent voice: "All this, I said to the young lads who are just beginning their journey in the service of the Almighty. A leader, however, must take a different approach."

In my imagination I can conjure up the image of Rabbi Meir'l as he looked deep into the eyes of his colleague Rabbi Elazar of Łancut.

Rabbi Meir'l continued: "Leaders should not announce their failings to all, lest they precipitate depression amongst their charges, or create a gloomy atmosphere that would undermine their own ability to lead. Indeed, the appropriate approach for leaders is indicated in a verse from the Torah: 'And when you convoke the congregation you shall blow long blasts and not short ones' (Numbers 10:7)." Rabbi Meir'l explained: "Moses—the paragon of Jewish leadership—was instructed to appear before the community as a *teki'ah*, an unbroken, pure blast of the *shofar*; not as a fragmented *teru'ah* blast." Thus according to Rabbi Meir'l, leaders should not broadcast their shortcomings, rather they should present themselves as shining examples for all to follow.

Meditating on the whispered words of Rabbi Meir'l of Przemyślany, I can't help but wonder whether his vision is appropriate for our day. Perhaps in our times leaders who honestly recognize their frailties and who are open about the challenges they face might provide more inspiration than an untainted—but unreal and essentially dishonest—person. The inner fragmentation of a leader is undoubtedly a challenge that should not be ignored. Leaders who conscientiously and scrupulously confront the vicissitudes of life, who tackle their shortcomings, who aspire to grow, develop and improve—surely these are the leaders we seek to emulate.

HOLIDAY LESSON
FOR

YOM KIPPUR

BY
RABBI MOSHE GOLDSMITH

A DAY OF ATONEMENT FOR ALL

HUMAN BEINGS ARE required to believe in Hashem—the Creator of the Universe; they are to refrain from worshiping anything or anyone else. If one *truly* believes in G-d, loves and fears Him, his (her) heart is overcome with embarrassment and pain after sinning. He (she) asks: *"How could I have forsaken the word of G-d?"*

True faith is marked by a constant awareness of the Divine Presence that surrounds us, a Presence which is tuned in to all that we do. This faith affords the realization that, ideally, that our soul is at so high a level, we are part of Hashem Himself. The Mitzvah of devotion and faith in Hashem is what Yom Kippur is all about.

The holiday teaches us that people can cleanse themselves of their sins through repentance; this means returning to Hashem. Our souls, spiritual entities, yearn to be as close to Hashem as possible, yet they are implanted in physical bodies which serve as a garment for the souls that are contained within. It is a task to keep them pure. Imagine trying to clean a stain on a white shirt—the stain is difficult to remove; it will almost always leave a mark. Similarly, by sinning, we stain the vestment of our soul. We cause it to dress in inappropriate garments, and it is likened to a queen dressed in rags.

Interestingly, the common symbols of mourning and repentance are sackcloth and ashes. These are a reminder that we have stained the apparel of our souls. It might seem, therefore, that one who has tainted the garment of his soul would always retain a mark on it. But no, on Yom Kippur it is customary to wear white garments that symbolize purity. G-d tells us: *"... it is on this day that atonement shall be made for you to cleanse you; you shall be purified from all your sins before Hashem."* (Leviticus 16:30)

Here the Torah reveals the awesome power of Yom Kippur—an amazing gift from The Almighty. By allowing us to confess our sins, exhibit true remorse, and determine to abandon our folly, he lets us begin again with a clean slate.

The word for *repentance* in Hebrew is related to the Hebrew word *return*. The Talmud (in Pesachim 54:1) teaches us that repentance was one of the seven gifts that proceeded the creation of the world. Thus, we were blessed with the opportunity to return to our true, originally pure selves. The prayer we recite each morning on awakening—*"Hashem the soul that you gave me is pure"*— is to remind us that every human being, Jew and non-Jew alike, is required to return to his true self. This is what the Day of Atonement is all about!

Interestingly, on Yom Kippur, at the afternoon *minchah1 service*, we study the book of Prophet Jonah, whose story raises some difficult questions. G-d orders the prophet to go to the Assyrian city of Nineveh (present day Iraq) and inform its people that them that their evil ways have come to His attention. Clearly, Hashem is hoping for their repentance.

Nevertheless, Jonah did not want to obey Hashem's directive and he boards a ship in an effort to escape it. The Mishnah[2] (tractate Sanhedrin 11:5) teaches us that a prophet who fails to report his prophecy to those for whom it is intended is liable to the death penalty at the Hands of G-d. Yet, even though Jonah's life is apt to be shortened because of his disobedience, he is determined to prevent the repentance of the people of Nineveh. Why?

According to Jewish tradition, Jonah knew that the people of Ninveh would heed his call for repentance, in contrast to the people of Israel who had heard the pleading of many prophets to reform themselves and still had not repented. In addition, Jonah knew that the banishment of the ten tribes of Israel was in the offing, and he wanted to prevent the immanent fall of the Kingdom of Israel, which he feared would be inevitable if the sinners of Ninveh seemed more worthy to Hashem by obeying Jonah's pleas for reform. Why, then, did Hashem force Jonah to relate a message to the people of Ninveh which would only bring harm to the people of Israel, his Chosen Nation?

Jonah's experience was meant to be an important lesson in the power of repentance. True repentance can cleanse any sin—even the most grievous of transgressions. One must never give of hope for the possibility of man's repentance and his return to Hashem, despite his previous actions. Through Jonah, G-d is teaching us that one day all the nations on earth can be expected to repent and return to Him.

Jonah's story is also a reminder that we must be a Light to the Nations. As a chosen people, our mission is to rectify mankind through our positive influence. Jonah tried to avoid his mission as a light to the nations by sailing away on

---

1 Minchah - the afternoon prayer service.
2 Mishnah - the first part of the Talmud; a collection of early oral interpretations of the scriptures that was compiled about AD 200.

a boat, but ironically, his interaction with the men on board demonstrates the relationship that must be developed between Israel and the nations.

Our sages teach us that there were representatives of all Seventy Nations on the ship. Each prayed to their false gods to calm the stormy sea, which threatened to overturn their boat, but their prayers went unanswered. Finally, when Jonah intervened and demonstrated, by jumping overboard, that G-d would then cause the storm to subside, he succeeded in introducing them to the True G-d, the G-d of Israel.

I while ago, I read that in the Book of Jonah, chapter 1, verses five, ten, and sixteen, we see a progressive fear of G-d as certain events proceed. In verse 5, we read that the seamen "feared and shouted to their gods;" in verse ten, that "they feared a great fear;" then finally, in verse 16 that "they feared a great fear of **Hashem**." I believe that this transformation demonstrates Jonah's ultimate success in fulfilling part of his Divine mission of elevating the nations by bringing them to the G-d of Israel, the G-d of the entire universe! This is a precursor to the fulfillment of the Messianic Dream when all the Nations will be transformed into worshipers of One True G-d.

This mission is also alluded to in the next part of the Jonah's story, when he is swallowed by a fish. In Hebrew, the word fish is spelle—Daled, Gimmel. The numerical value of the word is 7—the Daled is 4 and the Gimel is 3. This suggests that the 70 nations will attempt to swallow us up if, G-d forbid, we neglect our mission of being a light to the nations.

In conclusion, Yom Kippur has a personal side, which relates specifically to the people of Israel. In Leviticus 16:17 it says: *"And he shall effect atonement for himself, for his household, and for all the congregation of Israel."* The Torah stresses atonement for Aaron, for his house, and then finally for the people of Israel. G-d is teaching us that all of Israel is one nation responsible for one another.

We learn this from the covenant mentioned in Parshat Nitzavim. Nevertheless, we must not forget our responsibility to the nations. This is why we read the Book of Jonah on Yom Kippur during the *Mincha* service, when the fast is nearly over. Hashem wants the important message of Outreach to the Nations to be remembered as the Day of Atonement comes to an end. This message continues through the holiday of Succoth when Israel will bring 70 sacrifices for the nations. At the same time, we will also remember **who we are** with the celebration of the holiday of Shmini Azeret[3], which follows Succoth, and in which one sacrifice is brought, symbolizing a united Israel.

---

3 Shmini Azeret – Simchat Torah.

HOLIDAY LESSON
FOR

SUKKOT

BY
RABBI CHAIM RICHMAN

THE JOY OF HASHEM'S EMBRACE

T HE HEBREW CALENDAR is an exquisitely precise rendezvous with the Divine; it anticipates man's needs and provides the opportunity for personal growth. The sacred seasons sanctified by G-d grant us strength, encouragement and a deep connection with G-d in our lives.

Each of the three major festivals has a specific theme that challenges us to reach our spiritual potential. Although these are the pilgrimage festivals wherein the Nation of Israel goes up to the Holy Temple in Jerusalem, the messages conveyed by these holidays are for all of humanity. *Passover*, commemorating the Exodus from Egypt, is known as 'the time of our freedom' and is the holiday of emancipation when all people can realize their potential for redemption. *Shavuot*, the anniversary of the Sinai Revelation, is 'the time of the giving of our Torah' when each and every person can truly stand at Mount Sinai and receive the Torah anew.

And on *Sukkot*, the Feast of Tabernacles, we dwell in the *Sukkah* (Leviticus 23:42), which represents the protective shadow of the Divine Presence. Sitting within these 'temporary booths,' we are given the opportunity to recalibrate our relationship with G-d and make it real for the coming year. Sukkot is called the 'Time of our Joy,' as the Torah states, "And you shall rejoice on your festival (...) and you shall be only joyous" (Deuteronomy 17:13, 15). It is this true joy which is closeness to G-d, as King David testifies in his psalm, "But as for me, nearness to G-d is good" (Psalms 73:28). But what is really the source of this joy? How do we measure our closeness to G-d?

The entire month of *Tishrei*[4] is a process that enables the greatest intimacy with G-d. The awesome days of *Rosh HaShana* and *Yom Kippur* present unparalleled opportunities for renewal and growth. On *Rosh Hashana*, G-dliness is revealed in the world anew as we reaffirm the Holy One's sovereignty as King. We prepare to face His perfect judgment and in our prayers we give voice to our deepest wish for all of mankind: that all humans will recognize G-d and join together as a community in that recognition.

---

4 Tishrei is the first month in the Hebrew calendar. Tishrei usually occurs in September–October on the Gregorian calendar.

The intense sobriety of *Rosh HaShana* leads to the *Ten Days of Repentance*, enabling us to make amends for the entire year. And on the awesome *Yom Kippur*, the entire world is bathed in the light of forgiveness, as we resolve to rededicate ourselves completely to G-d's purpose.

But the climax of the *Tishrei* experience is Sukkot, as the cleansing of the Days of Awe brings us to a total recalibration of life. On Sukkot, the booths in which Israel live during these days symbolize her rock-steady, unshakable faith in the One G-d. It is fall now, just when the days are getting shorter and colder, and most people are coming indoors. It is no longer as pleasurable to sit outside as it was in summer. This is only felt when we move from the comforts and security of home, and take up residence in temporary dwellings, thanking G-d for His constant, enveloping presence. The knowledge of this presence is true joy!

Unconcerned with sunshine or warm weather, these temporary dwellings ostensibly do not appear to be "secure" in the physical sense as they may shake a little in the wind; their roofs are but thatches, open to the stars. But yet we sit within, unmoved and unaffected by what may be a hostile world—for like the booth, this world is temporary, and we are but temporary dwellers within her. Just as we are surrounded by the walls of this hut, so are we surrounded by the constant, protective presence of G-d Himself. The winds may shake and the elements may confront us, but the shadow of the Sukkah is the shadow of the Divine Presence.

Nonetheless, the secret of the Sukkah is even deeper than this.

After the cathartic experience of the Day of Atonement, the awesome time when justice is dispensed, just when we think we can't possibly get any higher—where could we possibly go?

Out of the house, and into the Sukkah.

After Yom Kippur, our human nature can leave us feeling vulnerable and unsure. It was unsettling standing before G-d in His capacity as the True Judge. Did I do it right? Was my repentance really sincere? Have I been judged favorably? Have I been sealed for life? And the most disquieting thought of all: Does G-d really forgive me? And lest one feel dejected, despondent or fearful that perhaps his judgment was not favorable, and he has lost that Divine connection— after the Day of Atonement he goes out into the Sukkah itself, symbol of Divine mercy, for instead of running away from the Holy One he flees directly into His presence, as it were.

On Sukkot we are in 'quarantine,' alone with G-d, surrounded by His light. In the Sukkah, we are overwhelmed by the realization of the depth of G-d's love and concern. It's the closest experience to being in the Holy Temple that one can have! Commenting on the juxtaposition of these holidays and the great Divine wisdom which plans for every human contingency, King Solomon was moved to write: "Go your way, eat your bread with joy and drink your wine with a glad heart, for G-d has already accepted your works" (Ecclesiastes 9:7).

Here is the real secret of the Sukkah: the Sukkah is the secret of G-d's embrace.

Let's say you meet up with someone who you know you've wronged. You spoke badly about him to others. Now, according to Torah law, you've got to tell this person what you did and ask him for forgiveness, before Hashem can forgive you. That's a hard thing to do: to go and admit to someone; I've wronged you.

But you summon the courage to confront him and apologize profusely for what you've done.

If he doesn't really know you or care about maintaining a relationship with you, and he doesn't appreciate how difficult it was for you to do this, he might just brush you off and say, 'Yeah, sure, it's fine, don't worry about it.'

If the fellow appreciates your sincerity and truly forgives you, he might shake your hand and say, 'Thank you, all is forgiven.'

If he is truly moved by what you've done, he might warmly take your hand in both of his and say something like, 'Please don't give it another thought, I absolutely forgive you.'

But if this person really, *really* loves you for who you are, and really forgives you with all his heart he will give you a big hug and say, 'forgive you? Forgive you for what? It never happened. I love you so much. I love you unconditionally. Don't ever forget that, not for a moment, and no matter what.'

He wants you to know how much he appreciates how difficult this was for you, how much he loves you and wants you to know that you have nothing to fear.

This is the secret of the joy of Sukkot. The walls of the Sukkah are the hug of G-d's loving embrace.

When we enter into the Sukkah, we are completely immersed in the shadow of the Divine Presence, we experience the totality of Hashem's compassion and love, and total forgiveness.

Another aspect of Sukkot is its unique connection to all the nations of the world. Of all the sacred seasons that G-d commanded Israel to observe, the festival of Tabernacles has the strongest implications for all humanity. Even today, vast numbers of gentiles identify with the holiday of Sukkot, and converge in Jerusalem just to be in the holy city at this time of year. It is as if their heart-strings are pulled by some invisible magnet, which draws them to the location of the Holy Temple during Sukkot.

The relationship between the nations and the holiday of Sukkot dates back to ancient times, and arcs through our own period to form a bridge towards the future, rectified world that we all yearn and long for, Israelite and Gentiles alike: the day when "the L-rd and His name will be One" (Zechariah 14:9).

In the time of the Holy Temple, during Sukkot a unique sacrifice was offered on the altar—with a unique intention.

Chapter 29 of the book of Numbers outlines the sacrifices which are to be offered over the span of the holiday. Counting the number of bulls which were offered over the seven-day period, we find that the total number was seventy. And in chapter 10 of the book of Genesis, there are seventy nations mentioned. These are the primordial nations, sometimes referred to as the "seventy languages," which represent all humanity. The Talmud (BT Sukkah 55: B) teaches that the seventy bulls that were offered in the Holy Temple served as an atonement for the seventy nations of the world. Truly, as the rabbis observed, "if the nations of the world had only known how much they needed the Temple, they would have surrounded it with armed fortresses to protect it" (Bamidbar Rabbah 1, 3).

We can already sense that inherent within the very nature of the holiday, an inexorable bond—as expressed through its offerings in the Holy Temple, the 'house of prayer for all peoples[5]'—links it to the peoples of the earth. Sukkot was mandated by the Creator Himself to be a holiday for all the world, and the festival calls out to all mankind to join forces with Israel in celebrating the acknowledging G-d's Presence in His world.

What a way to start the New Year! May it be sweet and full of blessing!

---

5 See Isaiah 56:7.

HOLIDAY LESSON
FOR

SIMCHAT TORAH

BY
RABBI NATHAN LOPES CARDOZO

THE UNYIELDING SEFER TORAH

SIMCHAT TORAH PRESENTS us with a rare paradox. On no other occasion do we celebrate our relationship with the Torah as we do on this day. We dance with it and sing love songs to it as if it was our beloved bride. Even after the holiday is over, huge festivities take place in Israel and the Diaspora when thousands of people turn to the streets carrying the Torah scrolls, while children holding lit torches accompany the festivities, and musicians leading huge parades turn it into a nearly mystical experience.

This, however, is most strange: the scrolls that we carry in our arms do not at all fit the times in which we live—they are completely outdated.

We live in a world of sophisticated technology; we walk on the moon, travel through space, communicate via satellite and make use of the Internet—all without batting an eye. Physicians transplant people's hearts, and replace or repair other parts of the human body with the greatest of ease. Any time now we will witness more scientific breakthroughs that will utterly surprise us, and before we know it, even more amazing inventions will usher us into a world we never dreamed was possible. Everything is moving and changing so rapidly that the term "speed" no longer has any relevant signifier.

Yet here we are, dancing with a script that is totally oblivious to it all. The text in this archaic scroll has not changed since the day Moshe received it at Mount Sinai. Furthermore, according to tradition, even the manner in which the Torah scroll is written has not been altered. It is still the human hand that must write the text; no word processor can take over. The quill has not been replaced, and nothing dramatic has happened to the formula used to produce the special ink. The parchment, as well, is prepared in the very same way as it was in the days of the prophets. If someone looked at the scroll we carry in our hands, and didn't know better, he would think we had discovered it in a cave where people thousands of years ago used to preserve their holy texts—such as the Dead Sea scrolls.

Jewish law always encourages integrating the latest scientific knowledge into our lives and has no problem with the newest developments in treating infertility, flying a spacecraft, and using technical devices to make it easier to observe

Shabbat. Yet, when it comes to the writing of a Sefer[6] Torah, no technological improvements are appreciated. They are basically rejected[7].

Ours is a future-orientated religion. We are not afraid of the latest technologies because they allow us to fulfill, in ways unimagined by our forefathers, the divine mandate to cure diseases, create more pleasant ways to live our lives, and make the world a better place. All this is beautifully expressed by our Sages, who direct us to become partners with God in the work of creation. But the very text that demands this does not allow for any changes in its content and bars us from making use of the latest technological devices when it comes down to its physical preparation and writing! What is the message conveyed by this paradox?

While living in a world that is constantly in a state of flux, where matters can change overnight, there must be a place of stability where we can take refuge. We need unshakeable foundations that won't shift like quicksand. Without such footing we would be lost and dangerously overwhelmed by the very technology we have created. While we benefit from all these new inventions, we also pay a heavy price and become the victims of great confusion. Technology and science often create moral problems that overwhelm us, and we begin to wonder whether it would be better to reject our moral standards in order to accommodate all the new possibilities that have opened up. Though many of us know this will only lead to more problems, others are calling for such radical steps, thinking it will bring improvement.

We need certainty but can no longer find it. The situation has become so critical that we realize we have reached a place where our human identity is at stake, unlike our forefathers who only had to deal primarily with problems related to ideology.

Looking at, and taking notice of, a Sefer Torah is therefore of great value. Here is an item that has not changed an iota. Its physical nature attests to its stability. It is the only thing in the world that would not give in to innovation. Its text informs us that while things indeed need to evolve and become more sophisticated, the basic moral positions in the Torah are not to be altered, and its physical

---

6 Sefer – book/scroll.

7 Although there are some slight changes in the way we produce all these components today, sometimes making things a little easier, basically the formula remains the same. In Ohr Yitzchak, the collection of responsa by Rabbi Yitzchak Abadi of Jerusalem, on Yoreh De'ah, siman 54, the author suggests ways in which a Sefer Torah can be written without the scribe actually writing the letters, making use of the latest technology. This suggestion has not been accepted by the vast majority of halachic authorities. I would indeed add that it is not in the spirit of Judaism, nor is it what a Sefer Torah should stand for, ideologically. This matter goes to the very root of the difficult question as to what extent ideology can play a role in halachic issues—a long and difficult topic beyond the scope of this essay.

representation as an "old-fashioned scroll" sends us that message. It does not want to accommodate everything, nor does it even want to accommodate itself. It is beyond time and space and hence disconnects itself from the so-called new developments that the passage of time always demands. It wants to remain itself, on its own terms, and therefore offers us a haven of stability and genuine identity in a stormy world. In that way, it reminds us of eternity, of another world in which enduring standards prevail and where there is tranquility; something we all long for.

A Sefer Torah teaches us that not everything old is necessarily old-fashioned. Making use of the word processor has in many ways led to a depersonalization of our lives. Running our world by remote control has not been good for our souls; and walking on the moon has not helped us to know our next-door neighbor any better. On the contrary, technological progress has robbed us of our own humanity.

It is therefore most meaningful that one item has maintained its constancy. It carries a text that has had a greater influence on the world than any other we know of. It has changed the universe as nothing else has; it encourages man to move, to discover and to develop. But it is written on parchment, by the hands of men, holding a quill, as if to say: "Be yourself. Don't get run over by the need for progress."

HOLIDAY LESSON
FOR

PASSOVER

BY
RABBI CHANAN MORRISON

Destroy Chametz, Gain Freedom

By the first day [of Passover] you must clear out
your homes of all leaven. (Exodus 12:15)

Why Clear Out Chametz?

WHY DOES THE Torah command us to destroy all *chametz* (leaven) found in our homes during Passover? It is logical to eat matzah; this fast-baked food has a historical connection to the Exodus, recalling our hurried escape from Egyptian slavery. But how does clearing out leaven from our homes relate to the Passover theme of freedom and independence?

Freedom of Spirit

There are two aspects to attaining true freedom. First, one needs to be physically independent of all foreign subjugation. But complete freedom also requires freedom of the spirit. The soul is not free if it is subjected to external demands that prevent it from following the path of its inner truth.

The difference between a slave and a free person is not just a matter of social standing. One may find an educated slave whose spirit is free, and a free person with the mindset of a slave. What makes us truly free? When we are able to be faithful to our inner self, to the truth of our Divine image—then we can live a fulfilled life, a life focused on our soul's inner goals. One whose spirit is servile, on the other hand, will never experience this sense of self-fulfillment. His happiness will always depend upon the approval of others who dominate over him, whether this control is *de jure* or *de facto*.

The Foreign Influence of Leaven

What is *chametz*? Leaven is a foreign substance added to the dough. The leavening agent makes the dough rise; it changes its natural shape and characteristics. Destruction of all leaven in the house symbolizes the removal of all foreign influences and constraints that prevent us from realizing our spiritual aspirations.

These two levels of independence, physical and spiritual, exist on both the individual and the national level. An independent people must be free not only from external rule, but also from foreign domination in the cultural and spiritual spheres.

For the Israelites in Egypt, it was precisely at the hour of imminent redemption that the dangers of these foreign 'leavening' forces were the greatest. At that time of great upheaval, true permanent emancipation was not a given. Would the Israelites succeed in freeing themselves, not only from Egyptian bondage, but also from the idolatrous culture in which they had lived for hundreds of years? To commemorate their complete liberation from Egypt, the Passover holiday of freedom requires the removal of all foreign 'leavening' agents.

CLEANSING OURSELVES OF FOREIGN INFLUENCES

In our days too, an analogous era of imminent redemption, we need to purge the impure influences of alien cultures and attitudes that have entered our national spirit during our long exile among the nations.

Freedom is the fulfillment of our inner essence. We need to aspire to the lofty freedom of those who left Egypt. To the Israelites of that generation, God revealed Himself and brought them into His service. This is truly the highest form of freedom, as the Sages taught in *Avot* (6:2):

Instead of "engraved (*charut*) on the tablets" (Exodus 32:16), read it as "freedom" (*cheirut*). Only one who studies Torah is truly free.

From *Silver from the Land of Israel*, pp. 151-153. Adapted from *Olat Re'iyah* vol. II, p. 244.

HOLIDAY LESSON
FOR

SHAVUOT

BY
RABBI DAVID AARON

A LOVE LETTER FROM THE DIVINE

AFTER THE MIRACULOUS Exodus from Egypt, the people of Israel traveled in the desert for 49 days until they reached Mount Sinai on the 6th day of the Hebrew month of Sivan. There they experienced the ultimate revelation and communion with G-d. They encountered G-d face to face, heard the voice of G-d and received the Torah and its commandments— the *mitzvos*.

Whereas Passover is the birthday of the people of Israel, this holiday, which is referred to as the holiday of Shavuot[8], can be likened to the Bar Mitzvah[9] of the people of Israel. It is a time to celebrate the *mitzvos*—the responsibilities implicit in the loving relationship we enjoy with G-d.

Recently a friend asked me if I would meet with his son, Sam, and help him prepare his Bar Mitzvah speech. I generally don't teach thirteen-year-olds, but I made an exception for my friend. So I got together with Sam and I began to share some insights into the Torah portion he would be reading in the synagogue on Shabbat. I actually got really into it, seeing how carefully he was listening, nodding his head ever so often. So I started to go even deeper and began to tell him some of the mystical meanings behind the passages he would be publicly reading. I was really impressed; he seemed to really understand me. After about an hour of all this deep talk I said, "Sammy, do you have any questions?"

He said, "Yeah, just one. Why do I have to obey all these commandments and adhere to all these rules?"

Well, I felt pretty silly. Here I was going in the deep end when he didn't even know what his Bar Mitzvah meant.

I asked him, "Sammy, do you like football?"

"I love it! I play it all the time."

"Do you know the rules?" I continued.

"Of course, you can't play if you don't know the rules."

"Why not?"

"'*Cuz* then there would be no game. You couldn't win or lose. There couldn't

---

8 *Shavuot* marks the giving of the Torah on Mt. Sinai.
9 *Bar Mitzvah* - a boy of 13 considered an adult and responsible for observing religious law.

be touchdowns, no out-of-bounds, no violations and no penalties. Without the rules it would just be chaos and no fun."

"Precisely, and that's also true about the game of life. Without rules and regulations it would just be chaos with no fun, no adventure and no challenges. You couldn't win or lose. Even though we all know the phrase: 'It's not whether you win or lose but it's how you play the game,' without rules, there is no way to evaluate 'how you play the game.' The Torah's commandments are the game rules of life and G-d is the referee."

In the end, Sammy got psyched for his Bar Mitzvah.

On Shavuot we celebrate getting the game rules of life, and on that day we rejoice because we became players in the game of life. If it wasn't for the rules there would be no game.

If there is no right and wrong, then what difference does it make what I do? If there is nothing to violate, there is nothing to fulfill. I can't even play a game of basketball without rules, let alone live my life! Without the Torah's game rules for living, the world is just a big chaos and the choices we make are meaningless.

The Torah, however, is more than just the rules of life. Torah is a living encounter with G-d. The revelation of G-d at Mt. Sinai wasn't just an opportunity for the people of Israel to receive G-d's laws but to experience G-d's love. What happened at Mt. Sinai was a personal, face-to-face encounter with G-d. It wasn't just about getting the laws that made the day important; it was about feeling the ecstasy of G-d's intimacy with the people of Israel.

The experience at Mt. Sinai was not only a revelation of G-d's truth, more importantly, it was a revelation of G-d's love. Torah was and continues to be G-d's love letter. It is the greatest gift ever because it embodies G-d's presence. When you learn the Torah you can actually feel G-d's closeness to you. The Talmud teaches that when G-d gave the Torah to the people of Israel He said, "I am giving you my soul in writing."

Imagine that one day you receive a love letter. You are at work and eating lunch at the employee cafeteria, and someone drops a letter in front of you. You see that it's a letter from the one you love. Do you rip open the envelope and start to speed-read through the letter? No, of course you don't, you save this letter. You're going to read it in a very special place because this letter deserves more.

Now imagine you're in that special place. You open the letter carefully, you start to read your beloved's words and you actually begin to hear her voice, and then you feel her presence.

If you're anything like me, you'll read the letter over and over again, because you know there's much more to this letter. The first time you read it you get the simple meaning. But then you read it even more carefully. You notice that she tells you about the weather and then she starts talking about her mother. What's the connection, you wonder. You then read the letter again and now you see that there are hints in this letter. You pay attention not only to what she says, but also to the way she's structured her sentences. Then you go over it again because you realize that it's even deeper than that. You even look at how she forms the very letters, because there are secrets in the nuances of the actual shape of her letters. You then start looking for the deeper subtle meanings.

Once you've analyzed every aspect, you carefully refold the letter, place it in its envelope and tuck it away for safekeeping. You save this letter because you sense the presence of your beloved within the sheets of paper.

Now let's imagine that someone else is reading that letter. Is that person going to feel the presence of someone else's beloved? No. He'd just get the letter's simple meaning, the information. But for you it would be different. You wouldn't just be reading the letter; you'd get involved in it. And through your involvement with the words, nuances, and deeper meanings, you'd meet your beloved.

This, in essence, is learning Torah. Through our involvement with the text, we hear G-d's voice, feel the Divine presence and experience G-d's love and relive the revelation at Sinai each day of our lives.

Therefore, the Torah embodies not only a way of life but also a way to love. The wisdom and commandments of the Torah empower us to love each other and love G-d. Shavuot is a day to celebrate the laws in love and the love in law.

From *Inviting God In,* by Rabbi David Aaron, © 2007 by Rabbi David Aaron. Reprinted by arrangement with Shambhala Publications, Inc., www.shambhala.com.

HOLIDAY LESSON
FOR

CHANUKAH

BY
RABBI MOSHE LICHTMAN

PRAISE GOD IN THE LAND

THE TALMUD (*Arachin* 10a-b) discusses the reasons why we recite *Hallel*[10] on certain holidays as opposed to others. We say it on Chanukah, of course, because of the miracles that occurred in the days of the Hasmoneans. Why, then, asks the *Gemara*[11], do we omit *Hallel* on Purim? After all, miracles occurred then, too! The Talmud offers three answers, all of which have important ramifications for our own times.

> (1) **R. Yitzchak** says, "[*Hallel* is omitted on Purim] because we do not sing praise for a miracle that occurred outside the Land (*Chutz LaAretz*)."

The *Gemara* goes on to explain that the Exodus from Egypt is an exception to this rule because it occurred before the Israelites ever entered the Land of Israel. After they entered the Land, however, *Hallel* is no longer said on miracles that take place in *Chutz LaAretz*.

Why is this so? Why should it make a difference where the miracle occurred? Do we have less of an obligation to thank God for the miracles He performs in *Chutz LaAretz*? The Maharsha (1555-1631) provides a beautiful answer, but first a word of introduction.

Why is the Land of Israel so special? Why do our Sages lavish so much praise on the Land and ascribe to it so many special qualities? Many leading rabbis answer this question based on a verse in *Deuteronomy* (11:12): *A land that the Lord your God seeks out; the eyes of the Lord your God are always upon it, from the beginning of the year to the end of the year.* That is, HaShem is directly involved in the affairs of the Land of Israel. He oversees everything that goes on here and provides its inhabitants with an extra measure of *Hashgachah P'ratit* (Divine Providence). In *Chutz LaAretz*, on the other hand, God appoints angelic ministers to supervise matters and care for the needs of its inhabitants. Therefore, Israelites who live in God's special Land are said to dwell in the Palace of the King, and they enjoy a closer relationship with HaShem.

---

10 **Hallel** is a collection of Psalms 113-118, which are said at joyous times. It is recited on Pesach, Shavuot, Sukkot and also on Chanukah.

11 Gemara - the second part of the *Talmud*, consisting primarily of commentary on the Mishnah. (Mishna - the first part of the Talmud; a collection of early oral interpretations of the scriptures that was compiled about AD 200.)

The Maharsha uses this concept to explain the difference between Chanukah and Purim. The miracles of Chanukah were a direct result of God's intervention, because they occurred on "His turf," so to say. The miracles of Purim, however, were accomplished through messengers, angelic intermediaries sent by God. And it is fitting to say *Hallel* only on miracles that God Himself performs.

(2) **R. Nachman** says, "The reading [of the *Megillah*[12]] is its *Hallel*."

That is, we really do say *Hallel* on Purim, just in a different form. Instead of reading chapters from Psalms, we read *Megillat Esther*.

As is well known, the miracles of Purim—as opposed to those of Chanukah— were hidden ones. HaShem did not alter any rules of nature at that time; He simply arranged events in such a way that the Jews were saved from imminent destruction. R. Nachman teaches us that such "miracles," as well, deserve some expression of *Hallel*.

(3) **Rava** explains that we do not say *Hallel* on Purim because the salvation was incomplete. After the Exodus from Egypt and the victory of the Macabees, we could truly proclaim, *Give praise, O servants of the Lord* (the first words of *Hallel*), because we were no longer servants of Pharaoh or Antiyochus[13]. We had achieved full sovereignty and complete freedom to serve God. After the downfall of Haman, however, we were still subjugated to Achashveirosh[14].

It is important to note that the 200-year period of Jewish sovereignty following the Chanukah episode was not Israel's most glorious era. Many of the Hasmonean kings were corrupt, murderous, and completely irreligious. Nonetheless, we say *Hallel* until this very day because the Jewish people gained sovereignty over their Land, and kept it for over two hundred years (see Rambam (1135-1204), *Hilchot Chanukah* 3:1).

Almost seventy years ago, a third of our nation was wiped out in the concentration camps of Europe. Three years later, HaShem (not an angel) arranged events (no, He did not perform any manifest miracles, just the hidden kinds)

---

12 Megillah – The Scroll of Esther/The Book of Esther in the Bible.
13 Antiyochus IV Epiphanes was a Hellenistic Greek king of the Seleucid Empire from 175 BC until his death in 164 BC.
14 Achashveirosh – King Ahasuerus in the Book of Esther.

in such a way that we regained sovereignty over our historic homeland, after nearly 2,000 years of exile. Based on the above, is there any doubt that we have an absolute obligation to thank HaShem for all that He has done for us?

Obviously, the preceding ideas have important ramifications on how we conduct ourselves on Yom HaAtzma'ut[15] and Yom Yerushalayim[16]. However, I believe there is a much more important lesson to be learned. We all know that actions are the best way to show thanks to someone who has done us a favor. Words can be cheap, but actions show that we really mean what we say. The same is true with respect to God. Although it is important to express our thanks to Him through the recitation of *Hallel* and the like, it is more important to show Him that we really mean it through concrete actions. If we really appreciate God's gift of the Land of Israel and the State of Israel, we must accept the gift before saying "Thank you" for it.

From *Eretz Yisrael in the Parashah* by Rabbi Moshe Lichtman.

---

15 Yom HaAtzma'ut is the national day of Israel, commemorating the Israeli Declaration of Independence in 1948.

16 Yom Yerushalayim is an Israeli national holiday commemorating the reunification of Jerusalem and the establishment of Israeli control over the Old City in the aftermath of the June 1967 Six-Day War.

HOLIDAY LESSON
FOR

PURIM

BY
RABBI CHANAN MORRISON

"Go Gather All the Jews"

URING THESE DAYS of Purim, in this difficult hour, many troubles
from without besiege and afflict the entire nation of Israel.

Yet our greatest anguish stems from troubles from within. We lack
internal unity, peace in the House of Israel. Let us recall those days and their
events as they are recorded in the Scroll of Esther—written, as it was, with
Divine inspiration. For the Divine spirit transcends the passage of time and
the transient ideologies of each generation. The eternal words *"Go gather all
of the Jews"* shall once again revitalize us and elevate us from our lowly state.

Is Unity Possible?

One may ask: Is it really possible nowadays to gather all of the Jews? Is it possible to unite all the different factions and parties? How will the bones scattered across the vast valley of exile—both material and spiritual—once again
form that entity known as *Klal Yisrael (The Whole of Israel)*, and put forth
its demands for strength, renewal, and redemption?

The answer is that there is a place where this dispersion, both physical and
spiritual, cannot rule over us. But you object: We see with our own eyes the
awful internal strife, Jews fighting Jews, brothers turning against brothers like
wolves and snakes. How then can one say, *"Go gather all of the Jews"*?

Whoever thinks that Haman erred when he said, *"There is one nation
scattered and divided"* (Esther 3:8), is mistaken. Indeed, the nation is scattered and divided; but nevertheless, it is 'one nation.' Nor should one question the possibility of a nation being simultaneously united and divided. The
world is full of wonders. This nation, whose very survival in history is replete
with wondrous wonders, demonstrates by its existence that it is essentially one
nation, despite its dispersion.

True, the malady of exile has divided us. But 'the Eternal One of Israel will
not lie.' The exile and all of its terrors must come to an end. Now that the wind
has begun to blow from the four corners of the earth, from both the troubles
surrounding us and from the spiritual revelation which stirs us to return and
be rebuilt in the land of our life—now we are nearing the realization that there

is a cure for the malady of our dispersion and division. In the final analysis, we are, and shall always be, a united nation. Israel shall once again rise to the eternal words, *"Go gather all of the Jews."*

THE HIDDEN SPIRIT

Yet the difficult question obstructing the path of redemption remains—the divisive discord that consumes us. The answer is that there are two sides to a person. Medical treatment utilizes the inner resources of vitality and health that lie hidden within. This inner spirit is so hidden that even the patient is unaware of its existence. Spiritual maladies and their physical manifestations infect only our baser aspects, that side of which we are aware. But our hidden, unknown side always bursts with energy, brimming with life and strength. This hidden repository of health has the power to heal the outer self, which can mislead one into thinking that he is sick and feeble, when in fact he possesses an energetic, healthy soul, full of life and vigor.

That which is true for the individual applies to a much greater degree to the entire collective. *Klal Yisrael* in particular is truly one nation: *"And who is like Your nation, Israel, one nation in the land?"* (I Sam. 15:19) We must admit our error in identifying the essence of Israel with its superficial appearance, with its outer, baser side. This self-image has made us fearful. We are conscious only of our dispersion and division.

The Hamans of every generation strike at us with their poisonous hatred. Especially in this transition period, they perceive our weak side, for it is visible and recognizable. But precisely through these tribulations we will come to realize that we possess a previously unknown, collective soul, a great national spirit whose existence we had forgotten. It abounds with vitality and possesses sufficient power to renew our lives as of old, and repel all of the Amalekites who wish to assault our weak.

This hidden Judaism, unknown even to ourselves, this great soul of a great nation, bearing both the suffering and the light of the world within it, will become known to us during these portentous times. The blessing of *"Go gather all of the Jews"* will emerge from its hidden place within the national soul. Every Purim we must appreciate the great inner repository of our blessedness and our essential trait of oneness, which will vanquish our divided side.

From a state of being unable to 'distinguish between cursed is Haman and blessed is Mordechai' will come a higher recognition—to find the unknown Jew within us. Brothers will know one another and join hands, and a mighty voice will be heard, *"Let us rise up and ascend to Zion, to the house of our God"* (Jer. 31:5).

First appeared in *Ha-Tor*, 5694 (1934). Adapted from Rabbi Pesach Jaffe's translation of Rabbi Kook's article in 'Celebration of the Soul,' pp. 126-129.

HOLIDAY LESSON
FOR

TISHA B'AV

BY
RABBI CHAIM RICHMAN

A TIME TO MOURN, A TIME TO BUILD

THE PERIOD ON the Hebrew calendar that begins on the 17th of Tammuz and ends with Tisha B'Av is known in Jewish tradition as 'the Three Weeks.' It is also referred to as *bein Ha-Mitzar'im*, literally meaning 'between the straits.' The expression invokes the image of a vessel passing through a narrow place, a path fraught with danger, which must be navigated with extreme caution.

The destruction of the Holy Temple and other calamities that have befallen Israel during these weeks have seared this period into the collective Jewish consciousness as a time of portent. The sages teach us that all of Israel's national and personal disasters, great and small, are reflections of the loss of the Temple. The Temple Mount is our uncontested and unparalleled spiritual center of the past, present and future. Torah teaches us that the Holy Temple is the source of the elusive peace that we all seek so fervently: "For in this place I shall place peace" (Hagai 2:9). Isaiah foretells an unprecedented peace which will be enjoyed by all mankind: "They shall beat their swords into plowshares (. . .) for My house shall be called a house of prayer for all peoples" (Isaiah 56:7).

Yet how do we actually regard the loss of the Holy Temple? The period of the Three Weeks is marked by ascending levels of mourning until the crescendo of the day of Tisha B'Av, when a unique and unparalleled *halachic*[17] reality is experienced. We are so completely focused on the loss of the Temple, that every individual Israelite becomes like one who is mourning, G-d forbid, the loss of a close relative.

Our tradition states that "when the month of Av arrives, we decrease our joy."

But in the quintessential, indefatigable and deepest level of the Jewish spirit, it is also reckoned as a time full of wondrous possibility and of future consolation. Indeed, this month of Av – the very mention of which causes the Jewish soul to cringe like the sound of chalk scratching against the proverbial blackboard of our history—is actually known as *Menachem Av* (the consoling father). From the very heart of darkness springs redemption, as according to

---

17 Halacha - is the collective body of Jewish religious laws derived from the Written and Oral Torah.

tradition the messiah is born on Tisha B'Av. Ultimately, the prophet Zechariah informs us that our days of mourning will be transformed into days of gladness (Zech. 8:19).

Tisha B'Av was never intended to be a day of perpetual mourning, but rather, to serve as a bridge to the future. Mourning is a means to an end; the yearning and desire which our mourning inspires is designed to motivate us to rebuild. Tisha B'Av is not about bemoaning the Temple—it's about bemoaning the world without the Temple; a world that has lost its light, its color, and its direction. Torah teaches that the Holy Temple is the secret of mankind's survival. It is the rectification of relationships—not only our relationship with G-d, but our connection with each other, with all people, and with all of nature; with the world around us.

The ultimate expression of Jewish conviction is anticipating the rebuilding of the Holy Temple. There can be no greater manifestation of the collective soul of Israel, than the desire to see the Temple become a reality. What will it take for the people of Israel to begin rebuilding the Holy Temple? Are we indeed moving closer to that day? Today we hear many excuses, such as; "Who are we to rebuild the Temple? We are not ready. The time has not yet come. The Temple is a thing of the past."

This is nothing new: The prophet Hagai, who exhorted his generation to rebuild the Temple, heard the very same excuses. "Thus said the L-rd, Master of Legions: This nation has said, 'the time has not yet come.' But I say, it is time for the Temple of G-d to be rebuilt!" (Haggai 1:2). The moving verses in the first chapter of the book of Haggai make it clear that the Holy Temple is the source of all blessing in this world, and its absence results in ruination for all. "And the word of the L-rd came by the hand of Haggai the prophet, saying: 'Is this a time for you yourselves to sit in your paneled houses, while this House is in ruins?' So now, thus said the L-rd, 'set your heart to consider your ways! You have sown much but bring in little; eating without being satisfied, drinking without quenching thirst, dressing, yet no one is warmed, and whoever earns money earns it for a purse with a hole.'"

These verses indicate that all the world's physical blessings emanate from the service of the Holy Temple, and its absence brings devastation. G-d tells us now, as He did then, that it is within our power to rebuild the Holy Temple: "Thus says the L-rd (...) set your heart to your ways! Go up to the mountain and bring wood and build the Temple! I will be pleased with it and I will be honored. You looked for much produce, but behold, it is little; you bring it home and I blow upon it. Why is this? Because of My Temple which is ruined, while you run, each to his own house" (Haggai 1:7–10).

A great spiritual revolution is taking place in Israel. More and more people identify with the values and spiritual goals that the Holy Temple represents for our lives. New polls reveal that more than half the people of Israel are ready to rebuild the Holy Temple. The Temple Institute has created nearly all of the sacred vessels needed to resume the Divine service, as well as priestly garments for the *kohanim* (men of priestly descent) that wish to show their dedication and readiness to serve in the Temple. The Institute is also working on computerized architectural designs for the actual building. Red heifers are being raised in Israel. The ancient recipe for the Showbread has been rediscovered. The list of positive developments and changes in Temple-related attitudes, accomplishments and achievements goes on. All of this brings Israel another step closer to the resumption of the Divine service.

The people of Israel are committed to both their heritage and their future. The past is always with us, but we stride towards our destiny. The renewal of Israel and the building of the Holy Temple is a process that has begun and is unstoppable. Israel knows intuitively that it is the Holy Temple she seeks. She can no longer accept a cycle of mourning and endless excuses that lead nowhere. The Nation is preparing to "rise up like a lion" (Numbers 23:24). We are moving closer to the day when we can truly say that Tisha B'Av is no longer relevant, without jaded cynicism or facetiousness but with true sincerity, for it will have turned into a day of gladness. This will be the day we have waited for, the day of the L-rd, the day when Israel and the nations walk in the light of G-d.

How will Zechariah's prophecy come to pass? This month will no longer be a month of desolation but a time of blessing. It is however much easier to mourn than it is to change the situation, and far less threatening. The mystical, dream-like, never-never land aspect of the Temple miraculously appearing one day out of nowhere has supplanted the Torah's call for the People of Israel to be a light for the nations. It is a charge that requires courage, conviction, and vitality, but most of all, a charge that requires the People of Israel to believe in themselves and in the righteousness of their cause. G-d brings about miracles, and the greatest miracles come through the determination of the People of Israel when they place their faith in G-d alone. It is Israel that will cause the *Shechina* (the Divine Presence), the source of all blessing, to return to the world and all the nations will stream to the Temple in Jerusalem, saying "Let us go with you, because G-d is with you" (Zechariah 8:23). Tisha B'Av will then be transformed to a day of gladness and rejoicing!

INTRODUCTION of the AUTHORS

RABBI
DAVID AARON

R ABBI DAVID AARON (www.rabbidavidaaron.com) is a visionary and a spiritual educator. He has taught and inspired thousands of people who seek meaning in their lives and a joyous connection to Judaism.

Rabbi Aaron is the founder and dean of Isralight and the Rosh Yeshiva of Yeshivat Orayta. He has authored several books including bestsellers like *Endless Light, Living a Joyous Life, The Secret Life of G-d, Inviting God in, The God Powered Life, Love is My Religion* and *Soul Powered Prayers.* His books have attracted international media attention including Larry King Live and E! Entertainment. He lives in Jerusalem with his wife, Chana, and seven children.

You will find Rabbi David Aaron's Torah lessons on pages:
63 (Toledot), 77 (Vayeshev), 193 (Behar), 219 (Korach) and 327 (Shavuout).

RABBI
DR. NATHAN LOPES CARDOZO

RABBI DR. NATHAN Lopes Cardozo (1946) is the founder and dean of the David Cardozo Academy and the Bet Midrash of Avraham Avinu in Jerusalem. Rabbi Cardozo is a sought-after lecturer on the international stage for both Jewish and non-Jewish audiences, and has written 13 books and numerous articles in both English and Hebrew. Rabbi Cardozo heads a Think Tank focused on finding new Halachic and philosophical approaches to dealing with the crisis of religion and identity amongst Jews and the Jewish State of Israel. Hailing from the Netherlands, Rabbi Cardozo is known for his original and often fearlessly controversial insights into Judaism. His ideas are widely debated on an international level in social media, blogs, books and other forums. His new documentary, Lonely but Not Alone, was premiered last March in Jerusalem, and his autobiography of the same name is due out in late 2016. Rabbi Cardozo's weekly Thoughts to Ponder, along with the audio and video of many of his lectures, can be found on the David Cardozo Academy's website: www.CardozoAcademy.org.

To receive Rabbi Cardozo's weekly insights,
free of charge, in Judaism and Religion:
nlc@internet-zahav.net

You will find Rabbi Nathan Lopes Cardozo's Torah lessons on pages:
189 (Emor), 197 (Bechukotai), 237 (Matot), 271 (Ki Teitzei), 285 (Vayelech)
and 319 (Simchat Torah).

RABBI
LEVI COOPER

RABBI LEVI COOPER, originally from Melbourne, Australia, is the spiritual leader of *Kehillat HaTzur VeHaTzohar* in Zur Hadassa—a mixed religious and secular neighborhood outside Jerusalem.

Since 1998, Rabbi Cooper has taught at the Pardes Institute of Jewish Studies, Jerusalem (www.pardes.org.il). He holds an LL.B., LL.M., and Ph.D. from the Law Faculty of Bar-Ilan University, and is a member of the Israel Bar Association. Rabbi Cooper is currently an adjunct professor in the Law Faculty of Bar-Ilan University and a post-doctoral fellow in the Law Faculty of Tel Aviv University.

Rabbi Cooper served in the IDF's Golani Brigade and continues to do Reserve Duty as a commander in an infantry unit. He is also a member of the Tzohar rabbis' organization; an educational advisor to the Jewish community of Istanbul, Turkey; an educator with Heritage Seminars; and he serves on the Readers' Association of the National Library of Israel.

He is also the rabbi of the Lavi Primary School. Rabbi Levi publishes a regular column in the *Jerusalem Post* on Hasidism. Since 2003 he has been a contributing editor for *Jewish Educational Leadership*—the journal of Bar-Ilan University's Lookstein Center (www.lookstein.org). His doctoral dissertation explores the interaction between Hasidism and Halakha, and his current research focuses on the evolution and normalization of Hasidic lore. His first book, *Relics for the Present: Contemporary Reflections on the Talmud* was published by Koren/Maggid in 2012. In his book, Rabbi Cooper explores the contemporary relevance of Talmudic passages from the tractate *Berakhot*. Volume 2, *Relics for the Present*, just came out

Rabbi Cooper is married to Sarah and they have 6 children together.

You will find Rabbi Levi Cooper's Torah lessons on pages:
73 (Vayishlach), 159 (Tzav), 203 (Bemidbar), 247 (Devarim)
and 303 (Rosh Hashana).

RABBI
YEHOSHUA FRIEDMAN

ABBI YEHOSHUA FRIEDMAN was born in 1948 in Cleveland, USA, about half a year after the establishment of the State of Israel. He grew up in a liberal suburban Jewish environment and graduated from the local public high school. He studied the Great Books curriculum at St. John's College in Annapolis, MD, leaving with a BA degree and realized that some of the smartest people in the world are not Jewish. Four years of reading, analyzing and discussing the great works of Western philosophy, literature and science left him thinking that civilization today is composed of Greek thought and the Jewish and Christian Scriptures and what followed from them. In the wake of the watershed of the 1967 Six-Day War in Israel he felt the need to address the Jewish roots which were not sufficiently discussed in general society. He was not alone, as a small movement of searching out Jewish sources was growing and leading other Jews to Israel. From 1970 to date, Rabbi Yehoshua has learned and taught Torah; raised a large family; been a part of founding the community of Kochav Hashachar in the Binyamin area north-east of Jerusalem; worked for a time as a computer programmer, and participated in various activities involved with what he calls the "spiritual foreign policy" of the Jewish people.

You will find Rabbi Yehoshua Friedman's Torah lessons on pages: 69 (Vayetze), 215 (Shlach) and 251 (Va'etchanan).

RABBI
MOSHE GOLDSMITH

R ABBI MOSHE GOLDSMITH was born and raised in Brooklyn, New York. He studied at BTA Yeshiva High School and completed a Bachelor's degree in Biology at Brooklyn College. From a very young age he felt a calling to go and settle down in the Land of Israel. Shortly after graduating college, he married his wife Leah and they made aliyah (immigrated) with the intention of joining hands with the nucleus of pioneers and establish a new community in Israel's heartland. Rabbi Goldsmith's love for Torah motivated him to join a rabbinical program in nearby Elon Moreh where he studied for thirteen years and received his *smicha* (Rabbinic ordination) from the Chief Rabbinate of Israel and a teaching degree. He has been very active in the community and was Itamar's mayor for over eight years.

Rabbi Goldsmith is a strong believer in the universal role that the people of Israel must play in being a light to the nations. He is an experienced lecturer on a wide range of topics and gives classes on a regular basis to Jews and non-Jews alike. At this vital time, he wants to raise awareness and support for Itamar by bringing the community's important message to the world. He believes this essential mission is vital for the future of Itamar and other communities in Judea, Samaria and Israel. This, he believes, will be done by bridging the gap between Jews and non-Jews—an important component of Tikkun Olam (rectifying the world).

www.TourItamarSupportIsrael.com
www.FriendsOfItamar.org
e-mail: leamoshe@netvision.net.il

You will find Rabbi Moshe Goldsmith's Torah lessons on pages:
167 (Tazria), 233 (Pinchas), 263 (Re'eh), 275 (Ki Tavo) and 307 (Yom Kippur).

RABBI
MOSHE D. LICHTMAN

RABBI MOSHE D. Lichtman was born and raised in Elizabeth, N.J. He studied at several Yeshivot in Israel. He received his rabbinic ordination (*semichah*) from the Chief Rabbinate of Israel and Rabbi Isaac Elchanan of the Theological Seminary of Yeshiva University. He also holds an MS in Jewish Education from Yeshiva University's Azrieli Institute.

Rabbi Lichtman made aliyah (immigrated) in 1991 and has taught in several post high school programs in Israel ever since. He currently resides in Beit Shemesh with his wife and eight children.

His "claim to fame" is undoubtedly his literary contribution to the Jewish world. Thanks to his efforts the broader English speaking audience worldwide can now benefit from the teachings of major works such as *Eim HaBanim Semeichah*, *An Angel Among Men (*, *A Question of Redemption* and *Rise from the Dust*. In addition, he has penned a highly popular original work entitled *Eretz Yisrael in the Parashah*, which demonstrates the centrality of *Eretz Yisrael* in the Torah. It is from this book that the articles in the current volume are taken.

The *Mishnah* in *Pirkei Avot* that teaches *"Bimkom she'ayn anashim hishtadel le'hiyot ish"* guides him in his writing almost exclusively about Eretz Yisrael and aliya. "When no one is filling a role, you must rise up and fill it," he explains.

Lastly, Rabbi Lichtman has lectured on several occasions to Jewish communities abroad, impressing upon them the importance of *aliyah* in our times. If you are interested in hosting Rabbi Lichtman as a scholar in residence in your community, please contact him through his website: www.toratzion.com.

You will find Rabbi Moshe Lichtman's Torah lessons on pages: 89 (Vayigash), 163 (Shemini), 207 (Naso), 241 (Masei) and 331 (Chanukah).

RABBI
GEDALIA MEYER

RABBI GEDALIA MEYER is living in the town of Maale Adumim in Israel. He comes from California where he studied sciences before getting interested in his Jewish roots and pursuing a rabbinic career. He has served for many years as a rabbi at four synagogues in America and Israel, most recently in his home community in Israel. He has also taught at several Jewish schools and yeshivot.

Rabbi Meyer has helped his wife, Suri, raising seven children. His interests include all manners of Torah subjects, with a special focus on the spiritual side. His current research interests include the historical development of Jewish spirituality and the ways in which it can merge with the latest developments of modern science. He is open to hear both old and new ideas and eager to share his own insights, however meager they may be, with others.

Rabbi Meyer is a founding teacher at Root Source, where he teaches "God: the Jewish Image - Video Lessons on the Jewish Journey to Understand God."

www.root-source.com/teachers/gedalia-meyer/
www.root-source.com/channels/god-jewish-image/

You will find Rabbi Gedalia Meyer's Torah lessons on pages:
41 (Bereshit), 109 (Bo), 137 (Ki Tisa), 227 (Balak) and 281 (Nitzavim).

RABBI
CHANAN MORRISON

RABBI CHANAN MORRISON grew up in Pennsylvania and graduated with a BA in Mathematics from Yeshiva University, New York. Wanting to pursue advanced Talmudic studies in Jerusalem, he spent the next seven years studying at Jerusalem yeshivot, including the famed Yeshivat Mercaz HaRav, founded by Rabbi Abraham Isaac Kook in 1924. He taught Jewish studies for several years in Harrisburg, PA, before returning to Israel where he settled down in a small community in the Judean Desert.

Rabbi Morrison is frequently featured in the Torah section of the Israel National News website, and his work can be read on his website: www.ravkooktorah.org. He has published three books about Rav Kook's writings: *Gold from the Land of Israel* (2006), *Silver from the Land of Israel* (2010) and *Sapphire from the Land of Israel* (2013).

The celebrated first Chief Rabbi of pre-state Israel, Rabbi Abraham Isaac Kook (1865-1935), is recognized as being among the most important Jewish thinkers of all times. His writings reflect the mystic's search for underlying unity in all aspects of life and the world. His unique personality similarly united a rare combination of talents and gifts. Rabbi Kook was a prominent rabbinical authority and active public leader, but at the same time, a deeply religious mystic. He was both a Talmudic scholar and poet, as well as an original thinker and saintly *tzaddik (righteous)*.

RABBI KOOK

You will find Rabbi Chanan Morrison's Torah lessons on pages:
59 (Chayei Sarah), 93 (Vayechi), 121 (Mishpatim), 211 (Beha'alotecha),
267 (Shoftim), 323 (Passover) and 335 (Purim).

RABBI
ZELIG PLISKIN

ZELIG PLISKIN IS an Orthodox Jewish rabbi, writer, lecturer, and author of more than 25 books, including *Gateway to Happiness, Conversations With Yourself, Building Your Self-Image and the Self-Image of Others,* and *Life Is Now.* He is known as Zaidy Zelig and has a grandfatherly attitude to bring out the best in others.

Rabbi Pliskin was born in 1946 in Baltimore, Maryland. As a young boy he attended Yeshiva Chofetz Chaim Talmudical Academy of Baltimore and later studied at the Telshe Yeshiva in Cleveland, Ohio. After his marriage to Raizel, they moved to Israel and he studied for five years at a Brisk yeshiva. He received his degree in Counseling Psychology at the State University of New York.

Rabbi Pliskin's father had been a student of the Chofetz Chaim at the Raduń Yeshiva in Poland and had written a biography of him. In 1974, after writing an article for *The Jewish Observer* about the life of the Chofetz Chaim, "The Profile of an Oheiv Yisroel," Zelig Pliskin was asked to write a book explaining the Chofetz Chaim's teachings. The result was his first book, *Guard Your Tongue.*

Several years following Rabbi Pliskin's move to Israel, the outreach organization Aish HaTorah asked him to speak on human emotions and relationships. Rabbi Pliskin now provides marriage counseling and works with individuals to encourage their personal growth and improvement. He remains closely affiliated with Aish HaTorah, and lectures both in Israel and in the United States.

Rabbi Pliskin lives in Jerusalem with his family.

Find Rabbi Pliskin's books here: www.artscroll.com
See more lessons from Rabbi Pliskin at www.aish.com

You will find Rabbi Zelig Pliskin Torah lessons on pages:
83 (Miketz), 147 (Pekudai), 177 (Acharei Mot), 181 (Kedoshim) and 289 (Haazinu).

RABBI
CHAIM RICHMAN

RABBI CHAIM RICHMAN is a founding member of the Temple Institute of Jerusalem and has served as one of its directors of nearly thirty years. Rabbi Richman was active in Jewish education in the USA before making aliya (immigrated) in 1982. He proudly served in an IDF combat unit. He is the author and translator of over ten books in English about the Holy Temple, as well as several original works of Torah commentary. As the head of the International Department of the Temple Institute, he has addressed audiences throughout the world, and has been interviewed extensively by the international media. For decades he has also been one of Israel's trailblazing rabbis in his outreach and teaching Torah to non-Jews who wish to draw close to the God of Israel.

Rabbi Richman reflects on his motivation in establishing the Temple Institute's International Department: "The Torah testifies that the Holy Temple in Jerusalem was the spiritual center for all mankind. All of Israel's prophets foretell that in the future, the Holy Temple will once again stand on Mount Moriah, and at that time all nations will worship there together.

In our time, there is a great spiritual awakening concerning the importance of the Temple. The Temple Institute views this awakening as Divinely-inspired, and actively seeks to share the desire and knowledge of the Temple with people around the world."

Towards this goal, the Temple Institute has established a unique International Department, whose purpose is to help bring the light of the Holy Temple to a world that is seeking the presence of G-d. The International Department exists in order to provide knowledge, inspiration and information to all those who share in this vision, and to provide the opportunity to support and actively participate in projects of the Temple Institute.

The International Department produces weekly Torah teachings by Rabbi Richman on internet video. They also arranges Torah-based tours and seminars in Israel with a unique focus on Jerusalem from an authentic Jewish standpoint. The Temple Institute's English language website: www.templeinstitute. org. Rabbi Richman can be reached directly at rabbirichman@gmail.com

You will find Rabbi Chaim Richman's Torah lessons on pages: 55 (Vayeira), 113 (Beshalach), 125 (Terumah), 295 (V'Zot HaBerachah), 313 (Sukkot) and 339 (Tisha Be'Av).

RABBI
SHLOMO RISKIN

R ABBI SHLOMO RISKIN is a noted teacher, author, speaker and visionary—
and his contributions to Israel and world Jewry over the course of the past
five decades have been instrumental in shaping today's Modern Orthodox
society.

As the founding rabbi of the Lincoln Square Synagogue in Manhattan,
Rabbi Riskin created a focal point for an exciting approach to Orthodoxy. He
served as a role model for religious social action, promoting the involvement of
women in religious learning, living and leadership, and thus became a major
spokesperson for Modern Orthodoxy.

In 1983, Rabbi Riskin moved to Israel to pioneer the settlement of Efrat,
which now numbers close to 12,000 people. Efrat is considered the most
thriving, vibrant and desirable bedroom community of Jerusalem.

Upon arriving in Israel, Rabbi Riskin founded a boys' High School in Efrat,
and started what would eventually become Ohr Torah Stone (www.ots.org.il):
a network of groundbreaking educational institutions; women's empowerment
programs; innovative leadership training; bridge-building outreach initiatives;
and proactive social action projects that today encompasses 3,000 students from
Israel and the Diaspora. The range of students comes from elementary school
to post-graduate programs for men and women. Despite the different scope of
ages, programs and locations, OTS institutions are all united in espousing the

vision and philosophy of their founder. This includes a deep love for Israel, tolerance of one's fellow man, knowledge and pride in Judaism and high level secular studies. Ohr Torah Stone is thus training a knowledgeable, caring and relevant leadership for the future.

You will find Rabbi Shlomo Riskin's Torah lessons on pages:
105 (Va'eira), 131 (Tetzaveh), 141 (Vayakhel) 155 (Vayikra), 171 (Metzora), 223 (Chukat) and 257 (Eikev).

RABBI
NAPHTALI "TULY" WEISZ

RABBI NAPHTALI "TULY" Weisz attended Yeshiva University (BA), Rabbi Isaac Elchanan Theological Seminary (Rabbinic Ordination) and the Benjamin Cardozo School of Law (JD). He also served as the Rabbi of the Beth Jacob Congregation in Columbus, Ohio.

Upon making Aliyah (immigrated), Rabbi Weisz founded Israel365 and is the publisher of Breaking Israel News. He is also the general editor of The Israel Bible. These innovative and popular websites serve to promote the Biblical significance of the Land of Israel to both Jewish and Christian Zionists all over the world. Rabbi Weisz is married and lives with his family in Ramat Beit Shemesh, Israel.

www.Israel365.com
www.BreakingIsraelNews.con
www.TheIsraelBible.com

You will find Rabbi Naphtali "Tuly" Weisz's Torah lessons on pages:
47 (Noach), 51 (Lech-Lecha), 101 (Shemot) and 117 (Yitro).